A THEOLOGY OF PEACEMAKING
A Vision, a Road, a Task

Mary Elsbernd

Briar Cliff College

UNIVERSITY
PRESS OF
AMERICA

Lanham • New York • London

Copyright © 1989 by

University Press of America,® Inc.

4720 Boston Way
Lanham, MD 20706

3 Henrietta Street
London WC2E 8LU England

British Cataloging in Publication Information Available

Library of Congress Cataloging–in–Publication Data

Elsbernd, Mary, 1946–
A theology of peacemaking : a vision, a road, a task / Mary Elsbernd.
p.   cm.
Bibliography: p.
Includes index.
1. Peace– –Religious aspects– –Catholic Church. 2. War– –Religious
aspects– –Catholic Church. 3. Catholic Church– –Doctrines. I. Title.
BX1795.P43E57   1989   88–31504 CIP
261.8'73– –dc19
ISBN 0–8191–7302–9 (alk. paper)

To my family
and
the Sisters of St. Francis
Dubuque, Iowa

ACKNOWLEDGEMENTS

In the beginning, the subject matter of this book was a new course assigned to me upon my arrival at Briar Cliff College. As I developed and taught the course, the need for an introductory undergraduate textbook on a theology of peacemaking became apparent. The actual satisfaction of this need through this book was possible only through the support of friends, colleagues and students.

Among these I would like to mention the Theology Faculty of the Katholieke Universiteit Leuven through whom I became schooled in excellent theological method and in the historical approach. The members of my religious congregation have encouraged me by their faith in me and in my work. I am concretely grateful for the proofreading skills of Sisters Marlys Becker, Kate Katoski, Kay Koppes, Anne Sedgewick, Joanice Theobald, and Raban Wathen.

Within the tradition of the small liberal arts college, Briar Cliff College offered me its personal and technical resources. I am grateful for the personal attention given me by a cooperative and perserverant library staff as well as patient and knowledgeable computor center personnel. The moral support of my colleagues and the financial support of the Faculty Development Committee remain a valuable asset, however the enthusiasm and the editing skills of Phil Hey were an invaluable contribution to this book's completion.

TABLE OF CONTENTS

INTRODUCTION

At its heart peacemaking asks each of us to do what we can, where we are, today , for peace. I am not an international mediator nor a picket line pacifist. I am a theology teacher at a small Franciscan Catholic college in northwest Iowa; and this book is my current contribution to peacemaking.

This contribution stands, however, within a larger context. In 1987 the persistent efforts of Briar Cliff personnel over the years brought about the introduction of an interdisciplinary peace studies minor into our curriculum. As part of that curriculum my neighbor from the English department teaches Literature of War and Peace; my colleagues from the History and Political Science department teach History of the American Peace Movement as well as International Organization and World Order. The Health, Physical Education and Recreation department offers a one-hour course in Non-competitive Games and the professor of physics also offers a one-hour course on Nuclear Energy. And so it goes--throughout the academic departments, we do what we can do here where we are today.

We celebrated the introduction of the peace studies minor on the fourth anniversary of the United States bishops' pastoral letter, *The Challenge of Peace* with the planting of a peace tree on our campus and the distribution of seedlings to plant wherever we called home. The planting of the peace tree linked our efforts to those earliest Sioux City inhabitants who reconciled conflict at a local peace tree. Chief War Eagle and his contemporaries did what they could for peace in their days. We entered into that Sioux City tradition by planting our peace trees.

Faculty, staff, administrators and students together form the Briar Cliff College peace and justice committee. Working together they have sponsored non-violent conflict resolution workshops on campus and have networked with other local peace groups. Other groups are developing a process for grievance and conflict mediation. Our students have walked for peace in the Soviet Union. Our graduates have worked as Peace Corp members and as Witnesses for Peace; They direct offices for peace and social concerns and are active members of their parish peace and justice committees as well as local peace organizations. I mention these few examples simply to reiterate that peacemaking asks each of us to do what we can do where we are. We are not extraordinary--in fact such peacemaking efforts might be expected legitimately of a Franciscan college.

This specific written contribution to peacemaking situates peacemaking within the Christian scriptural and historical tradition as well as a contemporary moral framework. Within this framework the personal and social, the local and international, the human and structural aspects of peacemaking are examined.

The first three chapters etch out the scriptural and theological contours for Christian peacemaking. Chapter One discusses the intended peace of creation and a compatible understanding of what it means to be a human person. Chapter Two sets forth the vision of peace depicted in scriptural images of Shalom, the New Jerusalem, and the Reign of God. Chapter Three describes Jesus as the literal embodiment of peace in the incarnation, in the saving action of reconciliation and in the gift of the indwelling Spirit to the Christian community.

The next three chapters examine three historical components of the Christian peacemaking tradition. The holy war tradition in Chapter Four is presented not as a divine mandate for violence as it has been misunderstood, but as one more instance in which human persons are confronted with the choice between self-justification and God's offer of salvation. The scriptural roots and history of Christian pacifism are treated in Chapter Five as well as the option for an incarnational pacifism which demands concrete peacemaking within the confines of our historical conditions. Chapter Six presents the historical roots of the just war theory with an analysis of its capability to facilitate moral decisions concerning war and peace in the nuclear age.

The final chapters sketch some contemporary cornerstones in Christian peacemaking. Chapter Seven treats the concept of peacemaking as more than the mere absence of war and the deterrent potential of war weapons. Chapter Eight takes up the integral relationship between justice and peacemaking both in its scriptural roots and in this current socio-political and socio-economic world. Chapter Nine moves from the requirements of justice to the challenges of development which Pope Paul has called the "new name for peace". Chapter Ten summarizes and highlights the essential components for Christian peacemaking today.

Although *A Theology of Peacemaking* is primarily a college level text, it is also suitable as a resource for adult professionals engaged in peace and justice education as well as an enrichment source for persons interested in the history and foundations of Christian peacemaking. The integrative nature of this book offers a solid basis for Christian formation in peacemaking.

Because the content is intended to facilitate the incorporation of peacemaking into daily living, a variety of additional resources supplement each chapter. Primary source readings from Roman Catholic magisterial teaching and a bibliography for further reading are included. Some films, discussion questions and integrating activities are also suggested. Finally, a set of scripture readings with reflection questions which correspond to the chapter topic are presented as a basis for a spirituality of peacemaking.

My research, reflection and teaching on a theology of peacemaking forged in me the conviction that peacemaking is a vision, a road, and a task. Peace is a vision both of who we are at our core beginnings and who we are called to become which urges a concrete embodiment in the present. Christian peacemaking is a road with its historical point of origin in the early Christian communities and its future destination in the end times reign of God; it is a road built by peace pilgrims as they do what they can do to reconcile, mediate or make peace. Peacemaking is a task integral to the Christian faith which proclaims the incarnation of Jesus, the reconciling activity of God in Jesus and the indwelling presence of the Spirit of Jesus in the Christian community. It is my hope that through these pages, the readers will uncover these convictions and will be enabled to do what they can where they are today for peace.

CHAPTER 1
IN THE BEGINNING

My favorite prayer as a high school student was the Peace Prayer of St. Francis. It was, I imagine, no small coincidence that a prayer card version of it was stuck behind the light switch by the telephone. During those proverbial teenage hours on the phone, the prayer for peace entered into my flesh and spirit. Perhaps it found there a kindred soul in primal longing for harmony and order.

In my more recent years, I often have been astonished at the cry for peace welling up from my being in moments of quiet, deep prayer. Coming as it did from a level beyond my consciousness, the desire for peace welled up from the most fundamental level of my person: the core where I am who I was created to be.

As I look back on these moments now, they seem to embody the human sense that in the beginning we are created in peace, for peace.

* * *

1. Genesis: In the Beginning

The peace of creation

The creation stories from Genesis were some of the later chapters in the Pentateuch to take written form. Before this, they were told for centuries around the campfires and hearths of the Hebrew people. In the present biblical form, the accounts of creation articulate the reflective understanding of generations of persons struggling with their beginnings: Where did we come from? What is the meaning of life? What is our place in the world around us? Has life always been like this?

The first chapters of Genesis are not on-the-spot documentaries of the creation event. They rather give words to a cumulative sense about the way things were--in the beginning when God transformed chaos and wilderness into creation and a garden.

The first creation story began with a description of pre-creation chaos as "formless wasteland", "darkness", "abyss" and a "mighty wind" (Genesis 1.2). God progressively ordered this chaos into a world of harmony and beauty. Light countered the darkness; the sky set limits for the watery abyss; the land and the seas shaped the formless void. Once the chaos was ordered on the first three days in the account, God created beauty within the structures on the following three days: sun, moon and stars; birds and sea monsters; animals, woman and man.

In the next verses, God established relationships of interdependency between man and woman, between human persons and all living creatures, and between all living things and the material world. Creation in the image of God suggested the author's conviction that in the beginning human persons knew a familial oneness with God. Thus, woman and man are ultimately responsible to continue the creative activity in God's name and manner. The Priestly author seems to indicate that desire for unity among human persons as well as with their God rests in their creation in the likeness of God. The solidarity of the human race is expressed in the common parentage of Adam and Eve. The Genesis creation account portrays a certain kinship with all things as created by the word of God. When it addressed the image of peace in the Bible, *Challenge of Peace* noted that the community and all

2

word of God. When it addressed the image of peace in the Bible, *Challenge of Peace* noted that the community and all creation provided the consistent context for peace[1] in the Hebrew scriptures.

While reading that God rested on the seventh day, the reader of Genesis can reminisce about a world created in interdependent harmony, order and beauty from the primeval chaos.

The second Genesis creation account begins not in chaos but in the wilderness. There, for the man and woman, God plants a desert-transforming garden, complete with four rivers, trees, wild animals and birds. This story speaks of human responsibility for the creation begun by God in agricultural imagery of cultivation and caretaking. Here God's commands and human name-giving to the animals are used to describe the relationships between the plants, the living creatures and human persons. The image of God's creation of the woman from man's rib highlights a sense of human unity through complementarity.

This cumulative Hebrew understanding reveals a sense of the human heart that in the beginning peace was a hallmark of creation. God's creation was an ordered cosmos, filled with the harmony of interdependent relationships and with the beauty of created things. The Hebrews understood that the desire to live in peace as one people came from creation in God's image and from the experience of mutual complementarity. In addition, this reflective intuition sensed human responsibility for the continuation of the created peace.

---

[1]National Conference of Catholic Bishops, *The Challenge of Peace: God's Promise and Our Response,* Washington, DC, 1983, #32.

The beginnings of disunity

Chapters of 3-11 of Genesis convey yet another insight. Women and men are responsible not only for the continuation of the created peace, but also for the breakdown of peace. Sin changes the peaceful unity of the man and the woman in the garden into a relationship of shame and blame (Genesis 3.7-13). The human desire to be "like gods" (Genesis 3.5) estranges the man and woman from their creator God (Genesis 3.8), from each other (Genesis 3.16) and from the land (Genesis 3.17-19). The peaceful, beautiful Garden of Eden is no more.

The story of the breakdown of peace only begins with the banishment from Eden. Cain murders his brother Abel, whom God especially favored (Genesis 4). Perhaps the reference (Genesis 6.1-4) to the "sons of heaven" intermarrying with the "daughters of men" illustrates the further crumbling of the ordered relationship between the divine Creator and human creatures. The story of Noah and the flood (Genesis 6-9) portrays to all creation the threat of a return to the watery abyss of Genesis 1.2. The cycle of primeval history ends with the Tower of Babel account. There one people speaking one language working on a common project--it is granted that the project appears to have been an exercise in egotism and self-deification--disintegrates into scattered peoples unable to communicate with each other (Genesis 11.1-9).

This twofold experience of human persons does not appear to have ended with the closing of primordial history in Genesis 11. The human heart can still thrill with stories of women and men who engage in peacemaking. It can still rejoice at the tearful embrace of two young women in a downtown cathedral after the pastor's reading and reflections on the story of the prodigal son. It can still admire the grit of the eighty-one year old Franciscan woman setting out on the 1986 trek across the United States for peace, simply because she believes in peace. It is still amazed by the professional men and women who take time out from their upwardly mobile careers to offer their skills

4

to the poor of the world. Even the event of Ronald Reagan and Mikail Gorbachev sitting down at a summit table for peace dares to rekindle the longing for peace.

Yet the human heart's desire for peace has its shadow side in the capability to damage peacemaking. There is in every human heart the potential to frustrate efforts at peacemaking. In John Knowles' graphic portrayal, *A Separate Peace,* international conflicts provide a mere backdrop for the personal wars being waged daily. Most people can recount a story of the lack of reconciliation because the memory of one of the parties has remained fixed at the point of estrangement. There are also the attitudes and patterns of society which encourage persons to see as threatening those of different ideas, other cultures, dissimilar backgrounds or diverse ideologies. How does one shake off the accumulated complacency which threatens peacemaking efforts when faced with multiple news accounts of terrorism, the unending reports of wars somewhere in the world, a myriad of television episodes portraying violence and the everpresent threat of nuclear destruction--in addition to daily doses of cynicism, coercion and pressure tactics?

Human life today, as in the beginning, knows the desire for peace as well as estrangement, disorder as well as harmony. It knows both the possibility of peace and the potentiality for its destruction.

God is a God of peacemaking

In the God of peace, however, there remained a note of hope. As consistent as the human choice to damage the created peace was the peacemaking and reconciling activity of God. In the final verses relating the human decision to be "like gods", a seamstress God made leather garments to improve upon the figleaf clothing efforts by Adam and Eve (Genesis 3.21). The God of creation continued to care for the creatures who had rejected their beginnings. Although Cain was banished to a nomadic existence away from God's presence because of his role in Abel's death, God promised full vengeance on anyone who would kill Cain (Genesis 4.15). After the flood's threat, God made a covenant through Noah with all living beings. The rainbow was the sign that the primitive chaos would never overcome the harmony of this new creation (Genesis 9.12-17).

In the writings of the later prophets (Isaiah 40-66; Ezekial 33-37) the theme of a new creation returns. As part of its development, Ezekial describes God's promise of a covenant of peace which reverses many of the results of the human decision in the garden. In Ezekial 34.25-30, instead of the enmity between the animal world and human persons, the new covenant of peace means so ridding the land of carnivorous beasts that people can sleep in the deserts and forests (Ezekial 34.25). Instead of an uncooperative land threatening famine, the covenant of peace means rain, fruit and crops (Ezekial 34.27,29). Instead of frustration and misguided attempts at knowing God, the covenant of peace means that the people will know their God (Ezekial 34.27,30). In this way Ezekial sketches God's desire to re- create those garden beginnings in a new covenant of peace and affirms the human sense that peace was the way of living in the beginning.

The biblical accounts of creation emerged from centuries of reflective living and storytelling. Through them a reader is left with the sense that creation brought a harmonious, a peaceful ordering of life out of chaos. This way of living was concerned with peaceful relationships between God, human persons and the whole world. God's promise of a new creation in peace after the great flood and in late prophetic literature also articulates the sense that peace was God's creation. In sharp contrast, primordial history as well as the whole biblical history of Israel attributes the disruption of the peace of creation to human decision. The human decision, however, does not negate the peace of creation but sets up opposing forces within the human heart and the human community.

2. A Christian Anthropology

As it is used in this chapter, the expression "in the beginning..." can also refer to the essential core of what it means to be a human person from a contemporary philosophical or anthropological approach.

The human person is multi-dimensional. When one admires an ornate cut-glass vase, one may not be consciously aware of the height, the depth, the width or its unique surfaces because the separate dimensions fit so well into one whole. It is similar with the human person. Although one can separate out various dimensions of the human person, all of the dimensions are simultaneously present and operative. No dimension is prior to another nor does any dimension carry more weight than another. All the dimensions together describe the human person.[1]

The human person is a subject. This subject dimension focuses on that "I" which is continuous throughout the various stages of personal growth and development. The "I" is aware of the self as self and is present to the self as self. In this experience the "I" recognizes the self as an object of knowledge. The subject dimension thus includes an openness to reality beyond the self as object of reality. The self-aware subject belongs to itself and yet is able to escape its own limits at a fundamental level of freedom. Fundamental freedom is the ability of the self to determine the meaning of its life in its wholeness. As such, it is distinct from the freedom of choice necessary to moral decision-making. The subject dimension of the human person or the self-aware I describes the capacity for intellectual activity and freedom.

---

[1]See L. JANSSENS, *Personalist morals,* in *Louvain Studies* 3 (1970) 5-16 and JANSSENS, *Artificial Insemination. Ethical Considerations,* in*Louvain Studies* 8 (1980) 3-29 for a more complete treatment of this anthropological understanding.

Vatican Council II included these elements in its description of the human person in the Church in the Modern World.[1] In their understanding, intelligence and freedom both evidence human participation in the divine image and provide the foundation for human dignity.

The human person is a corporeal--a bodily--person. The human person is not a subject or a spiritual entity which has a body. Rather the human person *is* an incarnate subject. It is highly improbable that readers can list among their acquaintances any bodiless person. This bodily incarnation makes a significant contribution to self-concept and self-realization. The condition and shape of a body plays a part in personal definition of abilities, activities and life choices. The human person is bodily.

The corporeal person stands under the needs and laws which apply to material things. For example, laws of velocity and force affect human persons in impact accidents. Needs for nutrition and oxygen influence intelligence and the capability for a productive life.

The human person is a sexual bodily person. As such, sexuality is not a possession: one does not have sexuality, rather one *is* sexual. Nor is sexuality only a corporeal fact. It is threaded through all five dimensions of the human person, providing a clear illustration of the essential interconnection of the dimensions of the human person. Self-awareness, relationality, historicity and fundamental equality in originality influence and are influenced by the corporeal sexual person. Persons do approach the whole of life as male or female.

---

[1]VATICAN COUNCIL II, *Pastoral Constitution of the Church in the Modern World*, in W. ABBOTT (ed.), *The Docuements of Vatican Council II*, New York, 1966, # 15 and #17.

The human body is the necessary means of human communication. Language, gestures and commonly accepted symbolic systems of meaning illustrate the body as a medium for communication. Saying "I love you", sharing an affectionate embrace, or giving a red rose communicates a human bond of a certain degree of intimacy. The body is the means through which the human person in its subjectivity grasps the objective knowledge and articulates the resultant understanding.

The *Church in the Modern World* holds that the human person is the epitome of the material world and that the body is "good and honorable". The body is not to be despised but rather is the way one glorifies God.[1]

The human person lives in relationships. The human person is a fundamental openness to external reality and to involvement or dialogue with that reality. The human person is in relationships to the material world, to other persons, to groups of persons and to God. These relationships can be characterized as associations of solidarity (a being with), of creation (a being by) and of service (a being for).

The human person lives in relationship to the material world, to all those things which provide the possibilities and limits within which human life takes shape. There is a solidarity with the material world in that the human person and the material world share the same earth, and labor under the same needs and laws.

Human persons not only create but are created by their material world. Smog and rain can shape personal life

---

[1]It is to be noted that this paragraph #14 from *Church in the Modern World* appears to presuppose a dualistic anthropology which subjects the inferior body to a superior soul. Such dualism is not consistent with a personalist anthropology.

attitudes on a temporary or a long-term basis. The geological potential of a specific area can determine what a people values as well as the socio-economic structures. The Iowa agri-economy places a high value on the market price of corn and hogs. The inability to resolve the current economic crisis in the Midwest illustrates the limited scope of these values and socio-economic structures.

By contrast the ecological movement and the stewardship programs in Christian churches recognize that a human approach toward this material world needs to be a posture of service in contrast to exploitation.

The Creator's command to the man and the woman in Genesis 1.28 describes their relationship to the material world with the Hebrew word equivalents of "to trample on, to subdue" and "to tread (e.g. grapes), to rule over". If the words remain separated from their context, one is left with a sense of brute mastery. The context of Genesis 1 and 2, however, suggests that the man and woman as God's representatives are given the task of continuing God's creative activity against the forces of chaos. Genesis 2.15 emphasizes the latter stewardship role, namely the cultivation and care of a garden. Verses 18-20 suggest human soldiarity with the animals, as God and the created human person begin their search for a suitable partner.

The human person also lives in relationship to other persons. There is one human family whose members share the same basic human rights, duties, needs and aspirations. This being with one another becomes the foundation of human solidarity. No one is truly human until all persons have access to what is neccesary for human fulfillment (*Church in the Modern World*, #26). The truth of this statement--albeit far from the actual state of affairs--rests in the fact of human solidarity.

1 0

The human person is to a large extent created by interaction with other persons. The actual physical creation of a child results from human intercourse. This creation by others continues through engagement with family, friends and acquaintances. A most striking example along these lines is the morally controversial experiment after World War II which withheld human interaction from infants while meeting their basic human needs. The babies died in the absence of ongoing creation through human interplay. There is truth in the pop psychological cliche of the 1970's, namely, we are shaped by those who love us and by those who refuse to love us.

Service to other persons flows from fundamental openness to a personal reality. Human persons are beings for others. Since this is true of all human persons, the notion of reciprocal service is a consequence. Every human person lays claim to a response from others. It is this fundamental human need which is the beginning point of the moral system of Emmanueal Levinas.[1] The response to concrete human needs is rooted in this fundamental being for others. The Old Testament prophets (Amos 5.10-12; Isaiah 1.21-23) measured the quality of community life by response to the concrete needs of those who were powerless to demand a response, namely the poor, the widow and the orphan. In the New Testament, Jesus reminded the disciples that the Christian life was about service to one another (John 13.1-17). In a similiar vein, Mother Teresa is often quoted as having remarked that the poor of the world will be the salvation of the rich. It is in the marginal folk that need most poignantly cries out for response. If such need is not

---

[1]See R. BURGGRAEVE, *The ethical basis for a humane society according to Emmanuel Levinas,* in *Ephemerides Theologicae Lovanienses* 57 April 1981) 5-57. See also R. BURGGRAEVE, *From Self-Development to Solidarity. An Ethical Reading of Human Desire in its Socio-Political Relevance according to Emmanuel Levinas.* Leuven, 1985.

1 1

given a response, it is unlikely that less urgent and less obvious need will even be noted.

From the beginnings of Genesis, human persons are described in relationship to others. In Genesis 1.27, God creates male and female persons. Genesis 2.18-24 relates the efforts to find a suitable partner for *'adam* which culminates in the creation of man and woman from the one generic human person. The collective sense of the reflecting Jewish community supports the understanding that the human person lives in relationship to other persons.

This same understanding appears in the anthropological theology of more contemporary church documents. The whole of the second chapter in the *Church in the Modern World* addresses the community of humankind. In this chapter solidarity with, creation by and service to others are mentioned.

Although technological advances have made human interdependence more obvious (#23), the second chapter maintains that human solidarity derives from what all persons share in common. Paragraph 29 lists these commonalities as a rational soul, creation in God's likeness, the same human origin, redemption by Christ and the same divine destiny.

The chapter finds in the Trinitarian unity of divine persons an analogy for the unity of the human community, for in the gift of self to others rests the fullness of human personhood (#24). This is to say that human relationships continue the creation of human persons.

Intimately connected to the continuation of human creation is the notion of service to others. In this connection, the *Church in the Modern World* (#27) highlights the obligations to promote human life and to provide help actively to any and all persons in need, for as long as "you did it to one of the least among you, you did it to me" (Mt 25.40).

Human persons are related to other persons not only in their singularity, but also as members of groups or structured social life. Human persons are members of national and ethnic groups, of religious and political bodies as well as social and job-related organizations. The social institutions of which a human person is a part play a role in the establishment of personal identity. "She is a democrat." "He is Hispanic." "They are Cathoics." Granted, such descriptions can degenerate into stereotyping labels; more positively, however, social institutions provide an introduction to as well as a support for the living of certain values and worldviews. To this extent, these groups to which the human person is related provide the experience of solidarity.

Social structures also provide contours within which persons can live and think. If there were not an agreed- upon system of linguistic signs and meanings, communication would be impossible. Yet the same language which makes communication possible shapes the human people who use it and in some way limits their grasp of the world. If there would not be an identifiable political system, public life in common would be severely hindered. In this regard, Hobbes' remark that life without government is nasty, brutish and short is not to be taken lightly. Yet again the very political system which makes public life in common possible, shapes its citizens and limits their ability to comprehend another way of structuring public life. The fact remains: no one stands outside of social structures nor can one. One can't be a generic anybody; one must be a specific somebody. To be a specific somebody includes the possibilities and the limits offered within the given social structures. Thus, human persons are created by the groups to which they are related.

In addition, the relationships of human persons to groups entail service. Classical moral thought spoke of general justice as the 'what is due' to the whole on the part of the individual person. Taxes, obedience to legitimate authority and some

13

exercise of personal abilities for the common good traditionally had been included among the dictates of general justice.

Contemporary moral theology prefers to use the more inclusive terms social justice and common good. These terms focus on the structures of the whole of social living and include the interrelationship of social institutions rather than only the specific person's obligation to the whole. The common good is described by the *Church in the Modern World* as "the sum of those conditions of social life which allow social groups and their individual members relatively thorough and ready access to their own fulfillment" (#26). As such, the common good involves the rights, duties, needs and legitimate aspirations of individual persons and social groups as well as efforts by persons and groups to provide such fundamental concerns. This understanding of the common good including human persons and institutional structures is the concern of social justice.[1] Thus, current moral theology conceives of the service aspect of the human person as relating to institutional groups in its contemporary complexity.

Beginning with the story of Abraham and Sarah, the Judeo-Christian scriptures are concerned with the formation of a people and their life in common. God's self-revelation to the ancestors is not for the purpose of individual religious experience, but for the establishment of a covenant with a people. The foundational Sinai covenant was concerned with the common life of the people. The same concern was evident in the good news of Jesus. Jesus came to a people, taught a people and sent the Spirit to a people. The Sermon on the

---

[1] See M. ELSBERND, *Papal Statements on Rights: a historical, contextual study of encyclical teaching from Pius VI to Pius XI (1791-1939)*, unpublished doctoral dissertation, Leuven, Belgium, 1985, 595-603. The dissertation is available through University Microfilms, Ann Arbor, MI.

Mount, the parables and the letters of the early church all pertain to living as members of Christian communities.

This consideration is not absent from current church documents. The *Church in the Modern World* holds that social institutions are essential for human development; in fact, human development is the purpose of societal structures (#25). The document further describes the service which the human person must render to groups in terms of responsibility and participation (#31).

Finally, the human person is in relationship to God. To be a human person is to be in relationship to the transcendent, that which goes beyond empirical proof. The articulation of the transcendent reality is a matter of religious expression, although the elements of creation, solidarity and service are threaded throughout the various religious traditions.

In the Judeo-Christian tradition, the human person is continually being formed by the hand of a creator God whose name Yahweh, "I-am-with-you" (Exodus 3.14), connotes a being for the people, that is, service. In Jesus, this transcendent God becomes Emmanuel, "God-with-us" (Matthew 1.23) or solidarity.

There is a mutuality about all of these relationships. The human person's experience and understanding of the transcendent begins a dialogue within which the transcendent can freely relate to that person. The Judeo-Christian covenant response to a loving God emphasizes service to the God whose love liberates (Exodus 20; Isaiah 11). Not only is Jesus God-with-us, but also those who believe become one with God in the Spirit of Jesus (1 Corinthians 12; John 14). Denying a transcendent dimension--or misunderstanding it- -does not change the reality that the human person lives in relationship to the transcendent.

The human person is historical in the sense that every particular human life occurs in a specific time and place. This specific decade in the United States provides a locus for certain values and worldviews which would not fit at another time or place. The fact of Hiroshima and Vietnam as well as the Peace Corps and African Aid are aspects of the American identity which cannot be consigned to oblivion. Technical advances in medicine and communications media create problems and potentialities unknown before this time. Contemporary life and its essential effect on ecclesial life were recognized by Vatican Council II in the watershed call to scrutinize the "signs of the times", to acknowledge, as well as to understand this world, "its expectations, its longings, and its often dramatic characteristics" (*Church in the Modern World*, #4).

Not only as part of a historical culture, but on a personal level, human life unfolds through a temporal series of particular choices and actions: personal options, career alternatives, attitudes and life preferences. One decision closes off some options and opens still others. The choice to be a teacher, for example, excludes other careers, but opens possibilities for continuing education and many contacts with people. One cannot be all things to all people all of the time in a kind of ahistorical illusion. Persons are temporized by their own specific determinations and values. The dimension of historicity affirms the concreteness of human life. It encourages the human person to put aside an ideal dream world for life and labor in the here and now.

It is this now of which Paul speaks: "Behold, now is a very acceptable time; behold, now is the day of salvation." (2 Corinthians 6.2). The here and now with its concrete irreconciliation and lack of grace is the material awaiting personal and cosmic efforts of redeeming love. This is in part the wondrous mystery of incarnation: in Jesus, the transcendent God becomes a historical reality. Especially since Jesus, "The joys and the hopes, the griefs and the anxieties of the men [sic] of this age, especially those who are poor or in any

16

way afflicted, these too are the joys and hopes, the griefs and anxieties of the followers of Christ. Indeed, nothing genuinely human fails to raise an echo in their hearts." (*Church in the Modern World*, #1). Jesus, as God-with-us, unfolded a specific Jewish existence through personal choices in a time when Rome controlled a small area which was home for shepherds, fishing folk and artisans. Jesus' living in this specific historical setting meant salvation for the people. Personal historicity in these times holds no less potential.

Human persons are fundamentally equal in their originality. This final dimension of the human person affirms a fundamental similarity of persons and a basic uniqueness of each person. Some philosophies described this shared sameness as 'human nature' or as the 'human condition'. In this connection the *Church in the Modern World* refers to a law written in the heart of every person (#16) and claims a "basic equality of all" based on a same nature, destiny and redemption in Christ (#29). This equality, it maintains, calls for an end to discrimination or violation of basic human rights. All of these terms recognize that the other is also a knowing, willing, feeling, acting subject just as the "I". The other is neighbor, colleague and equal.

Human persons, however, are original or unique. One person is not a carbon copy or a clone of all others or even one other. Even genetically identical twins are original persons because of their individual subjectivity, relationships and personal historicity. All persons have their own combination of talents, tendencies and skills or, in the thought of the *Church in the Modern World*, variations in "physical power and the diversity of intellectual and moral resources" (#29). The Genesis 1 affirmation of the goodness of the man and the woman in the wake of their creation appears to be an initial recognition of a fundamental worth and equality in personal originality.

This dimension argues that the human person, as well as being a subject, is also an other. As fundamentally equal in originality, the other claims a response of respect and recognition of the dignity due to equals. The mutuality of recognition and respect among persons fundamentally equal in originality provides a framework for social interaction. The response to equals, however, does not imply the exact same treatment but rather dealing with the other in a way appropriate to the originality of the person. A response arising from the sense that a hearing-impaired person is fundamentally equal in originality would seek ways to enhance interpersonal communication. The specific means, however, would probably not include the same methods used with hearing persons.

It is this dignity and respect of the other as fundamentally equal and original in needs which the story of the Good Samaritan salutes. The Samaritan saw in the robbed victim an equal whose specific needs called for compassionate action.

3. Implications for Christian Peacemakers

Toward the end of the last of his *Four Quartets,* T.S. Eliot reflects:[1]

> We shall not cease from exploration
> And the end of all our exploring
> Will be to arrive where we started
> And know the place for the first time.

We are reaching this end of all our exploring in seeking to understand the human person according to Scripture and a personalist anthropology. It is probable that this exploration has brought readers back to their own long- standing, intuitive

---

[1] T.S. ELIOT, *Little Gidding,* in T.S. ELIOT, *The Complete Poems and Plays, 1901-1950,* New York, 1952, 145.

understanding of what it means to be a human person. The first time freshness of this place would seem to rest not only in bringing intuition to conscious articulation but also in suggesting some specific implications for peacemaking.

The biblical stories affirm the sense of the human heart that peace is our original way of living. The human person is created for harmonious relationships and generous living. The grassroots peace movements and inner hunger for personal or international peace can be seen as contemporary expressions of that perennial sense of the human heart. Peacemakers welcome that age-old longing as the energy which can move persons, peoples and their leaders from whatever present state of unrest toward the hard work of peacemaking.

The Genesis accounts of disharmony brought about by freely chosen human sin challenges peacemakers to see the lack of peace as a human choice. God is a God of peace, not chaos; God is a God of loving relationships, not interpersonal discord. Individually and collectively, human persons making human choices continue to create the events shaping the current situation. This realization holds more promise than despair. If cumulative human choice for disharmony brought about this current historical situation, then it would seem that human re-choosing to continue the creation of God can bring about another historical situation, namely a world at peace. This remains the hope and the challenge for peacemakers.

Because peacemakers and other human persons are corporeal people, peace is not a mere feeling of interior well-being. Peace is an exterior, incarnate reality. It is not enough to seek the end to inner tensions and the personal management of conflict. Peace has an objective dimension which demands embodiment in concrete situations.

Similarly, peacemakers and other human persons are relational beings. In this light, peace is a relational reality. It is a quality of relationship between persons and between groups or nations. Peace is less about withdrawal from conflict and more about its resolution. Peace is legitimately concerned with peaceful conflict resolution and with skills for nonviolent resistance. The relational dimension also suggests that peacemakers need to gather together as persons and as groups for the promotion of peace. Such cooperation can allow all persons to offer their abilities to the fulfillment of the whole effort.

The historicity of the human person requires that peacemakers involve themselves in their own concrete time and place. Personal unrest and involvement, my family, my church and my community are the beginning points. Those specific givens--community apathy, personal fear, unjust laws, violent responses--call out for peace. It is often easier to dream of the end of international wars than to negotiate personal truces within the family or among colleagues. It is the precise circumstances of family and community with which the peacemaker is most familiar. Such expertise can advance effective alternatives and permanent commitment.

Finally, awareness that human persons are in part determined by the groups to which they belong and the times in which they live can facilitate an examination of the structures of living. There are structural ways of thinking, for example the division of reality into us and them, which we need to transcend if peace is to become a reality. There are presuppositions, for example the inferiority of certain ethnic or sexual groups, which need to be set aside if peace is to live. There are patterned behaviors, for example verbal abuse or silent withdrawal, which need to be avoided if peace is to function. An awareness of those structures of thinking or acting which damage peace can allow for their transformation into personal and social structures supportive of peace.

In the beginning, God created a peaceable world from chaos. The creator God is a God of peace who has entrusted the re-creation of a peaceable world to the peacemakers. The same creator God has written peace in our hearts and in the fabric of our being.

```
        P
        E
  P E A C E
        C
        E
```

Roman Catholic Church Documents
Official Roman Catholic teaching in the twentieth century has addressed issues in this chapter. The following selections are particularly pertinent.

Church in the Modern World, #12-17
What are the essential elements in the conciliar understanding of a Christian anthropology?

Church in the Modern World, #23-32
1. According to these paragraphs, what are the bases for the solidarity of all peoples?
2. What principles guiding Christian action toward other persons and groups of persons flow from the solidarity of peoples?

Challenge of Peace, #27-29
What are the three conditions outlined for the use of scripture when addressing a theology of peace?

Other Suggested Readings

BERGANT, D. *Peace in a Universe of Order,* in J.T. PAWLIKOWSKI and D. SENIOR (ed.), *Biblical and Theological Reflections on the Challenge of Peace* (Theology and Life, 10). Wilmington, DL, 1984, 17-29.

JEGEN, M.E. *A Buddist Peace Discipline for Christians,* in *Sisters Today* 58 (April 1982) 451-458.

TRAINOR, B. *The Politics of Peace. The Role of the Political covenant is Hobbes's Leviathan,* in *Review of Politics* 47 (July 1985) 347-369 is based on a radically different anthropology than the one presented here.

UNITED METHODIST BISHOPS, *In defense of creation. The nuclear crisis and a just peace,* in *Origins* 16 (May 29, 1986) 20-26.

Audio-visual Materials

The following are some of the audio-visual materials which are related to the chapter content. The list is not exhaustive, but is intended to give some initial suggestions for previewing.

1. **Book of Genesis: Creation** (Video; 14m; Genesis Project; 1980) depicts the first story of creation through realistic photograph and special effects.

2. **Cosmos** (video; 20m; Beyond War; 1984) presents a evolutionary process of creation and asks the question, is this marvel of creation to end in nuclear destruction.

3. **For Life. Christian Peacemaking in a Nuclear Age** (slides/tape; 29m; Sojourners; 1984) moves from creation beginnings through the history of human choices to kill and destroy. It ends with the hope that Christian people can and will turn death-dealing decisions to life-giving decisions.

4. **If the World goes away, where will the Children Play?** (video; 45m; Peace Productions; 1984) is an allegory which mimes the path from creation to uncreation with the message that peace must be human choice.

Introductory activities

The purpose of the introductory activity is to begin discussion on an understanding of peace as well as to allow the students/participants a chance to express what their previous experiences and understandings of peace have been.

1. What does it mean to be "at peace"?

2. What personal experiences brought the students/
participants to this class or workshop?
3. What is an experience of peacemaking for the students/
participants?

Discussion Questions

The purpose of the discussion questions is to encourage
students/participants to integrate the text and/or presented
material into their own thinking and living.

1. How do the biblical accounts of creation and the fall fit with
contemporary experiences of peace with which the class
began?
2. How does the understanding of what it means to be human
affect an understanding of peace?
3. Evaluate the personalist anthropology as presented with
other current, operative understandings of what it means to be
human.
4. What are other implications for peacemaking in addition to
the ones mentioned in the text?
5. Evaluate the creation accounts and a personalist
anthropology as the beginning points for a theology of peace.

Activities for application and integration

The following suggested activities provide opportunities for
students/participants to carry the concepts of this chapter
beyond the classroom. They are intended to clarify and
integrate understandings into their lived experience.

1. Collect ten to twelve advertisements from newspapers,
magazines or television. Analyse them as to the understanding
of the human person which is portrayed. Evaluate the
portrayed understandings for their potential for peacemaking.

2. Interview eight to ten persons on their experiences of peace.
Examine their responses for common experiences. Do these

2. Interview eight to ten persons on their experiences of peace. Examine their responses for common experiences. Do these experiences give some evidence for the "sense of the human heart" that human persons are created in peace, for peace?

3. After due thought, write a two or three page paper on your own understanding of what it means to be a human person. Compare it with the personalist anthropology presented. What are the implications for peace following from your own anthropology?

Spirituality Component

It is one thing to read and study about a theology of peace and quite another to become a person of peace. This spirituality component offers a series of Scripture readings with reflection questions which are closely aligned with the chapter topic. It is suggested that they be used for prayer and reflection over a series of days. The reader may wish either to find another Christian with whom the prayer and its fruit may be shared regularly or to journal one's growth in peacemaking.

DAY 1: Genesis 1.1-25
The creation story affirms the goodness of God's creation. How do I affirm that goodness?

DAY 2: Genesis 1.26-27
God is a God of peace. I am created in that image of God. How do I, how can I reflect the God of peace in my life?

DAY 3: Genesis 1.28-31
How can my stewardship of material things reflect the peace of creation?

DAY 4: Genesis 2:4b-20
How am I living in peace and harmony with the created world?

DAY 6: Ezekial 34. 25-31
How have I experienced God's covenant of peace with me and the people?

DAY 7: Genesis 3.1-21
Genesis 3 suggests that the cause of disharmony in the world and among human persons comes from sinful decisions. How have I experienced that disharmony due to my sinful decisons? How have I experienced God's care for me even in sin?

CHAPTER 2
THE VISION, THE CITY, THE ROAD

The first federal celebration of the birth of Martin Luther King caught me off guard. In the preceding January weeks, I witnessed the enthusiasm of a colleague who was instrumental in hosting a concert marking the event. In the Sunday edition of the local newspaper, I saw the pictures of Montgomery, Selma, Birmingham and read for the first time in years that moving speech, "I have a dream...". During the evening news there was a newsclip "I have a dream..." nudging my own dream-making intuition. In the evening the narrator of the Mt. Zion Baptist Consecrated Choir delivered an inspirited rendition of "I have a dream...". The power of the words, the passion of the speaker and the ongoing audience acclaims were impressing onto my heart the desire for a dream. I wanted a dream. I wanted a dream which could call me out of the future, draw me onward and enable me to live my life from its vividness. The next day I began to give words to this vision of peace as it is found in the Christian and Hebrew scriptures. May it be a vision capable of calling the Christian community onward to the reign of peace. May it realize the vision in its daily living.

* * *

1. The Biblical Vision of Peace

Biblical authors have written down a number of the visions of peace emerging from the communities of Israel and from the early Christian churches. The Biblical visions of peace focus on

27

three images, namely, shalom, the new Jerusalem and the reign of God.

Shalom

As a scriptural image of peace, shalom is more than the Hebrew equivalent of hello. Shalom addresses the fundamental order in human relationships with the physical world, other persons both individually and collectively, oneself and God. Peace reigns when the whole world and all its parts are in right relationship. Shalom evokes an image of harmonious interrelationships, order and cooperative interdependence.

The heart of shalom is the covenant relationship of Yahweh and the people:"they shall be my people, and I will be their God, with faithfulness and justice" (Zechariah 8.8). The whole of chapter 8 is a description of the Messianic reign of peace. The chapter ends (vv20-23) with the image of God's dwelling among the people and their mediation of that presence to the nations seeking the favor of the God of Israel. In Isaiah 2.2-5 it is the word of Yahweh among the people which instructs the nations to beat their swords into plowshares and their spears into pruning hooks. Shalom results when the peoples walk in the light of Yahweh. Thus a right relationship with God seems prerequisite to peace.

The image of shalom includes a sense of personal well-being. Personal well-being is not to be confused with 'peace of mind'. The Hebrew community did not separate the person into body, mind, soul, but rather envisioned wholeness, a well-being of the whole person. This well-being showed itself in a number of ways. People will grow old since their lives will not be shortened by war or famine or disease (Zechariah 8.4; Isaiah 65.20). There will be no sorrow or pain, for their causes will have vanished (Isaiah 65.19; Revelation 21.4). Not only will there be children born, but these children will live in peace and not die in wars or other destruction (Isaiah 65.23; Zechariah

28

8.5). In a reversal of the curse in Genesis 3.17, human labor and toil will not be in vain, but will bring forth fruitfulness (Isaiah 65.21-23; Zechariah 8.12). The passages in Zechariah 8 and Isaiah 65 present the picture of a long lasting secure home in which needs are met and a future of peace rests assured.

Shalom is not only personal well-being and right relationship with God. Shalom, as it is used in the Hebrew scriptures, is reflected in relationships of the socio-political community. The Hebrew authors address relationships between individuals. Thus Zechariah's description of the Messianic reign of peace admonished, "These then are the things you should do: Speak the truth to one another; let there be honesty and peace in the judgments at your gates, and let none of you plot evil against another in his heart, nor love a false oath" (Zechariah 8.16-17a). Even this passage, however, suggests that the more basic concern is the structures and quality of social life. Peace is a result of honest judgments in community disputes. There is no room for injustice when peace reigns.

In chapter 9.9b-10b, Zechariah describes the establishment of the reign of peace by a king:
> a just saviour is he,
Meek, and riding on an ass,
> on a colt, the foal of an ass.
He shall banish the chariot from Ephraim
> and the horse from Jerusalem;
The warrior's bow shall be banished,
> and he shall proclaim peace to the nations.

These verses have a twofold significance. First, peace is associated with political leadership. Shalom has socio-political visibility. It is not merely an inner personal harmony. The socio-political context of peace is also apparent in the frequent mention of right relationships among the nations--peace--in the visions of the Messianic reign (Isaiah 2.2-5; Zechariah 8.20-23 and 9.9-10). Matthew's beatitudes frame the

29

charter of the Christian life (Matthew 5.3-10) with reference to the reign of God.

The second significance of Zechariah's remarks rests in the description of the qualities of the peace ruler as a saviour from oppression, meek, riding an animal used not by warriors but by farmers and merchants. Thus Zechariah connects the reign of peace to justice instead of oppression, to meekness instead of violent domination, and to agriculture and commerce not industries of war. Thus, shalom makes itself visible in socio-political communities when truth, honesty and justice are encouraged by the social structures as well as by its leadership.

Shalom is also determinative of the whole cosmic order to which both Isaiah and the Book of Revelation refer as a "new heavens and a new earth" (Isaiah 65.17 and Revelations 21.1). It will be a time of cosmic harmony when "the wolf and lamb shall graze alike, and the lion shall eat hay like the ox" (Isaiah 65.25). Zechariah describes the cosmic order in terms of the vine and land sharing their crops, while the heavens provide the rain (Zechariah 8.12).

Thus even the heavens, the land and animals contribute to a harmonious ordering of all relationships. When Yahweh is the God of the nations, then shalom can be known in personal well-being, in socio-political life and in the cosmic world. This rich, wholistic image of peace has its origins in the Hebrew scriptures and provides a backdrop with which to understand peace as described in the Christian scriptures as well as in the *Church in the Modern World*, paragraph 39.

The new Jerusalem

The second biblical image of peace has its roots in both Jewish and Christian scriptures. Reference to a peaceful scene often conjures up in the contemporary American mind an idyllic natural scene complete with mountains, forests and streams. The city for Americans means business, traffic, entertainment opportunities, hectic multitudes. Few people head downtown to experience peace. Perhaps the apparent incongruity of a city, the new Jerusalem, as an image of peace is the heart of the vision.

The etymology of the name Jerusalem is not certain. *Jeru* is translated as *city of* or *foundation of*. *Salem* has popularly been connected with the Hebrew word *shalom*. Contemporary scholarship, however, sees a probable reference to an ancient god named Salem. The Genesis 14 story of Abraham's meeting with Melchizedek, king of Salem, links Israel's ties to Jerusalem back to its beginnings as a people. This connection is more firmly established in King David, who captured Jerusalem from the Jebusites and established it as the political and religious center of the Jewish people (2 Samuel 5.6-12). The kings of Judah dwelt there; the temple and the ark of Yahweh's presence dwelt there. When Israel turned from Yahweh to other gods, the glory of God left the temple (Ezekial 10.18-19) and the people were carried off into exile. During the exile Jerusalem was neither the religious nor the political center of the people. Thus, in the history of Israel, Jerusalem was a reality become symbol of Israel in its religious and political establishment.

It is against this background that the prophets describe the new city Jerusalem. As part of the description of the messianic reign, Isaiah includes the promise of the new Jerusalem created by the faithful God of Israel (Isaiah 65.18). Zechariah emphasizes that in the messianic age, God will bring the people home to Jerusalem and dwell there with them (Zechariah 8.8). Jerusalem is the mutual home of the Israelite people and Yahweh, their God. Thus, the new Jerusalem is the city of rejoicing and delight (Zechariah 9.9;Isaiah 65.18). In addition, Jerusalem is the home of God's word and instruction for the nations (Isaiah 2.2-3). The author of Revelation picks up on these themes in its description of the eschatological reign of the Lamb. In Revelation 21, Jerusalem is the new, holy creation of God. There God will dwell among the people. It is a city whose beauty and joy can only be envisioned. All nations and rulers shall walk by its light which is none other than the presence of God among the people (Revelation 21).

Jerusalem is a biblical image of peace. As a city, it requires the work of human hands building it with stone and mortar as well as creating a network of social relationships among the people. The new Jerusalem image stands as a reminder that peace requires human efforts in building structures and in shaping human relationships which enhance peace. The biblical image of the new Jerusalem is not mere spiritualism, but an endeavor of the political community.

As the creation of God, the peace of Jerusalem does not rely only on human effort. Peace is where God and the people dwell together in a relational and structural harmony resulting from interdependent effort. The new Jerusalem is not mere political expertise, but a Christian endeavor. The new Jerusalem as an image of peace seeks to bind human and divine efforts into an incarnational reality.

The Reign of God

A third scriptural image for peace, the reign of God (or in the gospel of Matthew, the kingdom of heaven) gives a primacy to God's role, highlights the centrality of Jesus and requires an ultimate decision from those to whom the reign of God is proclaimed. The reign of God is not estranged from some of the same notions as shalom and the new Jerusalem.

The image of peace as the reign of God gives a primacy to the place of God. It is God's reign in the human heart and in the whole world. The reign of God is identified with God's saving activity in history. The reign of God, therefore, is not a purely personal and spiritual event. Participation in the reign of God does require a personal conversion to God's will, but this conversion has definite effects in the historical situation. Paul describes the reign of God as a matter "of righteousness, peace, and joy in the holy Spirit" (Romans 14.17). The reign of God is salvation for the believer through the indwelling of God's Spirit. This saving activity of God manifests itself through communal living in peace, justice and joy. In this light, Paul adds, "Let us then pursue what leads to peace and to building up one another" (Romans 14.19). Although the context of these remarks--whether Christians can eat meat sacrificed to idols-- is quite foreign to the twentieth century, the verses still serve to connect acceptance of God's saving activity with the actual lived relationships of justice and peace. Peace is therefore an expression of the presence of God's saving activity.

Jesus is the singular presence of God's saving activity in history. The gospel of Mark begins with Jesus proclaiming the good news of God, "This is the time of fulfillment. The kingdom of God is at hand" (Mark 1.15). Jesus is the inbreaking of the reign of God. Jesus is the dawning of the end times when the peace of creation will be recreated in the fullness of human and cosmic acceptance. What Jesus lived and chose as a singular person, all peoples are called to live and to choose until the beautiful, peaceful, good creation of God has become the free intentional choice of the collectivity of human persons.

The inbreaking of the reign of God in Jesus is connected to some specific signs. Luke places the proclamation of Jesus in the synagogue of Nazareth at the beginning of Jesus' ministry as a kind of announcement of the forthcoming ministerial program (Luke 4.18-19):

> The Spirit of the Lord is upon me,
> because he has anointed me
> to bring glad tidings to the poor.
> He has sent me to proclaim liberty to captives,
> and recovery of sight to the blind,
> to let the oppressed go free,
> and to proclaim a year acceptable to the Lord.

Jesus' programmatic address at Nazareth centers on liberation and healing into wholeness. The latter touches on the function of the healing miracles in the gospels. It has already been seen that shalom means wholeness. The healing into wholeness which the miracles accomplished becomes a sign of the inbreaking of the final messianic reign of peace (Matthew 11.5) Likewise, the liberation of captives, the release of prisoners and the announcement of the jubilee year for debtors and renters meant a wholeness on a socio-political as well as a personal level. The rest of chapter four in Luke's gospel relates the stories of Jesus both announcing the good news of the reign of God (Luke 4.43) and healing demonics, Peter's mother-in-law and others with a variety of illnesses.

Chapter five adds yet another sign of the inbreaking of the reign of peace, the forgiveness of sin. In the story of the paralyzed man, Jesus makes it clear that the forgivenss of sin and healing are both signs that God is present on earth in Jesus (Luke 5.17-26). Matthew likens the reign of God to the king who forgave the debt of an official who did not reciprocate forgiveness for someone else (Matthew 18.23-35). In the reign of God present in Jesus, the peoples have been forgiven their debts. Not all have recognized the reign of God nor received forgiveness. After the resurrection, the peace of the risen Jesus is also associated with the forgiveness of sin (John 20.19-23). With the forgiveness of sin, Jesus illustrates the reconciliation of human persons with God and the recreation of the primal relationship of peace between creator and creature.

Finally the inbreaking of the reign of God is identified with doing the will of God. Jesus says, "I came down from heaven not to do my own will but the will of the one who sent me" (John 6.38). Or again, "Not everyone who says to me 'Lord, Lord' will enter the kingdom of heaven, but only the one who does the will of my Father in heaven" (Matthew 7.21). Jesus teaches the disciples to pray (Matthew 6.10):
your kingdom come,

>   your will be done
>   on earth as in heaven

The will of God seems identified with a reign of peace begun by the healing and forgiving ministry of Jesus.

The inbreaking of the reign of God in Jesus was not connected with the socio-political advent of Israel's reign over the nations, as had been expected of the Davidic messiah (Isaiah 9.1-6 and 11.1-9). Rather Jesus was a suffering servant, the unrecognized messiah whose punishment brings peace, whose wounds bring healing (Isaiah 53.5). Matthew addresses these unpretentious beginnings of the reign of God in Jesus through the parables of the mustard seed and the yeast (Matthew 13.31-33). The present but unacknowledged beginning of a single mustard seed for the mature shrub or a bit of yeast for the mass of dough is likened to the inauguration in Jesus of the reign of God in its fullness. Jesus, the suffering servant accustomed to infirmity (Isaiah 53.3), was spurned and rejected as the probable inbreaking of the reign of God. Yet Jesus did the will of God, forgave sins, healed persons into wholeness and brought peoples into liberation. In the life of Jesus, the peace of creation was recreated as a vision of how all peoples were invited to live.

The invitation into the reign of God as proclaimed by Jesus required a fundamental option of acceptance or rejection. In the parables about the reign of God, Matthew addresses the nature of this decision. The parable of the weeds and wheat illustrates that those who reject the reign of God are liable to judgement (Matthew 13.24-30 and 36-43). The parables of the buried treasure and the pearl of great price show that the reign of God requires total commitment (Matthew 13.44-46). The parable of the sower points out that the invitation requires understanding and a response.

The Sermon on the Mount and the beatitudes in particular describe what a response to this invitation entails:
>   Blessed are the poor in spirit,

> for theirs is the kingdom of heaven.
> Blessed are they who mourn,
>> for they will be comforted.
> Blessed are the meek,
>> for they will inherit the land.
> Blessed are they who hunger and thirst for righteousness,
>> for they will be satisfied.
> Blessed are the merciful,
>> for they will be shown mercy.
> Blessed are the clean of heart,
>> for they will see God.
> Blessed are the peacemakers,
>> for they will be called children of God.
> Blessed are they who are persecuted for
>> the sake of righteousness,
>> for theirs is the kingdom of heaven (Matthew 5.3-10).

The reference to the reign of God in the first and last beatitudes make it clear that the beatitudes are describing one who has accepted the invitation. An option for the reign of God involves conversion of heart. No longer is self-righteousness the norm but a radical trust in God's saving activity. Poverty of spirit, lowliness, hunger and thirst for justice as well as single-heartedness are attitudes which enable people to rely on God's righteousness. Sorrowing, mercy and peacemaking are the way God deals with human folk. In fact, peacemaking is viewed so much as divine activity that those who make peace are called sons and daughters of God. Those who accept the invitation to the reign of God are enabled to do what God does, with the knowledge that persecution is the most probable response from those who do not understand the invitation.

As a vision of peace, the reign of God suggests the integral nature of peacemaking to the gospel message. The inbreaking of the reign of God into this world in the person of Jesus meant peacemaking. Jesus did the will of God in healing broken bodies and spirits into wholeness. Today, as in the time of Jesus, apparently unpretentious people proclaim this gospel message.

Today, as in the time of Jesus, the message is met with rejection and persecution. Today, as in the time of Jesus, the gospel demands a response of conversion from self- righteousness and a commitment to do what God does: weap, show mercy and make peace.

The Judeo-Christian tradition in Scripture does present a vision of peace in the metaphors of shalom, the new Jerusalem and the reign of God. Peace is where basic human needs are met and human well-being in its social as well as personal aspects is encouraged. Peace is when social structures and personal interaction are founded on justice. Peace is a stewardship with the world and its resources. Peace is the active acknowledgement of the immanent presence of God dwelling in and among the peoples of the earth. The same God who calls the community from the future reign of peace to peacemaking in the cities today also inspires and even enables the human project. Precisely because the Christian tradition of peace makes room for the God of peace, the incarnate reign of peace emerges as a radically new creation beyond the coexistence and compromise which these times know. The establishment of this reign of peace is not yet fulfilled, but awaits its completion through the human community in which God dwells.

2. The Role of a Vision

For some time now poets and songwriters have given expression to the significance of a vision in life. The lyrics of *Happy Talk* from the musical South Pacific muse, "If you don't have a dream, how you gonna make a dream come true?" Diana Ross questions, "Do you know where you're going to?" Tim McAllister in the 1970's proclaimed more positively, "We'll just say that we've been to the mountain and caught of glimpse of all that we could be". On the other hand, when such a sense is absent, one can be described as aimless or directionless. As one author put it, "If you don't know where you're going, you'll probably end up somewhere else". Langston Hughes[1] said it this way:

> Hold fast to dreams
> For if dreams die
> Life is a brokenwinged bird
> That cannot fly.
>
> Hold fast to dreams
> For when dreams go
> Life is a barren field
> Frozen with snow.

When the activities which fill up one's day don't seem to be going anywhere, life itself appears listless, even wasteful. It is goals, dreams, a vision which give significance to daily living.

A vision can be a motivating force toward its realization. Students who have a clear image of their career goals are more able to put up with the inconveniences of course demands and the academic requirements. Their goals beckon them onward. A vision of the kind of person one wants to be can become the motivation behind rigorous health programs, personal growth projects or Lenten discipline.

For the Christian the same God who created us, dwells in human hearts, and calls us into the future. God's promise in creation is the vision which draws the peacemaker on into its realization. The biblical vision of peace as a socio-political event provides the motivation for involvement in peacemaking activities in the personal, social, national and international spheres.

A vision of peace, however, can be more than motivation. Indeed, it must be more, for overwhelming obstacles can paralyze motivation. It seems that the vision of a Martin

---

[1]L. HUGHES, *Dreams*, in *The Dreamkeeper and Other Poems*, New York, 1932, 7.

Luther King or a Ghandi did more than motivate. It was able to energize and empower thousands of people as they worked for equal rights. Even after their untimely deaths, that vision continues to draw persons into the power of love and nonviolent resistance. In some sense a vision has a life of its own and thus can inspire or energize.

For the Christian, the vision of peace as reconciliation or life in the city of God has its empowerment in the Spirit who dwells among and within the citizens.

A vision also functions something like a yardstick measuring present efforts as to their potential to embody the vision of peace. Will this tactic prepare the way for the incarnation of peace? Is this idea in keeping with peace or is it a short-term substitute, an ideology, a temporary movement? Is this attitude supportive of the vision or is it a private agreement, a compromise peace of sorts?

The peace described in Scripture is not an ethereal dream nor peace of mind. It rather stands as the reality of God's city constructed on justice. There, on the horizon of Christian life, it invites the peacemaker to walk toward it. As that objective reality the vision measures current efforts at peace. That is not all. The vision of peace also dwells in hearts as an energy, a power enabling its enfleshment in this day and age.

3. Implications for Christian Peacemakers

The experience of a tension between the Christian vision of peace and the present state of affairs is not surprising. Christianity is life at the intersection of apparent irreconcilability. Christians have died with Christ so as to live in Christ. The creator God dwells in the believers' hearts. Jesus is fully human and fully divine. Christians already live in God's life of grace and yet are sojourners on the way home to be with God.

In the attempt to resolve this fundamental Christian tension, there are three possible positions. The vision of peace can be interpretated as an endtime reality only, with little visible effect on the contemporary course of events. There will be a new city Jerusalem where shalom will reign and reconciliation will be the standard for relationships. But that is only a future hope remaining before the Christian much like the mechanical rabbit ahead of the pack of racing greyhounds. This position aims at reducing the Christian tension by emphasizing the futurity of peace and thus diminishing the stress for action on behalf of peace in the socio-political structures.

The other extreme position claims that the reign of peace is already fulfilled in the midst of millennial communities of Christians. Such communities are often small and isolated from socio- political structures and life. This position aims at reducing the Christian tension by emphasizing a past realization of peace in a particular religious communal manifestation. Thus, the norm for these Christians is separation, not involvement in contemporary efforts at enfleshing the peace of Jesus.

The final position dares continuously to struggle with the tension rather than reduce it. The vision of peace is an eschatological reality with present implications, even though immediate results may be less apparent. Through their baptism Christians are an eschatological people. Thus, the Christian life is a commitment to life at the intersection of divine and human, of already and not yet, of gift given and task mandated. Baptism celebrates the gift of God's indwelling life and the task of bringing the reign of God to completion. The baptized live in their very persons the tension of intersection.

In addition to the normal human tensions of body-person and person-in-community, the Christian embodies yet another dynamic tension not so readily acknowledged. Christians proclaim that this world is 'shot through' with the glory of God. They announce that God lives in and among the apparently human figures who walk the earth. The baptized are reminders that these are the end times into which God's reign of peace is inbreaking. Those who live this incarnation intersection seek to prepare the way for the fulfillment of a life into which they are already immersed.

When the vision of peace is viewed as an eschatological reality with present implications, the mystery of the incarnation itself is affirmed. The Christian vision of peace is a religious vision to be enacted in this historical world. The structures, the events, the 'stuff' of this world are taken seriously. The United States Bishops' pastoral on peace approached this position when it stated, "There is an urgent moral and political responsibility to use the 'peace of a sort' we have as a framework to move toward authentic peace..."(*Challenge of Peace* #189). The beginning point of Christian peace is the existent structures and events. The peacemaker cannot dismiss the decisions of the 1980's as so much refuse to be carried off in the weekly pickup service. Peace--true peace--can come out of this chaos only as it is reshaped by the hands of peace. It was human hands which created the events and structures in existence today. It will be incarnate hands which recreate these events and structures into carriers of peace. It is not enough that peacemakers form isolated groups to bemoan wars and rumors of wars. Nor is 'peace of mind' awaiting the final day sufficient. The biblical vision of peace begs, even demands, enfleshment in and through the 'stuff' of this world.

Thus, beginning with the situations in which they live and work, Christians through their baptism are called and empowered to make the reign of peace present in this world. God's reign of peace has its fulfillment in the future, but the people can hasten its dawning by building the road to meet it. The vision remains on the horizon ahead, beckoning, enabling and measuring the efforts of the peacemaker. But the road between here and there is not constructed. It may not even be surveyed. Can peacemakers become a road construction crew?

To build the road welcoming peace, the peacemaker must have a clear sense of the biblical vision of peace. Unlike the fixed and present point of reference from which a modern road crew surveys its direction, peacemakers chart their course from the vision ahead of them. It is more like the star by which the magi charted their course. All too often, there is no vision of peace to direct negotiations or peace conferences. A 'peace of sorts' is the outcome when wars and mediations are the beginning point of peace efforts. Interpersonal and international decisions require a vision of peace to shape the wilderness of living and attitudes into the road to the city of God. When such a vision recedes into absence, then--as the life image of Langston Hughes states--peace becomes broken and barren.

The vision, however, cannot remain only an external point of reference. God's vision of peace has to enter the lifeveins and the heartcore of the person until peace becomes the dynamic center out of which one lives. Peacemaking is then a way of life, not a program. Peacemaking becomes personal expression of conversion, not this year's movement. When that core is led by the biblical vision of peace, then peacemaking is an incarnational activity.

Once the vision is clear and internalized, the possibility emerges that one can and is willing to act on behalf of peace, to be an advocate of peace. Peacemaking is not passivity; it is the ability to respond to a vision. As such it is directed outward toward persons and situations. Peacemaking is less about feeling good inside than it is about establishing honest relationships with the persons and groups which make up life's environment.

The biblical vision of peace has been firmly established in a socio-political context which includes not only social relationships but socio-political structures itself. At some point, peacemaking becomes insufficient when it occurs within a network of human relationships which are oblivious to those structures causing the destruction or absence of peace. It is good to care for the recurrent illness of a friend, but would it not be better to seek the cause of the recurrence. Likewise, the Christian peacemaker must address the structures which promote disharmony and inequity.

Today's crisis of peace results in part from the failure to measure specific steps or tactics in light of the vision. Few people would disclaim a desire for peace. How many people, however, examine a particular action or attitude in terms of its potential for peace? How often are the daily annoyances and frustrations approached with an eye on peace? How often are the conflicts among family and friends resolved so that peace may reign instead of coexistence? How many proclaim peace, then fill their days with a pace that jangles nerves and frays tempers?

Challenge of Peace addresses this tendency in its discussion of nuclear deterrence when it states, "Each proposed addition to our strategies system or change in strategies doctrine must be assessed precisely in light of whether it will render steps toward progressive disarmament more or less likely." (#188) It is granted the perceived goal appears to be disarmament, which is not necessarily equated with the biblical vision of peace. The statement, however, does recognize the necessity of examining specific steps in light of the overall goal. To acclaim a vision and then act in daily decisions without regard to it is tantamount to heading north by moving southeast.

Given the incarnational nature of Christian existence, there is a fundamental ambiguity in living toward the vision of peace. The road is not finished. An incomplete vision strives for fulfillment in an unfolding history through imperfect agents. Each of these elements adds to an ambiguity which protects the peacemaker against smug self-righteousness. The grays of this ambiguity can encourage listening hearts and humble revision of plans. Incarnational ambiguity is

43

complicated by sin, the conscious choice to be unloving in concrete situations. The choice of self-interest with the subsequent neglect of others is a reality which the vision of peace will judge as inappropriate for the city of God. Thus, the path of the peacemaker seems one of reconciling and being reconciled the whole way toward the vision.

Road construction takes months, as any summer traveler is doomed to discover. Building the way for completion of peace requires the patient plodding of a pilgrimage. Causes and even peace programs come and go. Perhaps the vision is not clear; sometimes it is worn like jeans and not wombed like the unborn child; or the programs are inconsistent with peace itself; other times the vision becomes privatized or self-righteous; but sometimes it just takes too long. Contemporary culture has come to expect instantaneous results and immediate visible effects. It is not surprising that peace takes too long. Or is it? How many years has it taken the peoples of the earth to get to this point of unpeace? Why should it take less time to recreate peace?

The reign of peace is not about easy answers; it is rather about the long process of a vision becoming enfleshed. God grant us the patience to see the vision and to become it.

```
          P
          E
P   E   A   C   E
          C
          E
```

Roman Catholic Church Documents

Official Roman Catholic teaching in the twentieth century has addressed issues in this chapter. The following selections are particularly pertinent.

Church in the Modern World, #39
1.What are the elements of the endtime reign of God as described in this paragraph?
2.What are some concrete things one can do to begin to prepare the way for this reign of peace to become a reality?

Other Suggested Readings

BOSS-KOOPMAN, G., HOOGERWERF, S.D., and WHITE, R.A. *Christ is our peace.* Lansing, IL, 1982, 1-8.

BRUEGGEMANN, W. *Living toward a vision,* in E.A. POWERS, *Signs of Shalom.* Philadelphia, 1973, 101-110.

BRUEGGEMANN, W. *Living toward a vision: Biblical reflections on Shalom.* Philadelphia, PA, 1976.

KOMONCHAK, J.A. *Kingdom, History and Church,* in P.J. MURNION, *Catholics and Nuclear War. A commentary on The Challenge of Peace.* New York, 1983, 106-115.

POWERS, E. A. *Signs of Shalom.* Philadelphia, 1973.

Audio-visual Materials

The following are some of the audio-visual materials which are related to the chapter content. The list is not exhaustive, but is intended to give some initial suggestions for previewing.

Shalom. God's vision of peace (filmstrip; 20m; Alba) presents the biblical understanding of shalom as peace, harmony, justice and wholeness for the individual and for society. Shalom is presented as a vision of the world as God intends it to be: all creation living in creative harmonious relationships.

The Time has Come (film; 27m; NARMIC; 1982) documents the June 12, 1982 march for peace in New York City.

A Church at the Service of Peace (Slide/tape; 23m; Joliet, IL Social Concerns Office, 1983) is an overview of the vision of peace presented in the U.S. Catholic Bishops' Pastoral Letter *The Challenge of Peace.*

Introductory Activities

The purpose of the introductory activity is to begin discussion on an understanding of peace as well as to allow the students/participants a chance to express what their previous experiences and understandings of peace have been.

1. Describe your vision of peace.
2. What has been your experience of peace.

Discussion Questions

The purpose of the discussion questions is to encourage students/participants to integrate the text and/or presented material into their own thinking and living.

1. In what way, if any, do the Scriptural images of peace differ from contemporary peace activities?

2. What are the risks in living a life of shalom?

3. Evalute the peace testimonies of Christian churches today.

4. What creates tension for the Christian community between the vision of peace and the situation today?

5. What might make Christians today less comfortable with an urban vision of peace like the new city Jerusalem than the Israelites in the scriptures?

6. What role have visions or goals played in your life or the lives of persons you know? What does the input on the role of the vision of peace say to your experience?

Activities for Integration and Application

The following suggested activities provide opportunities for students/participants to carry the concepts of this chapter beyond the classroom. They are intended to clarify and integrate understandings into lived experience.

1. Make a portfolio of articles from newspapers or magazines which suggest a vision of peace. Critique these visions according to the scriptural vision of peace.

2. Prepare a report (or a research paper) on peace in the Hebrew Scriptures or the Christian Scriptures.

3. Prepare a script and audio-visual materials for a five minute presentation on the vision of peace for a specific audience.

Spirituality Component

It is one thing to read and study about a theology of peace and quite another to become a person of peace. This spirituality component offers a series of Scripture readings with reflection questions which are closely aligned with the chapter topic. It is suggested that they be used for prayer and reflection over a series of days. The reader may wish either to find another Christian with whom the prayer and its fruits may be shared regularly or to journal one's growth as a peacemaker.

DAY 1:Isaiah 2.2-5:
This is Isaiah's vision of peace. What is my vision for a peaceful world?

DAY 2: Isaiah 52.13-53.12
This passage is from what is traditionally called the fourth suffering servant psalm in the book of Isaiah. What has been your experience of personal suffering bringing peace to others?

DAY 3: Isaiah 65.17-25
God's peace includes personal, material and political gifts. How do I experience personal, material and political peace in my life today?

DAY 4: Matthew 5.1-8
How in my life's relationships can I be a peacemaker?

DAY 5: Revelation 21.1-7
Which elements from this vision arouse a desire for God's vision of a world in peace?

DAY 6: Zechariah 9.9-10
This vision of peace includes an end to war. Which war in my own life do I seek to end? How can a meek saviour, riding an ass aid me in making my peace truces?

DAY 7: Zechariah 8.4-8, 12, 16-17
Toward the end of this passage, Zechariah tells us what to do to bring about the peace he envisions. How can I see myself implementing one of his suggestions.

CHAPTER 3
JESUS IS OUR PEACE

It is a crisp night with huge floppy snowflakes ambling their way into soft sculptured mounds in the yard outside. But I am inside in my favorite chair fascinated again by the lights on the Christmas tree. After the joyful noises of the day's events, I relish the silence pregnant with peace in the closing moments of Christmas day. My mind wanders through the 'peace of Christmas': that stranger's smile, warm greetings from the neighbors we hardly ever see, the songs everyone knows, a self-made gift from a dear friend. Even the newspapers are filled with stories of peace on earth and good will to those usually forgotten. The fleeting nature of such happenings brings out cynicism in some, but not in me. I am awed yearly that the celebration of Jesus' birth nearly 2000 years after its occurrence can still bring peace to this old earth--even if it is only for a few days in the darkest, coldest season of the year. Yet I maintain that the reason peace returns each year at Christmas rests more in whom Jesus is than in Jesus' words about peace. I find in that peace the hope and the promise that, throughout the year, Christians can be the peace which is Jesus.

* * *

1. Jesus: The Incarnate God

Christmas celebrates a central tenet of the Christian tradition. Jesus is the fullness of divinity and the fullness of humanity. Neither the humanity nor the divinity of Jesus

49

negates the other. Throughout the ages people have grappled with this wondrous mystery and probed its significance for Christian living. The evangelists Matthew and Luke find it significant to include the human ancestry of Jesus in their infancy narratives (Matthew 1.1-17; Luke 3.23-28), although they both testify that the conception of Jesus was the work of the Holy Spirit (Matthew 1.18-20; Luke 1.35). According to these authors, both Joseph (Matthew 1.19-24) and Mary (Luke 1.26-37) sought to understand what this child meant.

Throughout the ages the Christian faithful have continued to wrestle with the fact of an incarnate God in Jesus. Although the divinity of Jesus (Docetism) or the humanity of Jesus (Arianism) was at times overemphasized, Christians continued to affirm that Jesus was fully human and fully divine.

The *Church in the Modern World* gives words to this phenomenon:

> He (Jesus) who is "the image of the invisible God" (Col.1.15), is Himself the perfect man. ... Since human nature as He assumed it was not annulled, by that very fact it has been raised up to a divine dignity in our respect too. For by His incarnation the Son of God has united Himself in some fashion with every man (sic). He worked with human hands, He thought with a human mind, acted by human choice, and loved with a human heart.[1]

---

[1] The above quotation from paragraph 22 includes the following footnote:"Cf. Second Council of Constantinople, can. 7:'The divine Word was not changed into a human nature, nor was a human nature absorbed by the Word.' Denz. 219 (428). Cf. also Third Council of Constantinople: 'For just as His most holy and immaculate human nature, though deified, was not destroyed (*theotheisa ouk anerethe*), but rather remained in its proper state and mode of being': Denz. 291 (556). Cf. Council of Chalcedon: 'to be acknowledged in two

This paragraph begins to suggest some of the implications of an incarnate God for daily Christ living. Because Jesus is fully human and fully divine, the transcendent dimension of earthly reality is affirmed.

Human persons today are carriers of the divine. The divine Spirit of Jesus dwells in human hearts (John 14.23-26) urging that the incarnation of God in this world be completed (John 14.10,12). From John's perspective the works of Jesus are the faithful embodiment of God's loving presence among the people. The disciple is called to continue these works of Jesus. The story is told of soldiers passing through Italy at the end of World War II. In a village, they came upon a statue of the Christ which the wartime ravages had left without hands or feet. One of the soldiers made a sign reminding the passersby, "Today Christ has no hands or feet but yours". Such an attitude testifies that the incarnation was not only a past event involving one person, Jesus, in whom God was radically embodied. Rather the Christian community continues to be the body of Christ; the divine dwells in and among the people of God. Inasmuch as the transcendent God is present in the Christian community, the incarnation of God persists.

The incarnation proclaims not only that human persons are bearers of the divine, but also that the whole world shares in that potential. The biological food chain is a somewhat elemental witness to that fact. In the letter to the Romans, Paul recalls the potential of creation to "share in the glorious freedom of the children of God" (Romans 8.20-22). In a similar

---

natures, without confusion, change, division, or separation.' Denz. 148 (302)."

recognition of creation's potential to show forth the divine,
Gerard Manley Hopkins[1] writes:
The world is charged with the grandeur of God.
It will flame out, like shining from shook foil;
It gathers to a greatness, like the ooze of oil.
Crushed. Why do men then now not reck his rod?
Generations have trod, have trod, have trod;
And all is seared with trade; bleared, smeared with toil;
And wears man's smudge and shares man's smell: the soil
Is bare now, nor can foot feel, being shod.

And for all this, nature is never spent;
There lives the dearest freshness deep down things;
And though the last lights off the black West went
Oh, morning, at the brown brink eastward, springs--
Because the Holy Ghost over the bent
World broods with warm breast and with ah! bright wings.

Hopkins is quick to point out, however, that this potential is not
always recognized. Generations have trod upon the obvious
reflection of the divine. It is seared, bleared, smeared and
smudged until it smells of human effort. In fact, humanity has
shoe-ed itself against the bare, divine grandeur. Creation can
be exploited as well as reverenced. The human transformation
of the world can be death- dealing as well as life-giving.
Human efforts in the universe can embody immediate egotism
as well as the transcendent God. Jesus the incarnate God
endures as the persistent claim that the whole of created reality
is theophany, the 'stuff' which mediates the transcendent God.
Or, in Hopkins' words, still "the Holy Ghost over the bent
world broods with warm breast and with ah! bright wings".

The person of Jesus which the Christian tradition describes as
fully human and fully divine seems to call into question a life

---

[1]G.M. HOPKINS, *God's Grandeur*, in W.H. GARDNER and
N.H. MACKENZIE   (eds.), *The Poems of Gerard Manley
Hopkins*, London, 4th edition,   1967, 66.

approach which clearly highlights opposites. It is so easy to augment what separates black from white, female from male, young from old, East from West that the lifestance itself can degenerate into a field of 'us' versus 'them' maneuvers. 'They' are inferior; 'they' are threatening 'our' way of life and should be avoided; 'they' cannot be trusted. Jesus was not either divine OR human, but rather lived the Christological tension of human AND divine. It would seem that the disciples of Jesus too must seek to embody that same tension of seeming opposites.

This could mean that a disciple gives at least as much reign to the divine dimension of Christian living as to the human. It could also mean some attitudinal adjustment toward those others who don't share the same worldview or lifestyle as the disciple. Or this could mean the active promotion of unity in parishes, neighborhoods and peace groups despite differences and difficulties. Not long ago, the Diocesan Council of Catholic Women and the Association of Women Religious of Sioux City, Iowa joined in hostessing an evening of reflection, Women Gathered for Peace. One of the striking features of the evening was the diversity of opinions articulated and listened to around one common table--without raised voices or clenched fists. Women belonging to Beyond War talked with women belonging to the Blue Army. Quaker women brought their long pacifist tradition to the table with women who could call this their first exposure to peace thinking. But there they were, women talking together around tables in spite of diverse views and different opinions. The tension of opposing viewpoints seeking common ground and common action appears to be more in keeping with the mystery of Jesus the incarnate God than groups promoting programs which exclude those of other persuasions.

2. Jesus: The Reconciliation of God

The incarnate one, Jesus, is the reconciliation of God. Jesus is the one who overcomes the historically accrued divisiveness between God and human persons, between human groups, as well as between human persons and the created world. In Jesus the human choices against the created peace in the beginning are overturned. In Jesus God is reconciling humanity, indeed the whole world, into the harmony of the beginning.

The New Testament presents a recurrent cluster of ideas in its descriptions of reconciliation. The reconciliation which means peace is God's action through Jesus Christ (Romans 5.1; Ephesians 2.13; Colossians 1.20) in an earthy fleshy body (Romans 5.9; Ephesians 2.15; Colossians 1.20). In Jesus God promises faithful love to those who reject God's mercy. In the television miniseries Jesus of Nazareth by F. Zeffirelli Jesus announces God's reconciling action: "The distance between you and God is vast. No human steps can cross it. Here is the good news: you don't have to cross it. God is coming to save you, even the most wretched. Do not shut the door in the face of God." In this announcement, Jesus proclaimed the absence of God's wrath toward sinful humanity. In it Jesus announced a new reality: human life is not about appeasing a vengeful God, but about responding to God's saving love in Jesus. Although the whole of Jesus' ministry proclaimed this new reality, it was particularly concentrated in the death of Jesus on the cross (Romans 5.8; Ephesians 2.13-14; Colossians 1.21). Jesus entered the human condition including death.

As an incarnation of the holy, Jesus embodied not only God's love for all peoples, but also the depth of human love's response for God. Jesus did not shut a door in the face of God. Instead Jesus modeled a life without hostility toward God or others. In Jesus the disciples witnessed the possibility of a personal relationship with the God whose love had crossed over the gulf made by sin. The whole life and death of Jesus showed how human persons through faith can live reconciled with God. Jesus accomplished reconciliation because Jesus is reconciliation.

Prior to Jesus, enmity reigned: enmity between the peoples and God (Romans 5.10; Ephesians 2.12-13; Colossians 1.21), between the major divisions of peoples at that time,(Galatians 3.28), and within all of the natural world (Colossians 1.20). The death of Jesus brought peace with God (Romans 5.1) and access in the Spirit to God (Ephesians 2.18; Colossians 1.22). For Paul the wonder of Jesus' reconciling activity was that Jesus died for sinners, thus proving God's immense love for all those whose human choices had separated themselves from that love (Romans 5.6-8). Since Jesus' death no longer were people enemies of God, for God in Jesus had come to dwell in their midst and in their hearts through the Spirit of Jesus.

The Torah, the Jewish law, had insisted that the Jews live in separation from the Gentiles who did not know the covenant. Through death on the cross for all Jesus broke down this enmity which kept Jew and Gentile apart. It was not, however, by making Jews into Gentiles or Gentiles into Jews. Rather in Jesus there is one new creation who is neither Jew nor Gentile. In Jesus one new person was created from those who had been two (Ephesians 2.15-16). This meant peace between those who had been enemies. Such an understanding is consistent with Paul's presentation of justification by faith apart from the Jewish law or Gentile wisdom. Jesus, however, was not only the reconciliation between Gentile and Jew, but also between male and female as well as slave and free. Through faith in Jesus, symbolized by Christian baptism into Jesus, all Christians are one in Jesus (Galatians 3.27-29; 1 Corinthians 12.13; Colossians 3.11).

The letter to the Colossians expands the reconciliation effected through Jesus' death on the cross to all things on earth and in heaven (Colossians 1.20). Again this application is consistent with the portrayal of the cosmic Christ in the letter as a whole. The reconciliation through Jesus' death makes peace with God (Romans 5.1; Colossians 1.22), with Jew and Gentile (Ephesians 2.15), and with everything (Colossians 1.20).

The final recurring element in this concept of Jesus as the reconciliation of God offers an understanding of Christian life. The new Christian community is reminded that, although they are already reconciled in Christ, they must strive to be reconciled (Romans 5.9; Ephesians 2.22; Colossians 1.23). In keeping with the incarnational nature of Christianity, this unity in Jesus needs to be enacted within the community. Two recurring characteristics of such a Christian community appear to be a peaceable life together and love of those who call Christians enemy (Matthew 5.38-45; Romans 12.9-21). There is no place for disunity among people made one in the Jesus who overcame these divisions. The apostle Paul continues. Not only has God in Jesus overturned the enmity of the people toward God, toward each other and the whole world, but God also made those in Christ ministers of reconciliation (2 Corinthians 5.19-20). All those who are the body of Jesus Christ continue to be agents of God's reconciling activity in the world. Reconciliation in Christ Jesus is not a one-time accomplishment but an ongoing process which Christians complete by their living.

It is against this background of Jesus as the reconciliation of God that one can interpret the words of Jesus. After the beatitudes, the Sermon on the Mount treats of six antithetical statements: "You have heard that it was said, ...But I say to you,..." (Matthew 5.21,22ff). With these comments the authoritative understanding of Jesus is contrasted with the popular interpretation of the Law. What the Law had established as restrictions on disproportionate vengeance, Jesus radicalizes as the demands of interior conversion to the message of reconciliation. Two of the antitheses are of particular interest since they specifically address reconciliation and response to coercion.

In the section on murder Matthew 5.23-24 presents the situation of a worshipper who recalls that someone is holding a grudge against her. Jesus urges her to leave her cultic activities and to seek reconciliation, even though she apparently is not at fault. The reader is left with the sense of the urgency of reconciliation with one's neighbor: it takes precedence over cultic ritual and it requires initiative even when one is innocent of disharmony. The same urgent injunction is repeated in verses 25-26 with an example of legal litigation.

The second antithesis touches on the subject of retaliation. Jesus not only requires an end to retaliatory activity in the face of physical violence (Matthew 5.39), legal cases (5.40), forced (military) conscription (5.41), and personal imposition (5.42), but also obliges active non-resistance to such infringement on self- interest. Neither retaliation nor resistance is an appropriate response to those who have been reconciled to God in Jesus.[1]

Instead the message of Jesus promotes a response which makes a positive contribution to the demise of the cycle of violent actions and counteractions. The disciple of reconciliation is to initiate reconciliation regardless who is at fault in the breach of relationship. The follower of Jesus responds to imposition by originating more that what was demanded.

Jesus as the reconciliation of God confronts the Christian community with a number of dimensions. Reconciliation claims both human and divine roles in peace. Although

---

[1]P. PERKINS, *Reading the New Testament. An Introduction*, New York/Ramsey, NJ, 1978, 97-99 briefly states the following explanations given to Jesus' ethical teaching: literal requirements, a perfectionist ethic, an impossible ideal, archaic moral statements, demands irrelevant to the contemporary situation, fundamentally amoral worldview and commands which must be rejected for a self-fulfilled life. See also J. LAMBRECHT, *The sayings of Jesus on nonviolence*, in *Louvain Studies* 12 (Winter, 1987) 291-305.

reconciliation is the work of God in Jesus, it is in the human body and death of Jesus that reconciliation is effected. In addition reconciliation is the creation of something new (2 Corinthians 5.17; Ephesians 2.15), the creation of one new entity from those who had been two. Thus, the enmity between God and humanity is overcome in Jesus. Jew and Greek, male and female are in Christ one new creation. Lastly, reconciliation is not a static accomplished fact, but an objective beginning which awaits completion in and through the ongoing human ministry of reconciliation.

3. The Risen Jesus

God's reconciling activity in Jesus was most evident in the death- reconciliation event. Through the resurrection of Jesus God gave the divine response to human suffering as well as to injustice and violence.

Jesus entered into suffering and death believing in the God whose life he embodied and whose faithful love he revealed. God's response to the human attempts to terminate divine life and love made incarnate was the fullness of a new way of living: resurrection. The resurrection of Jesus is God's response not only to this one specific instance of suffering and death, but also remains God's response to centuries of death-dealing activities in wars, collective human misery and solitary personal pain. The Risen Jesus stands as a testimony that the God of Jesus is definitively for life, for unexpected life even through pain and death.

The God of Jesus presents the believer with the possibility of choosing to embody that which is life-giving even when the personal or institutional forces of the environment are death-dealing.

The resurrection victory over death invites the disciples of the Risen Jesus to encourage the development of gifts and talents rather than to withhold confirmation. The resurrection urges the support of others in their life ventures instead of institutional individualism. Jesus' victory over death dares disciples to love one another faithfully in lieu of apathetic non-response. The resurrection encourages a joy of living in place of a stern shouldering up of obligation. Jesus' victory over death promotes career choices which serve life among the human community instead of individual gain or social erosion. The resurrection presents the Christian today with a reason to believe that life-giving decisions remain real options in spite of cumulative choices to the contrary.

Life-giving options would be more attractive if they did not entail personal cost or dying. But the Risen Jesus recalls that the life which is God's gift comes through suffering and death, not in spite of such pain. The Risen Jesus not only proclaims that life has overcome death, but also how death has been overcome, namely through the path of suffering (*Church in the Modern World*, #22; Matthew 16.24-26; Romans 8.17-25). A life which encourages others' talents could mean setting aside efficiency or even one's own expertise so others can become skilled. A life supportive of others may mean going against certain institutionalized ways of treating others. Faithful love gives a priority to what is best for the beloved even when it is not personally convenient. Careers oriented to service of the human community rarely result in wealth or status. Living in the hope of the resurrection comes no easier for the Christian disciple today than it did for Jesus in the agony of the garden.

The resurrection is not only about life's victory over death. It is also about the divine response to violence and injustice. Violence and injustice were the fabric of the trial and crucifixion of Jesus. The resurrection proclaims the limited jurisdiction of violence and injustice. The response of God to the unjust violence unleashed on Jesus was neither anger nor revenge. Rather, the Spirit of Jesus was handed over to the disciples that they might continue the ministry of reconciliation.

The Spirit[1] --the gift of peace--the ministry of Jesus: such was the divine response to violence and injustice.

In the gospel of John, the death of Jesus is reported with a singular expression, Jesus "handed over the spirit" (John 19.30). Scholars hold that John intentionally used this atypical expression for dying to point out that the Spirit was passed on to the Christian community through the death of Jesus. Jesus had promised the Spirit to the disciples (Luke 24.49; John 14.26) and after the resurrection the Spirit came upon those who had experienced the Risen Jesus (John 20.22; Acts 2.4). The gift of the Spirit was to a group of persons gathered together, and the Spirit transformed the group into a community.

In his letters Paul suggests some aspects of this Spirit-guided community. The presence of the Spirit means the life of the Christ, the Risen Jesus (Romans 8.2-11). Life in the Spirit is the way Christians participate in the risen life of Jesus. God raised Jesus from the dead and gave the Spirit to the believers as a promise, as the first phase of their own salvation and risen life in Jesus (Romans 8.23). The gift of the Spirit is not only the yet to be completed beginning of redemption, but living in the Spirit also makes believers children of God and heirs to God's reign (Romans 8.14-17). Community life in the Spirit of the Risen Jesus is characterized by "love, joy, peace, patience, kindness, generosity, faithfulness, gentleness, self- control" (Galatians 5.22-23).

In the aftermath of the crucifixion the Spirit of Jesus was the divine gift to the community of believers. The divine response to violence was the Spirit of patient endurance, love and peace. The divine response to the injustice of the crucifixion was to inspire a human community with the very Spirit of God. Yet today the Spirit of Jesus dwells in the community and is able to

---

[1]*Challenge of Peace*, #52-54 also treats of the interrelationship of these three.

transform individuals or groups into a unity of justice, love and peace.

In the resurrection accounts the gift of the Spirit and the gift of peace are closely linked. The constellation of new life, the spirit of God and the peaceful ordering of things has already shown up in the creation story in Genesis, chapter 1. Their reappearance here together in the context of the resurrection suggests nothing less than a new creation in Jesus. Jesus promises the Holy Spirit and gives peace as a farewell gift before the death and resurrection (John 14. 25-27). Later in the same gospel, Jesus greets the fearful disciples, "Peace be with you". Then breathing on them, Jesus says, "Receive the holy Spirit" (John 20.21-23).

The author of Ephesians 4.1-6 reflects that the one Spirit is the origin of communal unity and that peace is that which binds the community together. Peace is a visible manifestation of the gift of the Spirit in the new creation which is the Christian community. If Jesus is the reconciliation of God, it is then consistent that the Spirit of Jesus would evidence a presence of peace and that this peace would be the peace of creation and of the end times. The God of the Risen Jesus is the Creator and the God who reigns in the new city, Jerusalem. If Jesus is the reconciliation, then it is understandable that the divine response even to violence and injustice would be peace.

Just as this Spirit was the life principle of Jesus, the incarnation and reconciliation of God, so is this Spirit of Jesus the life principle of the body of Christ now. It is in the Spirit that the disciples are the one body of Christ.[1] The believers joined by the one Spirit of Jesus are both the incarnation and the reconciliation of God in the world today. In the death and resurrection, Jesus handed over the Spirit to the community of believers that they might be who Jesus was and that they might continue the ministry of Jesus.

---

[1]*Church in the Modern World*, #22 develops this idea.

Again mention of the Spirit and peace is often connected with the ministry which Jesus passed on to the disciples. In John's gospel Jesus' commission to be ministers of reconciliation is joined with the blessing of peace and the gift of the Spirit (John 20.21-23). In the gospel of Matthew, Jesus' greeting to the women on the first day of the week was "Peace". With the greeting the Risen Jesus gave them the ministry to proclaim the good news to the eleven (Matthew 28. 9-10). When Jesus encounters the eleven in Galilee, this ministry is universalized to include all nations. The Risen Jesus promises to remain with the eleven as they baptize "in the name of the Father, and of the Son, and of the holy Spirit" and teach the good news (Matthew 28.18-20).

In the Acts of the Apostles, the Pentecost experience of the disciples urged the proclamation of the good news of Jesus (Acts 2). In Paul's understanding the ministries of those joined together in the one body of Christ came from the one Spirit (1 Corinthians 12.4-11; Cf. Romans 12.4-21). Throughout the Scriptures the ministry of Jesus given to the disciples is connected with the Spirit of Jesus which they have received. The ministry of Jesus was the ministry of reconciliation.

The God of Jesus responded to the death-dealing rejection of incarnate love by inviting and in-spiriting the human persons who rejected Jesus to become who Jesus was: incarnate love and the good news of reconciliation. What a genius of human psychology! What a persistent belief in the goodness of created humanity! What an indestructible love of human persons!

4. Implications for Christian Peacemakers

People have attempted to ground their peacemaking efforts in the words of Jesus. Such an effort is less than satisfying for a number of reasons. The first century authors of the Christian Scriptures simply did not address war and peace as a social issue because it was not a concern.[1] It follows that the interpretation of specific texts on peace is necessarily a decontextualization from their original setting. Because war and peace were not of prime consideration in the first century, even references to peace were relatively few. In addition, the words of Jesus divorced from the person of Jesus are not able to substantiate a univocal position with regard to peace. For there are as many decontextualized references which seem more supportive of war and violence. Some examples include the statement of Jesus that he came to bring not peace but the sword (Matthew 10.34), that wars would mark the end times (Mark 13.7), and the violence in the cleansing of the temple (John 2.15).[2]

A theology of peacemaking will have firmer foundations when it is established on the person of Jesus. If Jesus is understood as the incarnation of God, as the reconciliation of God, and as the one raised by God from a violent death, then peacemaking is established as the continuation of the Jesus-event. Faith in this Jesus does have here and now implications for Christian living.

The ministry of Jesus was to be the incarnation of God's love accomplishing reconciliation among those estranged by sin.

---

[1] V.P.FURNISH, *War and Peace in the New Testament*, in *Interpretation* 38 (October 1984) 363-379, especially 379 gives the reasons for this lack of concern as the relatively peaceful political conditions in the Roman empire at this time, the lack of access to political power usually afforded minority groups and the Christian expectation that the reign of God was coming soon.
[2] G.H.C.MACGREGOR, *The New Testament Basis of Pacifism*, Nyack, NY, revised edition with *The Relevance of an impossible ideal. An Answer to the views of Reinhold Niebuhr*, 1954, chapter 2: "Does the New Testament sanction war?" interprets these and other difficult texts from a pacifist understanding.

63

When Jesus handed over the Spirit to the disciples, Jesus handed over the ministry of reconciliation. Since it is vivified by the Spirit of Jesus, the Christian community not only is commissioned but also has the ability to continue the ministry of Jesus. Consequently it can be expected that Christian peacemakers are the home of peace and reconciliation initiatives even when they are not the cause of the disputes.

Peacemakers seek to incarnate God's response to death and violence. Living in the Spirit, peacemakers make choices which promote physical, emotional and spiritual life. Peacemakers seek responses to violence which engage the oppressor in the ministry of reconciliation. When peacemakers model themselves on Jesus, they must also expect that reconciliation will be achieved through suffering and even death. That seems to be the path historically repeated, for peace is the fundamental tension in which the peacemaker participates.

In Jesus the reign of peace has burst into this world, but it is not yet completed. The disciple who already lives the resurrected life of Christ is not yet transformed by divinity. It is this fundamental tension which is the agony and the ecstasy of the peacemaker. The peacemaker knows the agony of possibly compromising negotiations, petty infighting and personal lapses of fidelity. But the peacemaker also knows the ecstasy of the Spirit's insights in otherwise dismal processes and in a surge of hope when the last effort has just failed miserably. Participation in this fundamental tension between the already and the not yet preserves the peacemaker from despair in the face of what remains to be done and from simplistic optimism in human potential.

Yet a final implication for the peacemaker is a reliance on a community of believers. Most obviously persons find assurance in others when their own confidence is gone. For the Christian peacemaker the Spirit of Jesus was given to the community gathered together; and it is in that same gathered community that the peacemaker can expect to find anew the gifts of the Spirit.

On yet another level, the completion of the reign of peace depends on no one individual but on the whole of humanity. This has positive and negative elements to it as the following example illustrates. A group of some twenty-four students read *Challenge of Peace* in a class I was teaching. As I read their comments, I was surprised at the consistent affirmation they gave to the document. Here was a group in which peace could find a welcome reception. Yet there was the gnawing sense that the group stopped with the articulated desire for peace and had not given evidence of action on behalf of peace. One may speculate that they had not given much thought to the issue of peace prior to reading the document. Or perhaps they reflected a more or less universal desire for peace but had not yet tackled the more difficult problem of how to realize this desire in their concrete lives. Or perhaps they were not willing to put time and energy into peace activities.

These speculations do give some insight into the less positive elements of peacemaking as it involves the whole of humanity. Since peacemaking is a communal activity, it requires the cooperation of many persons. One individual cannot bring about peace, for peace is in between persons and groups. But when there are large numbers of people involved, there are ample opportunities for debates on methods of peacemaking; there are people at all different stages of awareness; and there are a multitude of levels of commitment to action on behalf of peace. In spite of that, the gift of peace, the presence of the Spirit and the ministry of reconciliation were given to a community of persons.

The Jesus who is the reconciliation of God has handed over the ministry of reconciliation to the Christian community. This is not merely a nice ideal, but it is a reality awaiting incarnation in the human community.

Roman Catholic Church Documents
Official Roman Catholic teaching in the twentieth century has addressed issues in this chapter. The following selections are particularly pertinent.

Church in the Modern World, #22
1. How is the incarnation a peace event?
2. How is Pentecost (the coming of the Holy Spirit) a peace event?

Church in the Modern World, #32
Through the incarnation, Jesus lives in solidarity with the whole of humanity. What does this suggest as the relationship of the Christian to other persons?

Challenge of Peace, #52-54
1. How is the peace of God made present in Jesus?
2. What does Jesus' life show us about the lifestyle of a peacemaker?
3. What do the words of Jesus tell us about a lifestyle of a peacemaker?

Other Suggested Readings

FURNISH, V.P. *War and Peace in the New Testament,* in *Interpretation* 38 (October 1984), 363-379.

HAMMER, P.L. *The Gift of Shalom.* Philadelphia, 1976. Romans 5 and 8 is treated on 28-32 and Luke 2 on 101-106.

LAMBRECHT, J. *The sayings of Jesus on nonviolence,* in *Louvain Studies* 12 (Winter, 1987) 291-305.

MCCOLLOUGH, C.R. *Theological Understandings of Shalom,* in E.A. POWERS, *Signs of Shalom.* Philadelphia, 1983. See specifically 132-136.

MACGREGOR, G.H.C. *The New Testament Basis of Pacifism. The Relevance of an impossible ideal. An Answer to the views of Reinhold Niebuhr.* Nyack, NY, 2nd ed., 1954. See Pacifism, especially Chapter 1: The Problem; Chapter 2: Does the New Testament Sanction War?; Chapter 3: The Way of Jesus in Personal Relationships; and Chapter 4: The Wider Application of the New Testament Ethic: Jesus and War.

PEIFER, C.J. *Peace According to St. Paul,* in *The Bible Today* 21 (1983) 170-175.

PHAN, P. *Toward an Anthropology of Peace,* in *Theological Studies* 32 (summer, 1985) 125-129. It is a digest of A. RIZZI, *Riflessioni per un'antoroplogia della pace,* in *Rassegna di Teologia* 24 (January/February, 1983) 1-14.

SCHNEIDERS, S.M. *New Testament Reflections on Peace and Nuclear Arms,* in P.J. MURNION (ed.). *Catholics and Nuclear War. A Commentary on The Challenge of Peace. The U.S. Catholic Bishops' Pastoral Letter on War and Peace.* New York, 1983, 91-105, especially 101-105.

SWAIM, J.C. *War, Peace, and the Bible.* Maryknoll, NY, 1982. See especially Chapter 3: Prophet to the Nations and Chapter 4: Prince of Peace.

YODER, J.H. *He Came Preaching Peace.* Scottsdale, PA, 1985.

Audio-visual Materials

The following are some of the audio-visual materials which are related to the chapter content. The list is not exhaustive, but is intended to give some initial suggestions for previewing.

Faces of my brother (film; 5m; Maryknoll; 1973) A short film on "who is the third world?" which provides a glimpse of the sisters and brothers in the human family.

Blessed are the peacemakers (filmstrip; 8m; Treehaus; 1983;). The violence we meet in the world and our share in responsibility for it are related to the Christian tradition of reconciliation.

Visions of Peace. Lessons from Scripture (filmstrip; 9m; Treehaus; 1983). Shows the continuity and development of the notion of peace from the Hebrew Scriptures to the life and teachings of Jesus. It includes peacemaking through non-violence and reconciliation.

I caught a glimpse of Christ today (7m; filmstrip; Menonite Central Committee Canada; 1982). Tells the story of MCC Canada volunteers and SALTers who work with native people, the elderly, youth, inmates, problem children and others.

Introductory Activities

The purpose of the introductory activity is to begin discussion on an understanding of peace as well as to allow the students/participants a chance to express what their previous experiences and understandings of peace have been.

1. In the 70's Simon and Garfunkel did a commentary on peace and the celebration of the incarnation of Jesus with the song, Seven o'clock news/Silent night. Play the song or put together a similiar sound collage for today featuring a background of Christmas music for newsstories.

2. Initiate a discussion about the peace of Christmas. What is meant by the peace which people talk about at Christmas? What is most comforting about Christmas peace? What is most difficult about the message of the peace which Jesus incarnated?

Discussion Questions

The purpose of the discussion questions is to encourage students/participants to integrate the text and/or presented material into their own thinking and living.

1. What are some differences between the peace of the world and the peace of Jesus?

2. Comment: Christians are called to be peacemakers, not only because Jesus spoke of peace, but because of who Jesus was?

3. What are some instances in which people categorize others into "us" and "them"? What needs to be done to overcome these divisions?

4. How, practically speaking, can Christians be ministers of reconciliation?

5. Can you give examples of persons whose lives witness to the presence of the Spirit of Jesus?

6. Can you give examples of persons who have responded to violence and death with love, trust and faith in the basic goodness of others, even those making life difficult for them? How does this work in real life situations?

Activities for Application and Integration
The following suggested activities provide opportunities for students/participants to carry the concepts of this chapter beyond the classroom. They are intended to clarify and integrate understandings into lived experience.

1. Keep a record of stories of others and incidents in daily living which were "successful" peacemaking or reconciling responses to situations. Occasionally reread the stories looking for common patterns or "keys to success".

2. Carefully read the daily newspaper around the Christmas holidays for stories on peacemakers and peacemaking. Evaluate the stories in light of the chapter content.

3. Prepare a sermon or homily on peace using the Christmas season texts (or the other suggested Scripture readings in this chapter).

4. Prepare the sound and/or audiovisual collage suggested as the basis for the introductory activity.

5. Interview a person(s) who is/are involved in peacemaking activities about the part Jesus and the Christian message play in the peacemaking. Is faith in Jesus and the Christian message necessary to persever in action on behalf on peace? If it is not necessary, how is it helpful?

Spirituality Component

It is one thing to read and study about a theology of peace and quite another to become a person of peace. This spirituality component offers a series of Scripture readings with reflection questions which are closely aligned with the chapter topic. It is suggested that they be used for prayer and reflection over a series of days. The reader may wish either to find another Christian with whom the prayer and its fruits may be shared regularly or to journal one's growth as a peacemaker.

DAY 1: Luke 2.1-14
Luke associates the glory of God in the highest at Jesus' birth with peace. Is this my experience of peace? What does it tell us about peace?

DAY 2: Romans 5. 1-8
Jesus is our peace. What does that mean in my life?

DAY 3: 2 Corinthians 5. 18-21
Paul tells us that we are reconciled to God in Jesus and therefore we must "be reconciled". How do I experience this ministry of reconciliation?

DAY 4: Ephesians 2: 13-19
Who or what in my life is the "opposite" that wishes to become one with me in the reconciliation of Jesus?

DAY 5: John 14. 23-31
The peace of Jesus is not the peace of the world. How do I experience the truth of verse 27?

DAY 6: John 20. 19-21
The Risen Jesus gives peace to us with a mission to others. What is your peace mission today?

DAY 7: Romans 8: 9-28
How do I experience my life in the Spirit of Jesus?

```
        P
        E
P  E  A  C  E
        C
        E
```

CHAPTER 4
THE HOLY WAR TRADITION

When our church celebrated the feast of Timothy and Titus this week, we rang out the eucharistic liturgy with the rousing hymn, "For all the saints". The verses brought me face to face with a tradition in the Roman Catholic Church which uses the imagery of warfare and soldiers to describe the Christian life. The hymn is well punctuated with phrases like "You, Lord, their Captain in the well-fought fight...Oh may your soldiers, faithful, true and bold...And when the strife is fierce, the warfare long". The tradition is not recognized as legitimate by Christian pacifists. Those of a less pacifist persuasion remain perplexed by the origins and the theological meaning of warfare as an image of Christian life.

As a ten year old, I remember that a certain uneasy anticipation colored my preparation for Confirmation. I was not sure that I liked being slapped on the check to show that I was now a soldier of Christ, but yet the vision of accepting the slap bravely attracted me as the first step toward Christian heroism. The affectionate pat of the kindly bishop did not measure up to my expectation, and I joined the ranks of those wondering about warfare and Christian living. My studies in Scripture and church history nurtured those questions in later years. Today I conclude that the traditions of holy war and God the warrior must be acknowledged as a first step in examining the appropriateness of this image for Christian life today.

* * *

1. Yahweh Sabaoth and the Holy War

Yahweh Sabaoth[1] is a military image of God in the Hebrew Scriptures which is variously translated as God the mighty warrior, Yahweh the Great Soldier, God of hosts or Yahweh of the armies. The image is threaded through the whole of the Scriptures beginning with the Exodus. After the successful escape from the Egyptian armies at the Reed Sea, the victory song of the exodus proclaims:

> The LORD is a warrior,
> LORD is his name!
> Pharaoh's chariots and army he hurled into the sea;
> the elite of his officers were submerged in the Red Sea.[2]

The image highlights God's sovereign power and superior strength. God's gracious intervention on behalf of the people, Israel is also included in the image. In the ensuing conquest episodes, Yahweh Sabaoth is pictured as intervening for Israel against their enemies. Already in the desert, Israelite success against the Amalekites was attributed to Yahweh's warring against Amalek, who apparently attacked the encampment without cause (Exodus 17.16).

The first Mosaic speech in Deuteronomy insists that the wars which Yahweh waged on behalf of the Israelites were connected to their undeserved election by that same Yahweh (Deuteronomy 4.34). When entering the promised land, the people of God were reminded: "For it is the LORD, your God,

---

[1]The following articles are particularly helpful on this point: D. BERGANT, *Yahweh: A Warrior-God?*, in *The Bible Today* 21 (May 1983) 156-161; F.D. KIDNER, *Old Testament Perspectives on War*, in *Evangelical Quarterly* 57 (April 1985) 99-113; R.J. SKLBA, *'A Covenant of Peace'*, in *The Bible Today* 21 (May 1983) 149-155.

[2]Exodus 15.3-4. *The New American Bible* translates the Hebrew name, *Yahweh*, as LORD and the Hebrew title, *Sabaoth*, as GOD of hosts

who goes with you to fight for you against your enemies and give you victory" (Deuteronomy 20.4; cf. Numbers 10.9).

This image is also found in the psalms. Psalm 84 sings to Yahweh, the Great Soldier who is battlement and shield. Psalm 24 describes Yahweh the mighty Warrior as valiant in battle. From the beginning the God of the armies intervened in history to save the chosen ones and to right injustice. Israel, in turn, understood the image as an exhortation to place their trust in Yahweh Sabaoth rather than in their own efforts to save themselves from their enemies.

The image of God as a warrior is intertwined with the notion of holy war.[1] The books of Joshua and Judges are filled with holy wars of conquest. The following recurring elements can be identified. A call to follow God occasioned the holy war. From the onset the holy war was an act of faith in the God of Israel. The scriptural record talks of leaders filled with the Spirit of God like Gideon (Judges 6.34) and Saul (1 Samuel 13.3) who "sounded the horn" and Israel responded to God's offer of salvation from their enemies. In the pre- monarchical period, the twelve tribes were joined in a loose confederacy, but when they were assembled for war by a charismatic leader, they became the "armies of the living God" (1 Samuel 17.26).

In the monarchical era, charismatic leadership in response to Yahweh's call became separated from political leadership offered by a king. During this era, however, the king consulted the priest or the prophet who was the voice of God before waging war in Yahweh's name (1 Samuel 27.4-19; 2 Samuel 5.19-23).

Because Yahweh in the Ark of Covenant was in the war encampment, the camp was a holy place similar to the temple. Ritual cleanliness (Deuteronomy 23.9-14), prayer, fasting, and

---

[1]We are indebted to the classic treatment of the holy war by G. VON ROD, *Der heilige Krieg in Alten Israel*, Zurich, 1951.

sacrifices which sanctified the soldiers were practiced (Joshua 3.5). This sanctification was a consecration or a setting apart from the mundane and secular routine for a holy purpose, much like the consecration of Levitical priests. In fact this parallel is highlighted when Ahimelech the Levitical priest gave David and his band the consecrated bread and weapons from the place of worship so that they could carry out their mission of war (1 Samuel 21.1-10). The soldiers were called and consecrated by Yahweh for a cultic ritual battle.

The troops were encouraged (Joshua 10.19) and told not to fear but to have trust in Yahweh (Joshua 10.8,25). Those who were not ready to enter into the holy war were released to go home (Judges 7.2-4). The holy war took place under Yahweh's prior verdict: "Do not fear them, for I have delivered them into your power" (Joshua 10.8). The battle begins with a ritual call for Yahweh Sabaoth's help, such as a trumpet blast or a shout in a procession with the Ark of the Covenant (Joshua 6). The battles themselves were minimally described (Joshua 10.20), for the victory belonged to Yahweh (Joshua 10.14,42). Yahweh's atypical tactics like hailstones (Joshua 10.10) or lengthening the day (Joshua 10.13) served as reminders that Yahweh was sovereign and that the victory was due to Yahweh's efforts. With Yahweh on the Israelite side, the enemy lost heart (Joshua 10.2) and was totally defeated.

Israel expressed its conviction that the spoils belonged to their victorious Warrior God by imposing a ban: all things were given over irretrievably to Yahweh Sabaoth. Precious metals were transferred to the temple treasury and all living things were given over to God through killing them. Death removed all living things from human use, since the victory was God's doing and not Israel's skill. An attentive reading of such accounts, however, leads to the conclusion that the ban was not always practiced with the indiscrimination which the notion implies. Sometimes the Israelites did not obey the ban (Joshua 7.16-28). Sometimes livestock was spared (Deuteronomy 3.7; 1 Samuel 27.9). Sometimes marriageable young women were spared (Judges 21.10-12). Sometimes women and children who could be easily integrated into the tribal order were spared (Deuteronomy 20.14). Sometimes a family (Joshua 6.25) or a city (Joshua 9) were spared.

In spite of the blatant bloodshed waged by the armies of the living God in the name of Yahweh, the wars of conquest were understood as an expression of Yahweh's gracious intervention on behalf of the chosen people in times of national crisis. Through their experience of the end of other false cultic systems, Israel experienced God's living concern that they be able to live a holy life in the presence of their God without harassment from other nations and their gods. In the unanticipated victory over nations more numerous than they, Israel experienced a cosmic and national sovereignty deserving of their trust. The ban introduced the notion that innocent victims in war suffer along with evildoers and non-believers by virtue of human solidarity.

The sanctification, rituals and absolute dependence on Yahweh which occasioned the holy war image in the Hebrew Scriptures cannot be equated to humanly devised violence in the name of a religious ideology within a contemporary setting. Since such a mistaken connection is sometimes made, questions surrounding the appropriateness of the image of the warrior God seem legitimate.

Both Yahweh Sabaoth and the holy war are images used by the people of Israel to give expression to their experience of God and of divine intervention in their communal history. The image appears to have connections with ancient near eastern literature of the same era which depicted the gods doing battle with chaos.

Early literature both within and without the community of these early ancestors addresses the struggle of order and of good with chaos and evil. Already the early verses of Genesis identified the God of Israel as the one who creates the good order out of chaos. The image of Yahweh Sabaoth extends this good ordering activity of God into historical reality where the warrior God continues to restrain the evil of oppression and to maintain uncontestable sovereignty in order. Yahweh Sabaoth is not a distant God who largely ignored earthly adherents nor an extraworldly God who knew nothing of human life. The God of Israel dwelt with Israel and was actively involved in their fortunes and future.

The image of Yahweh Sabaoth is not only an extended literary expression of a cosmic creator God; it is also connected to the specific history of this specific people. The event which formed Israel as the people of God was the exodus: the liberation from oppression in Egypt to freedom in a land of promise. Through this event, the God of their ancestors was revealed as Yahweh, the God who liberated them from slavery and who led them in the conquest of the land promised to their ancestors. Both the exodus and the conquest were experienced as beyond the possibility of human calculation or intrigue and as more than the sum total of collective efforts. This 'more' and this 'beyond' were understood in faith as the intervention of a God who was personally committed to their well-being as a people --a God who acted on their behalf through wars and battles. It is likely that victory bore witness to the sovereignty of Yahweh over other gods, over their adherents, over evil oppression and even over the cosmos itself. Since the Israelites experienced the presence of God in every aspect of their lives as the myriad of laws attest, it becomes somewhat understandable that this God was experienced as present in their wars.

Even though the Israelites have imaged God as a warrior, God in fact is not a warrior. Yahweh Sabaoth, like all images for God, is a human attempt to give human words to a human experience which actually transcends all these efforts and articulations.

In later writings the Israelites seem to have understood that Yahweh Sabaoth was an image which could be transformed to articulate more accurately the experience which originally gave rise to it. In the period of the exodus, the conquest and the judges, the image of the warrior God called Israel to total faith in Yahweh who intervened to rescue them from oppression and who subjugated all evil to divine power. Trustworthiness, justice and intolerance of wrong were the hallmarks of Yahweh Sabaoth.   These threads remained through the monarchical and prophetic transformation.

Samuel was the judge and prophet to whom the Israelite people came to beg for a king like the other nations (1 Samuel 8.5). With realistic ambiguity, Samuel described a king both as a charismatic leader chosen by God to save Israel as the judges had done (1 Samuel 9) and as a political ruler chosen by a people who lacked trust in Yahweh (1 Samuel 8). The two aspects co-existed in tension throughout the period of the monarchy. One tradition maintained that Yahweh would never withdraw the divine benevolence from the king (2 Samuel 7.14-16), while the other tradition held that the ultimate criterion of divine judgement was trust in Yahweh. Political astuteness, economic prosperity or victory over national enemies were secondary to trust in God's ways.

This criterion is the background to the messianic prophecy in Isaiah 7. The prophet tests the faith of King Ahaz with the request to ask Yahweh for a sign like the charismatic leader Gideon did (Judges 6.36-40). Isaiah is asking the politically distraught Ahaz to place his trust in Yahweh. But Ahaz cannot rise to the occasion and instead chooses to trust human calculations and military alliances. Isaiah responds with the promise of a messianic king who will trust Yahweh without reserve. Isaiah 22.10-12 later repeats this charge to the whole nation:

> You numbered the houses of Jerusalem, tearing some down to strengthen the wall; you made a reservoir between the two walls for the waters of the old pool. But

you did not look to the city's Maker, nor did you consider
him who built it long ago.
On that day the LORD,
    the God of hosts, called on you
To weap and to mourn,
    to shave your head and put on sackcloth.

The prophetic tradition of which Isaiah was a part continued to
call Israel to faith in Yahweh in the face of the royalist claim
that Yahweh's election of Israel and its king remained firm no
matter what Israel did or how they failed to believe in Yahweh.

The prophetic tradition and the demise of the monarchy
transformed the image of Yahweh Sabaoth. Yahweh Sabaoth
was no longer a god who subjected Israel's enemies, but was
experienced as a God who hated all deceit even in the ranks of
the people of Israel. Again and again, the prophets raise
Yahweh Sabaoth's lament that the people will not listen to the
words of truth (Jeremiah 29.17-18), that false prophets speak
lies (Jeremiah 23.15-16), that Jerusalem is a City of Falsehood
which knows only oppression and wickedness (Jeremiah 6.6-7),
and that the Temple itself houses wrongdoers and sacrifices of
deceit (Malachi 1 and 2). The victory of enemies over Israel
was understood as God's defeat of the evil perpetuated by
Israel's disregard of the law, of religious ritual and of moral
activity (Isaiah 13.4-5). The evil in Israel's enemies would also
be rooted out by Yahweh Sabaoth (Isaiah 10.5-19). Yahweh
Sabaoth upheld the good and conquered evil no matter who
had instigated it in human history (Isaiah 2.11-16).

In the period of the exodus and the conquest, the image of
Yahweh Sabaoth expressed Israel's conviction that their God
intervened personally to save them from oppressive nations.
In the period of the monarchy and prophets, the image,
Yahweh Sabaoth, came to articulate God's demand that justice
be done to the poor, the widow and the orphan even when that
demand accused the elite of Israel (Isaiah 1.21-28; Amos 5.7-
15).

These writings express, in addition, the conviction that war and violence would be avenged--even when waged against the oppression and injustice hated by Yahweh Sabaoth. At times excesses in righting injustice are understood as the cause of the punishment (Jeremiah 50.33-34). Other times the punishment derives from war in itself (2 Samuel 12.9-10) or from the rejection of Yahweh Sabaoth by the punishing nations (Jeremiah 50.31-32). There is, however, the underlying sense that resort to warring activities results in similar retaliation.

Interestingly this transformed image of Yahweh Sabaoth numerically mushrooms in wisdom literature and in prophetic literature in comparison to the historical and pentateuchal writings. Rarely (as in Isaiah 13.4-5 and 31.4-5) is Yahweh Sabaoth imaged at the head of armies in these later writings. Rather the title becomes an image for the opposition of Israel's God to arrogant trust in human efforts (Jeremiah 19.3), to deceit (Jeremiah 23.16), and to injustice (Amos 3.14-15).

In the beginning when the Israelite nation trusted God, the image Yahweh Sabaoth expressed their absolute dependence on Yahweh whose engagement in their historical situation saved them from their enemies and protected them from injustice. Trustworthiness, justice and intolerance of evil in their historical unfolding remained the characteristics of Yahweh Sabaoth, but these same three characteristics became the criteria of divine judgement against Israel itself. Did Israel live their trust in Yahweh in daily choices? Did they do justice to the poor in the concrete events of their lives? Did they avoid evil in specific decisions? One can conclude that the transformation of the image Yahweh Sabaoth during the period of the prophets and the monarchy served to articulate Israel's experience of God more clearly.

2. Images Coming from Warring Activities in the Christian Scriptures

The image, Yahweh Sabaoth, shows a minimal carry over into the Christian Scriptures. It is used once in the Christian scriptures in addition to a quotation of Isaiah 1.9 in Romans 9.29. In the single new instance (James 5.4) Yahweh Sabaoth is described as the God who hears the cries of the oppressed. There are, however, passages which reflect war and soldiers.

The Book of Revelation 19.11-21 presents the Word of God and the Lord of Lords leading the armies of heaven out to do battle against the beast and the armies of the kings of the earth (Cf. 16.16). This passage draws on an apocalyptic tradition of a final cosmological battle in which the Messiah triumphs over the powers of evil before the reign of God is established. Elements in the passage draw on Isaiah's description of the Messiah of God. Isaiah 11 also characterizes the Messiah as possessing faithfulness (v.5), justice (v.4,5), and knowledge of God (v.2), as well as wielding the rod of his mouth (v.4). The new God-given name (Revelation 19.12,16) draws on Isaiah 62.2; the winepress image (Revelation 19.15) reflects Isaiah 63.2 and the sword from the mouth (Revelation 19.15,21) suggests Isaiah 49.2 (cf. Hebrews 4.2).

The presence of the qualities attributed to Yahweh Sabaoth also suggest a reliance on this tradition. For example, the Book of Revelation introduces the rider on the white horse as "Faithful and True" (Revelation 19.11), whose standard in judgement and in warmaking is justice. Any interpretation of this passage, therefore, must take into account its apocalyptic literary style, its messianic background as well as Israel's experience of God which had been articulated in the image Yahweh Sabaoth.

These verses articulate the faith conviction that Jesus is the historical embodiment of God's justice and God's true revelation as well as the faithful disciple who trusted Yahweh through death itself. This image of the Risen Jesus serves to encourage Christians to trust in God's justice and truth when they are faced with suffering and death.

In Pauline and Deuteropauline letters an image of the Christian life derives from soldier's gear or a military lifestyle on three occasions. In the context of preparedness for the Second Coming of Jesus, Paul encourages the Thessalonians to be alert, "putting on the breastplate of faith and love and the helmet that is hope for salvation" (1 Thessalonians 5.8). This brief comment is expanded in a general Deuteropauline appeal to the Ephesians to put their trust in God when the world tempts them to evildoing (Ephesians 6.10-17). These verses repeatedly insist that faith in God--even as evil threatens--is the heart of Christian living. The armor of God, a belt of truth, the breastplate of righteousness, footgear of readiness for the gospel of peace, a shield of faith as well as a helmet of salvation make it clear that the author is describing the Christian life and not a military expedition.

In a similar appeal to Timothy, the Deuteropauline author begs, "Bear your share of hardship along with me like a good soldier of Christ Jesus. To satisfy the one who recruited him, a soldier does not become entangled in the business affairs of life" (2 Timothy 2.3-4). This description suggests that salvation has separated Christians from the affairs of this world. Christians are called to follow Jesus Christ their leader unreservedly.

Since the authors of these letters do derive occasional images from the garb and loyalty of military personnel, radical aversion of early Christians to everything military can not be maintained. In fact, all of the soldiers who appear in the gospel accounts are portrayed in a positive light. The statements, however, can not be construed as a pro-military stance either. Rather the authors drew on the ordinary experience of the Christian communities with regard to the life of the soldier to describe two aspects of Christian living, namely God's benevolent care of the disciples and the Christian's response of total faith in Christ.

The sword is the only part of the soldier's gear which is mentioned in the gospels. It appears in two sayings and in the account of Jesus' arrest in the garden. In the latter, one of those with Jesus uses the sword to inflict injury. Jesus' response varies. In the synoptic gospels, Jesus chides those who came with swords and clubs for the arrest of a robber (cf. Mark 14.48). The remark may suggest that the presence of such weapons is a misunderstanding of who Jesus is. Matthew's account adds the reminder to the militant disciple that those who use the sword will die by the sword (Matthew 26.52). In John's gospel, however, Jesus tells Peter to put away the sword and let things happen according to God's plan instead of turning toward human plans (John 18.11). In Luke's account, Jesus heals the sword-inflicted injury with the comment, "Stop, no more of this!" (Luke 22.51).

According to the text of the arrest, Jesus disavows the use of violence because Jesus was not a robber and because Jesus was convinced that the arrest was God's will for human salvation. One can, therefore, legitimately wonder whether weapons are appropriate IF one is dealing with a robber or IF an arrest is less clearly a salvific intervention.

These questions, however, do not address the more foundational reality of who Jesus is: Jesus is our peace and reconciliation with God. From this fundamental perspective, the appeal to weapons described in this situation reflects the all too human attempt to take matters into our own hands. Jesus, in contrast, is revealed as the one who trusts God unreservedly even through death. Such trust stands in marked contrast to human efforts at self-salvation and the weapons which that requires. Consequently, the comments of Jesus, "Stop, no more of this" (Luke 22.51) and "Shall I not drink the cup which the Father gave me?" (John 18.11) take on crucial, clarifying significance. The arrest is a paradigmatic encounter between trust in God and trust in human efforts.

In Luke's gospel the just described arrest is separated by another sword saying only by the agony in the garden (Luke 22.39-48). Taken together the sword sayings form bookends for the agony in the garden. Luke 22.35-38 alone records this sword saying:

> He said to them, "When I sent you forth without a money bag or a sack or sandals, were you in need of anything?" "No, nothing," they replied. He said to them, "But now one who has a money bag should take it, and likewise a sack, and one who does not have a sword should sell his cloak and buy one. For I tell you that this scripture must be fulfilled in me, namely, 'He was counted among the wicked'; and indeed what is written about me is coming to fulfillment." Then they said, "Lord, look, there are two swords here." But he replied, "It is enough!"

This saying is best understood in connection with what follows immediately, namely the agony and arrest as well as its explicit connection (v. 35) to the missionary journeys.

In both chapters 9 and 10 Luke describes Jesus' mission to the disciples to preach the reign of God. In both chapters the disciples return jubilant over their success. Between these two missionary journeys the transfiguration account occurs-- surrounded on either side by two passion predictions. The missionary journeys in Luke are interwoven, therefore, with foreshadowings of the passion-death- resurrection event of Jesus in sharp contrast to the disciples' apparent success. The arrest, it has been noted, highlights the human struggle to trust in God or to trust in human efforts. Like the account of the arrest, this sword saying also suggests the backdrop of opposing, fundamental understandings of who Jesus is: Is Jesus the one who trusts God through death or is Jesus a popular messianic figure who consolidates human efforts at saving themselves?

With this background let us look at the saying in Luke 22.35-38. More than anything else Luke 22.35-38 illustrates the disciples' misunderstanding of Jesus, the messiah of God. The disciples and the larger Jewish community expected a political messiah who would liberate Israel from foreign domination. As long as this was the dominant understanding, the disciples of a Jesus popularly perceived as a messiah like King David were welcomed and provided for as they announced this good news of liberation.

Beginning with the agony in the garden it would become increasingly clear that Jesus was not a political messiah but a suffering servant. With this revelation the people would turn away from Jesus and from Jesus' disciples. It is this rejection which Jesus is addressing in Luke 22.35-38. No longer will the disciples be welcomed and their needs satisfied. Instead they will be rejected and actively persecuted. The disciples' response, "Lord, look, there are two swords here" indicate that they are taking Jesus literally and do in fact understand Jesus as a messiah who will seize political power. Somewhat naively the disciples proclaim their willingness to take part in a political uprising with their two swords. They will engage their human abilities for salvation. Jesus' response comes as a sigh in face of their misunderstanding. Only the death and resurrection will be able to convert the mistaken notion that trust in human effort is sufficient. The verbal exchange here will be acted out in the arrest with real swords to illustrate the extent of the disciples' trust in human effort.

Interestingly enough the passage sandwiched between these two incidents depicts Jesus in an agonized soul search to trust God ("Still, not my will but yours be done"), while the disciples' sleep suggests they have no need to struggle with trusting God.

The only remaining passage in the Christian scriptures which specifically mentions a sword (Matthew 10.34-36) begins with the difficult statement of Jesus, "Do not think that I have come to bring peace upon earth. I have come to bring not peace but the sword." The use of 'division' for 'sword' in the parallel text of Luke 12.51-53 hints at the fact that the early Christian community surrounding Luke understood sword as a metaphor and not as a literal weapon. The author of the Letter to the Hebrews most clearly articulates the understanding: "Indeed, the word of God is living and effective, sharper than any two-edged sword, penetrating even between soul and spirit, joints and marrow and able to discern reflections and thoughts of the heart" (Hebrews 4.12). The following verses in both Luke and Matthew elaborate on the division which the word of God in Jesus precipitates in families.

The place of the Matthean parallel, namely Jesus' address to the disciples setting out on their missionary journeys, suggests such division will result no matter who announces the word of God. It is recalled that the sword saying in Luke 22.35-38 also referred to the missionary activity of the disciples. Jesus' remark, therefore, is not a statement about waging military war, but rather an astute judgement about the rejection of God's word in Jesus and in the disciples.

The division which results from the presence of the word of God in human history appears also in the apocalyptic discourses in Mark (13.12) and in Luke (21.16). This points to an early Christian association of the sword with the final cosmological battle (cf. Revelation 19.21). The prophet Micah in his lament over Israel specifically links family division with the issue of trust in God (Micah 7.5-7).

This brief sword saying of Jesus in Mark, therefore, states that God's word in Jesus and in the disciples' own missionary activity divides those who accept from those who reject it. Such specific choices are part of the final cosmological confrontation between the Word of God who trusted God through death and all those who prefer to place their trust in human efforts. These sword passages confront the Christian with the question: In whom do you trust? This question, I suggest, remains paramount to a theology of peace.

The cleansing of the Temple from the gospel of John continues to perplex those who image Jesus as the peaceful messiah. Only in John's version of the temple cleansing (John 2.13-17; cf. Matthew 21.12-13; Mark 11.15-17; Luke 19.45-46), Jesus makes a whip of cords to drive out the money-changers and the traders of sacrificial animals. The effectiveness of an impromptu cord whip fashioned from available materials against animals and their traders can be legitimately raised. Although this added detail in John has provoked a variety of interpretations, concentration on the whip alone distorts John's point.

John's second chapter could be entitled *The Dawn of the Messianic Age.* The chapter is composed of two smaller units, the Wedding Feast of Cana and the Cleansing of the Temple. Using traditional messianic imagery of a wedding banquet, John announces that Jesus is that new era where God lives intimately with the people. The hour in John's gospel refers to Jesus' glorification, that is, the fulfillment of the messianic era. When Jesus protests Mary's request with "My hour has not yet come" (John 2.4), Mary shows herself to be the faithful disciple whose trust in God's word hastens that messianic era.

Jesus' response to the Jewish demand for the meaning of this sign was, "Destroy this temple and in three days I will raise it up" (John 2.19). This response also points to Jesus' glorification in the death- resurrection event. The absence of merchants from the Temple was part of the vision of the new messianic age (Zechariah 14.21). The Cleansing of the Temple reiterates the point of the messianic wedding feast by relocating the dwelling place of God from the temple buildings to the body of Jesus, the crucified and risen Jesus. Located within this context, the whip of cords could be a faint hint of that final cosmological battle which births the reign of God in its fulfillment.

88

When these passages which use the images of war and soldiers are taken together, they delineate the early Christian community's conviction that the person and message of Jesus inaugurated the final messianic era. The usual apocalyptic language for this event envisions a final battle between the living God and the rulers of the earth, between those disciples whose trust is in God and other people who trust human efforts. This ultimate struggle takes place in the daily lives of the disciples: in whom do we place our trust? Do we wear the armor of God, or do we raise the sword to force our salvation?

3. Religious Wars

Even though later writings in the Hebrew scriptures and the Christian scriptures demilitarized the image Yahweh Sabaoth, Christian history periodically drew on a literal understanding of holy war to fortify its own warring instincts. Yahweh Sabaoth is an image of God who asked for absolute trust, who deplored injustice and who intervened on behalf of the oppressed. God is not an armored warrior with drawn sword. The failure to distinguish God from the image and the failure to understand what the image Yahweh Sabaoth signified made it possible to wage ideological wars in the name of God and Christian religion.

Ideological religious wars found a model in Joshua's conquest of the promised land. These wars were encouraged and sponsored by churches giving voice to the command of God.[1] The rectification of injustice and the liberation from oppression paled into fanatic religious zeal, flamed afire with phrases like, "Cursed he who holds back his sword from blood"

---

[1]URBAN II, *The Call to the first crusade, November 26, 1095,* in C.J. BARRY, *Readings in Church History. Vol. I. From Pentecost to the Protestant Revolt,* Westminster, MD, 1965, 328: "Wherefore, I pray and exhort, may not I, but as the Lord prays and exhorts you ... I speak to those who are present, I proclaim it to the absent, but Christ commands."

(Jeremiah 48.10b).[1]   In wars of this nature, the division between 'us' and 'the enemy' is simplistically clear.[2] The culmination of all these characteristics is the disregard for any restraint.[3]   Thomas Aquinas addresses the logic behind this disregard in the Summa Theologica (II II, Q 11, Art. 3):

> I answer that, With regard to heretics two points must be observed: one, on their own side; the other on the side of the Church. On their own side, there is the sin, whereby they deserve not only to be separated from the Church by excommunication, but also to be severed from the world by death. ... On the part of the Church, however, there is mercy which looks to the conversion of the wanderer, wherefore she condemns not at once, but after the first and second admonition, as the Apostle directs: after that, if he is yet stubborn, the Church no longer hoping for his conversion, looks to the salvation of others, by excommunicating him and separating him from the Church, and furthermore delivers him to the secular tribunal to be exterminated thereby from the world by death.

---

[1]Contemporary biblical scholarship generally recognizes the verse as a later scribal error.

[2]URBAN II, *Call*, 328: "What shall I add? On this side will be the sorrowful and the poor, on the other the joyful and rich; here the enemies of the Lord, there His friends."

[3]Archbishop DAIMBERT, Duke GODFREY, and Count RAYMOND, Letter to Pope Pascal II, September, 1099, in BARRY, Readings, 329-331: "And if you desire to know what was done with the enemy who were found there, know that in Solomon's Porch and in his temple our men rode in the blood of the Saracens up to the knees of their horses. ... Therefore, we call upon you of the Catholic church of Christ and of the whole Latin church to exult in the so admirable bravery and devotion of your brethren, in the so glorious retribution of the omnipotent God,..."

With this background, let us briefly survey the ideological religious wars in Christian history. In the barbarian invasions Christians offered the barbarians the choice between baptism or death by sword.

Pope Urban II inaugurated the Crusades in 1095 with an appeal for all Christians to join together to rescue the holy land from the infidel. The chronicles of the crusades are filled with tales of brutality deemed appropriate for unbelievers who were already condemned to eternal damnation.[1] One wonders what literary or actual connection contemporary religious crusade movements, such as Campus Crusade, have with the original bloodthirsty wars against infidels.

When the crusades failed in the East and returned to Europe, their fanatic zeal for religion and hatred for heretics returned with them. The crusader approach to deviations from the true faith were unleashed first against the Albigensians in France and then against any heretics by the infamous Inquisition. The motive was a kind of concern for the salvation of the heretic and those others which might be influenced.[2]

Beginning in the sixteenth century, the Reformation period loosed a one hundred year period of religious wars among various Christian states and religions. Each was convinced that God willed the defeat and extermination of the heretic, that is, their religious and political enemy. These wars were fueled by the concept of an inviolable contract between God

---

[1]R.H. BAINTON, *Christian attitudes toward war and peace. A historical survey and critical re-evaluation*, Nashville/New York, 1960, 111-114 offers several instances.
[2]BAINTON, *War*, 116. The Synod of Toulouse in 1229 prohibited the owning of property by heretics or those suspected of heresy. See BARRY, *Readings*, 541. contemporary religious wars in Ireland and the Middle East as well as in a fundamentalist mentality.

and the political leader to establish a theocratic state. The elect were to persuade or to constrain the ungodly so that the Christian commonwealth might flourish.

The notion of 'God on our side' allowed any excess for the preservation of certain values. Today, this approach lingers in some contemporary religious wars in Ireland and the Middle East.

The holy war mentality is grounded in an arrogant self-righteousness that the values, the lifestyle and the belief systems espoused are not only legitimate but also the only right values, lifestyle and belief systems. Because 'our' way is right, it is good and favored by God. Alternative values, lifestyles and belief systems are wrong, evil or inspired by the Evil One. This approach to differences facilitates the construction of 'the enemy' and a unifying goal for 'us', namely the destruction of an external evil threat to 'our' good life. Because the enemy threatens what is good, right and willed by God, any means to defend or to pursue 'our way' is legitimate and obligatory.

There are at least three consequences to this mindset. First, there is a tendency to identify personal or national interests with the will of God. This inclination can be observed in individual comments that a given course of action or event is surely the will of God. Groups, however, also make the same self-assured claim to embody the untainted will of God with regard to ethical choices, economic endeavors or political decisions.

Second, violence in the pursuit of these personal or national interests becomes a God-given right and duty which is outside the usual moral, social or legal limitations. Moral principles of proportion or discrimination are bypassed as in the nuclear deterrence build-up. Legal norms can be circumvented for national security as in the 'Iran scam'. Long-standing social conventions, such as civilian immunity or basic human rights, can be evaded in light of the disruption which their observance would cause to 'our way'.

Third, the preference for violence and the option for aggression takes precedence over collaboration and negotiation in settling disputes. The approach prefers definite winners and losers to the more arduous settlement in which all win. It seems that the decision to launch an attack on Lybian military and civilian installations in April 1986 can illustrate this preference. The vocabulary used to describe athletic victories or even the events themselves accentuate a win-lose, we-they perspective. Advertising for household and personal products also uncovers an aggressive approach. The use of drill sergeant routines to advertise toilet bowl cleaner and cold remedies glorifies domineering techniques.

When the preference for violent solutions to disputes is joined to a number of other attitudes, the result is militarism. Militarism flourishes when nationalistic reverence fosters an anti-international perspective, when authoritarianism and unquestioning loyalty are valued as ends in themselves, when ethnocentrism diminishes a humanitarian outlook, and when war is glorified. Militarism is equated with the military service only insofar as military structures and training accept and inculcate these attitudes. The current trend in advertising, however, indicates that militarism may become a favored perspective from which to approach all aspects of life.

This survey illustrates the consistent tendency of human persons to misunderstand the God of Israel, Yahweh Sabaoth, and to abuse the 'holy war' tradition to suit immediate needs. The image of Yahweh Sabaoth emerged from Israel's experience, namely the God of their ancestors intervened to liberate them from oppression. In time the image was detached from these initial historical events, although it continued to articulate God's intolerance of injustice and evil as well as the call to trust God completely. History has shown the preoccupation with the original locus of Israel's experience, namely the wars of conquest, but in a reversal of Israel's historical role. God was used to legitimate these pursuits of national interests. Instead of human persons seeking to embody God's will on earth, God is expected to endorse human will. At other times, human persons set out to make the world safe for God in a kind of 'we're in control and we know best' approach.

4. Implications for Christian Peacemakers

What does the holy war tradition mean for Christian peacemakers in the twentieth century? First, as Christian peacemakers, we must acknowledge that holy war and Yahweh Sabaoth are part of our Christian heritage. Although at its root this tradition is a call to radical trust in a benevolent God, it has been misunderstood and abused throughout history. We cannot re-write this history, but we must recognize that it is ours. In fact we, personally and communally, retain the immoral possibility of using God for our own advantage and of simplistically identifying our causes with God's will for the world.

Second, Christian peacemaking is situated within the perennial struggle of two fundamental approaches to life: acceptance of God's reconciliation in Jesus or self-justification. We choose to place our trust in God or to place our trust in our own efforts. We can welcome what is benevolent, just and good; or we can exercise controlling and self-serving options. If peacemaking is the result of our efforts alone, we will fail. If, however, we seek to embody the peace God offers in Jesus, then our peacemaking activities will be sustained into the endtimes.

Third, the holy war traditions remind Christian peacemakers that this on-going struggle between two foundational worldviews takes place in our own daily reality. The story of Jacob wrestling with a divine being (Genesis 34) discloses a thought-provoking model. As dawn ended the match, Jacob was not defeated but bore marks of the encounter in a life-long limp. Trust in God does not annihilate us, but keeps us from arrogantly relying on ourselves alone. It is not God's way versus our way, but our embodied life choices bear the marks of our encounter with God. As Christian peacemakers, we incarnate justice even when it is personally inconvenient; we enflesh good even when unobserved; and we embody trust in our God even when we can't see the result.

The holy war tradition correctly understood does leave a legitimate question for Christian peacemakers: can oppression and injustice today be justification for resort to violent warfare? The answer does not come without reflective struggle. To the extent that the kind of holy war unleashed against injustice resembles a crusading or militaristic solution, the answer is no. This, however, does not imply a do-nothing response. The personal or structural oppression must be transformed into an environment in which all have access to personal and communal development (Cf. *Church in the Modern World*, #26).

Such a transformation must be guided by the conviction that God is God of all persons (Amos 9.7; Jeremiah 18.7-8). God is not against 'them' and for 'us', but against injustice and evil wherever it appears. Since God is the God of all, collaborative resolutions in which all win would be preferable.

The means used to bring about the transformation must be proportionate to the injustice and may not contradict the intention of promoting justice for all. In other words, the means used to end oppression may not be oppressive. In this context one can correctly ask whether violence is by nature oppressive and therefore a contradictory means to eliminate oppression. Equally difficult is maintaining an intention directed toward justice which excludes vengeance or retaliation.

Yet another consideration touches on the fundamental human value, life. Violent warfare threatens not only this basic value for individuals, but also the foundational structures which make the socio-political and economic life of the community possible. In light of these realities, the use of violent warfare to transform injustice and oppression could be considered only in those situations where the existent situation is already destructive of life for individual persons and of those very structures for life in the community.

The holy war tradition at first appears to be the dark side of our Christian peacemaking tradition; in fact, it has been used as such. A longer look at this tradition, however, puts the Christian peacemaker at the heart of the age-old struggle to accept God's salvation for us or to create a salvation of our own making; to place our trust in the God of creation or in our own efforts alone.

```
        P
        E
  P E A C E
        C
        E
```

Roman Catholic Church Documents
Official Roman Catholic teaching in the twentieth century has addressed issues in this chapter. The following selections are particularly pertinent.

Challenge of Peace, #31 and #40-43
1. What is the Holy War tradition in the Hebrew Bible trying to express?
2. What are some of the military images used in the New Testament?
3. For what is war in the New Testament an image?

Other Suggested Readings

BAINTON, R.H. *Christian attitudes toward War and Peace. A Historical and Critical Re-evaluation.* Nashville-New York, 1960.

BERGANT, D. *Yahweh. A Warrior-God?*, in *The Bible Today* 21 (1983) 156-161.

BLANK, J. *Gewaltigkeit-Krieg-Militardienst in Urteil des Neuen Testaments*, in *Orientierung* 46 (1982) 157-163.

KIDNER, F.D. *Old Testament Perspectives on War*, in *The Evangelical Quarterly* 57 (1985) 99-113.

MCSORLEY, R. *New Testament Basis of Peacemaking.* Washington, DC, 1979. See particularly chapters I, II, and III.

MARSHALL, I. H. *New Testament Perspectives on War*, in *The Evangelical Quarterly* 57 (1985) 115-132.

SKLBA, R.J. *'A Covenant of Peace'*, in *The Bible Today* 21 (1983) 149-155.

SWAIM, J.C. *War, Peace, and the Bible.* Maryknoll, 1982, chapter I.

VonRAD, G. *Der heilige Krieg im Alten Israel.* Zurich, 1951.

Audio-visual Materials

The following are some of the audio-visual materials which are related to the chapter content. The list is not exhaustive, but is intended to give some initial suggestions for previewing.

1. **War and the Christian Conscience,** (filmstrip, Klise) begins (frames 1-25) with the history of holy war in Israel and through the Crusades.

2. **Image of the Enemy** (video; 8m; Beyond War II; 1986) explains how we create and magnify 'the enemy' in our minds and how these projections inhibit communication or understanding. We are capable of cooperating rather than confronting.

Introductory Activities

The purpose of the introductory activity is to begin discussion on an understanding of peace as well as to allow the students/participants a chance to express what their previous experiences and understandings of peace have been.

1. What are some examples of 'holy wars' from history or contemporary experience?
2. Are there any evidences of a holy war tradition in worship or symbols in Christian churches today? Are they appropriate?
3. How would you explain Jesus' statement: "I have come not to bring peace but the sword."

Discussion Questions

The purpose of the discussion questions is to encourage students/participants to integrate the text and/or presented material into their own thinking and living.

1. What are the characteristics of God the warrior?
2. What are the elements of the Holy War?

3. Do the images of God the warrior and holy war raise any questions for contemporary Christian life? Is there a place for a 'holy war' mentality today?

4. Can the injustice or oppression experienced by a people ever be sufficent reason for resort to war or violence?

Activities for Application and Integration

The following suggested activities provide opportunities for students/participants to carry the concepts of this chapter beyond the classroom. They are intended to clarify and integrate understandings into lived reality.

1. Study your church's hymnal for songs which use military or soldiering images (Cf. Battle hymn of the Republic and For all the Saints). Evaluate these hymns for their appropriateness in Christian worship.

2. Research the current wars in Ireland and the Middle East to assess the extent that these wars could be termed 'holy wars'.

3. Choose a daily newspaper or a weekly periodical and clip out the headlines which use war related terminology over a six issue period of time. Group the headlines according to topic, i.e., military conflict, sports, entertainment, etc. Summarize and draw conclusion from your findings.

Spirituality Component

It is one thing to read and study about a theology of peace and quite another to become a person of peace. This spirituality component offers a series of Scripture readings with reflection questions closely aligned with the chapter topic. It is suggested that they be used for prayer and reflection over a series of days. The reader may wish either to find another Christian with whom the prayer and its fruit may be shared regularly or to journal one's growth as a peacemaker.

DAY 1: Exodus 15.1-8
Is this image of God as a warrior out of place for a peacemaker in 1980's or can it give us some insight about our God?

DAY 2: Joshua 5.13-15
Who or what in my life has been sent to me as aids in my struggle against evil?

DAY 3: Joel 4.1-12
Here Yahweh God is speaking to the nations who oppressed his people Israel. Why is Yahweh declaring war on the nations?

DAY 4: Matthew 10.34-39 and/or Luke 12.51-53
What is my experience of the division which the message of Jesus brings?

DAY 5: Luke 22.35-51
Here are two instances in which the disciples of Jesus turn to the sword? What is Jesus trying to teach them through word and action?

DAY 6: John 2.13-17
What does John want to teach the reader about Jesus through this passage?

DAY 7: Revelation 19.11-16
What are the characteristics of the Divine Warrior described here? How do these images fit with your experience of Jesus?

CHAPTER 5
THE CHRISTIAN PACIFIST TRADITION

A recent television advertisement began as a wildwest shootout, but the confrontation was ended with the gift of flowers. This commercial brought me back to February, 1986. While the evening news chronicled the Philippine elections, along with millions of Americans I watched and wondered how long before a full-scale shootout would erupt there. All the elements were present: an oppressive minority regime led by an aging Marcos and the disgruntled masses inspired by a charismatic Aquino. But that was not the way it went. Instead of a violent revolution--flowers, carried by thousands of unarmed women and children. These mass demonstrations prevented the rebel military troops and Marcos' militia from ever meeting head on. It was a remarkable scene: we were witnessing the triumph of non-violence. I wonder how much of the significance of this event escaped us. In the Phillipines, oppression was ended through non-retaliation. A military battle was transformed into a peaceful celebration by thousands of flowers. A nonviolent solution to injustice took place in the twentieth century as the world watched via television. The Christian scriptural tradition on enemy love was embodied in this nation's people.[1] This event challenges us in the twentieth century to take another look at the Christian pacifist tradition.

* * *

---

[1]R. MUSTO, *The Catholic Peace Tradition*, Maryknoll, NY, 1986, 214-219 addresses the role of the Catholic Church in this nonviolent revolution.

1. Christian Pacifism and the Scriptures

Peace is threaded through the gospels from the angels' announcement of Jesus' birth "Peace on earth" to Jesus' post-resurrection greeting, "Peace". The connection between peace in the gospels and the pacifist lifestyle, however, does not know universal agreement. Any study of the scriptural basis for pacifism touches on some foundational questions,[1] the answers to which shape the interpretation of the scriptures and in turn pacifism itself. Is the peace spoken of in the gospels an image of salvation, much as the Good Shepherd is an image for Jesus; or is peace the concrete reality of redemption in Jesus with implications for daily living? Is the era of gospel peace now or at the end of time? Is peace an impossible ideal given the sinful nature of human persons, or is it the characteristic ethic of believers who have welcomed God's reconciliation in Jesus? The pacifist orientation holds that peace must be a concrete reality, that it is constitutive of Christian belief, and that now is the time of gospel peace. Those who answer these questions differently reject the possibility or the practicality of pacifism.

There are other significant questions, however, which pacifists answer differently among themselves. What is the relationship of the gospel to public, socio-political life? In other words, is the gospel an incarnational reality or only a spiritual one? Another question centers on the locus of peace: does peace dwell in the human heart or does it change the structures and patterns of relationships? Finally, is peace God's unilateral gift or is peace an interactive reality: a divine gift and a human task? The responses to these questions shape two

---

[1]G.H.C. MACGREGOR's classic *The New Testament Basis of Pacifism* and R. MCSORLEY's *New Testament Basis of Peacemaking*, Washington, DC, 1979 focus on the apparent scriptural contradictions between pacifist and war texts in the scriptures.

distinct approaches to pacifism[1] which I have come to call separatist pacifism and incarnational pacifism. Let us look at these in turn.

A separatist pacifism understands the gospel peace as a God-given spiritual reality dwelling in the heart of the true believer. These pacifists attempt to re-present the early Christian community in literal adherence to the pacifist words of Jesus and to the pacifist lifestyle of the early Christian communities. What Jesus said and did takes on an importance, apart from the person of Jesus.

Those early Christian disciples expected the imminent return of the Risen Jesus. Consequently they absented themselves from involvement in the social order, for they understood themselves as citizens of the end times reign of God. Their relationship to the Roman Empire was foreshadowed by and not distinguished from the military and ritual exemptions afforded the Jewish inhabitants of the empire. Insignificant in number and in socio-political or economic power, the Christians lived the way of Jesus, namely non-retaliation to evil and non-resistance to injury. Today separatist pacifism becomes a way of living an explicit Christian response to the gospel message: love one's enemy, do good to those who persecute, turn the other cheek and offer no resistance (Matthew 5). It expects to encounter misunderstanding and cross purposes in an evil world just as Jesus did.

This way of living is the end times reign of God already present. Separatist pacifists, then, understand themselves as citizens not of this world, but of the eschatological reign. Their heavenly citizenship separates them from those whose cares

---

[1]An approach recognizing the plurality of pacifist traditions is not new, although these categories and descriptions are original. For other descriptions of pacifism, see J. YODER, *Nevertheless: The Varieties of Religious Pacifism*, Scottsdale, PA, 1972.

are with this world. Peace is not connected to human effort; it is God's intervention in the lives of those who accept God's salvation and word in the scriptures. The pacifist does not labor toward structures and relationships which promote peace. Rather the focus is on individual acceptance of the peaceful way of living and on the preservation of heavenly citizenship from the onslaught of evil. At best the role of the separatist pacifist in the world is to witness individually to God's saving action.

Pacifism, so understood, characterizes Christian groups which have withdrawn from society into various separatist and millenial communities throughout the eras. But one does not have to absent oneself from the world physically. This approach to Christian pacifism can also show itself in a certain spiritual or personal separatism. An abiding sense that the world is lost and the believer's salvation is independent from that forsaken world encourages individual distancing from the fate of the world. An understanding of peace as an interior individual gift from God promotes harmony only in personal and spiritual relationships. The belief that peace will come only with an end times divine intervention absolves the pacifist from striving toward peace in social institutions and structures. Consequently the conviction that the Christian is to absorb evil passively now only to be vindicated in the last days approaches a victim (or doormat) mentality. The credence that personal peace and salvation takes place apart from the world and other people fosters disregard of the structures and institutions in the family of nations.

In contrast incarnational pacifism finds its roots in the person of Jesus: the presence of God-with-us. The incarnation of God in Jesus confirms the fundamental goodness both of this world and its people. The ancient conviction of the world's goodness and the creation of woman/man in God's image is now affirmed. The incarnational pacifists demonstrate their conviction of the world's goodness and mirror the divine presence in their living. Christian pacifists love those who would count them enemies, for God loved them while they were yet sinners (Romans 5.10). Wherever God dwells with the people, peace is an already present reality. The incarnation, in addition, attests to the decidedly material nature of peace and challenges the incarnational pacifist to embody peace similarly.

Just as the person of Jesus reconciles divine and human, the pacifist reconciles opposition and conflict into a new reality. The passive absorption of evil and violence is not sufficient; rather the pacifist actively promotes peace where there had been hostility. This creation is a new way of relating, indeed, a new social order. The ancient conviction of our descent from common parents suggests a human solidarity and oneness brought to new fulfillment in Jesus' handing over of the Spirit to us: this life in the one Spirit of Jesus means a new creation, a new social order.

Incarnational pacifism does more than bear witness to God's gift of peace; it is an agent of social change participating in building the new city of God. This sense of one human family created and redeemed by one God preserves pacifism from an elitist, God-is-on-our- side perspective. Just as Jesus' living with us modeled loving relationships not dependent on family ties, religious position, political preference or social distinction, the pacifist active love reflects the resocialization of one converted to the divine way of loving.

The incarnational pacifists refuse to cooperate with evil and with structures promoting violence. Such an alternative way of living is not without suffering. They understand that the loving acceptance of suffering can mean unexpected life for them as well as for their oppressors, just as Jesus' assent to the passion and death meant resurrection and salvation.

This approach to pacifism rooted in the person of Jesus is built on several convictions: 1) this world and all its people are created good; 2) peace is a process begun in Jesus and continuing into the end times--through the efforts of Christian pacifists; 3) pacifism is an active commitment to transform enmity and hostility; 4) the locus of peacemaking is the flesh and blood world, including social structures; 5) the incarnation of Jesus intimately involved God in the whole world. Consequently the gospel does address socio-political life.

In addition the pacifist must be engaged in creating patterns of relating and structures of common life capable of bearing and revealing God's reconciling love. Rooting Christian pacifism in the reconciling person of the incarnated Jesus discourages the literal re- creation of first century pacifist lifestyle. The first century form of pacifism was an appropriate Christian response to the first century historical situation. The living, dynamic Christ requires an appropriate Christian response to the contemporary historical situation. The traditional pacifist scripture passages understood within this framework provide a strong foundation for incarnational pacifism.

The sections of the Sermon of the Mount on non-retaliation and love of enemies form one traditional scriptural foundation for Christian pacifism:

> You have heard that it was said, 'An eye for an eye and a tooth for a tooth.' But I say to you, offer no resistance to one who is evil. When someone strikes you on [your] right cheek, turn the othe one to him as well. If anyone wants to go to law with you over your tunic, hand him your cloak as well. Should anyone press you into service for one mile, go with him for two miles. Give to the one who asks of you, and do not turn your back on one who wants to borrow.

> You have heard that it is said, 'You shall love your neighbor and hate your enemy.' But I say to you, love your enemies and pray for those who persecute you, that you may be children of your heavenly Father, for he makes his sun rise on the bad and the good, and causes rain to fall on the just and the unjust. For if you love

those who love you, what recompense will you have? Do not the tax collectors do the same? And if you greet your brothers only, what is unusual about that? Do not the pagans do the same? So be perfect, just as your heavenly Father is perfect. (Matthew 5.38-48)

This passage ends a series of reinterpretations of laws from the Torah attributed to Jesus. This immediate context as well as the larger context, namely Jesus' address on Christian discipleship in chapters 5 through 7, point to an understanding that the Christian way is a departure from the world's usual approach to conflict. Verses 38-42 not only put an end to retaliation,[1] but also replace retaliation with an active loving response: "turn", "hand", "go", "give". Verses 43-48 maintain that this loving response does not distinguish between friend and enemy. Why? God's love does not depend on human response. Because Christian disciples mirror this love of God in the circumstances of their lives, their incarnation of love is dependent on God's love of them, not the response of others. The passage ends with the challenge to imitate the life-giving, love- giving perfection of God.

Matthew succinctly presents non-retaliatory, dynamic love both as possible for those who have been converted to God's way of relating and as having visible and concrete implications in the socio-political order. The references to being taken to law and to enforced labor come out of the Roman system of occupation, while the prescriptions for lending were present in Jewish law.[2] The location of these teachings on non-retaliation and love of enemy in Matthew's Sermon on the Mount (cf. Luke's Sermon on the Plain) demonstrates the

---

[1]Even the original law of talion was intended to limit revenge by calling for parity, according to D. SENIOR, *Invitation to Matthew*, Garden City, NY, 1977, 70.

[2]MUSTO, *Catholic*, 24 and W.F. ALBRIGHT and C.S. MANN, *The Anchor Bible Matthew*, Garden City, NY, 1971, 42.

centrality of the teaching in the communities of the synoptic gospel authors.

Writing even before the synoptic authors, Paul is no stranger to similar teachings on enemy love. Already in his first Letter to the Thessalonians (about 51 CE) Paul's closing exhortation reads, "See that no one returns evil for evil; rather, always seek what is good [both] for each other and for all" (1 Thessalonians 5.15).[1] A few years later, in defending his apostleship to the Corinthians, Paul describes his ministry in terms of non-retaliation: "When ridiculed, we bless; when persecuted, we endure; when slandered, we respond gently" (1 Corinthians 4.12b-13a).

In chapter 12 of the Letter to the Romans, Paul gives his fullest expression to the Christian teaching on love of enemies With this chapter Paul begins his ethical exhortation to the young Christian community in Rome. In the first two verses of the chapter, he reminds the Romans that their bodies are living sacrifices and that their new existence means a way of behaving which is different from the worldly behavior around them. Separating this introduction from the quotation on love of enemies is a description of the gifts for ministry within the body of Christ. Verses 14-21, then, are Paul's foundational instructions on the Christian community's ministry to the broader community in which they lived.

> Bless those who persecute [you], bless and do not curse them... Do not repay anyone evil for evil; be concerned for what is noble in the sight of all. If possible, on your part, live at peace with all. Beloved, do not look for revenge but leave room for the wrath; for it is written,

---

[1] D. SENIOR, *Jesus' Most Scandalous Teaching*, in J.T. PAWLIKOWSKI and D. SENIOR (eds.), *Biblical and Theological Reflections on The Challenge of Peace* (Theology and Life Series, 10), Wilmington, DE, 1984, 55-72, discusses the Pauline and Petrine love of enemies passages cited here on 61-64.

"Vengence is mine; I will repay, says the Lord." Rather "if your enemy is hungry, feed him; if he is thirsty, give him something to drink; for by so doing you will heap burning coals upon his head." Do not be conquered by evil but conquer evil with good. (Romans 12. 14,17-21)

In the context of chapter 12's introductory verses, Paul squarely places this teaching on love of enemies as a characteristic Christian ministry determined by reconciliation with God in Jesus. Paul is convinced that the Christian way is countercultural (vv. 2 and 20); it is not the usual response among unbelievers.

Yet another formulation is found in the first Letter of Peter: "Do not return evil for evil, or insult for insult; but, on the contrary, a blessing, because to this you were called, that you might inherit a blessing" (1 Peter 3.9). Scholars maintain this letter is a baptismal sermon for a Christian community experiencing persecution. The link to Christian initiation instructions attests to a foundational character of the teaching on non-retaliatory love of enemy. The specific historical situation facing the community, namely persecution, makes the spiritualization of this notion an inaccurate interpretation.

These words encapsulated the earliest Christian memories of Jesus' response to the violence of the last hours. In the garden Jesus halts the disciples' turn to the sword when faced with the armed band of arrestors. When abused by the guards in John's gospel, Jesus does not retaliate, but presents two alternatives: a clarification of the wrong for which he was hit or an end to the abuse (John 18.23). Again during the trial in John's gospel, Jesus remarks that, if he were an earthly king, his followers would be fighting. But such action does not belong to the way of Jesus (John 18.36). On the cross Jesus asks forgiveness for those who knew not what they were doing (Luke 23.32-34). There is no record of fear or hostility in Jesus' responses to violence; instead the way of Jesus was non-retaliatory love. The conversion of enemy hearts--the Pharisee Nicodemus

(John 19.39), the thief (Luke 23.42-43), the Roman soldier (Mark 15.39)--suggests the transforming potential of such non-retaliatory love.

In addition to presenting Christian love as non-retaliatory, the Christian scriptures describe love as self-sacrificing particularly as modelled in the person of Jesus. Drawing on a liturgical hymn, Paul refers to the self-sacrificing love of Jesus who did not find equality with God something to cling to, but rather gave it all up and became a human person even to death on a cross (Philippians 2.6-8). In the Letter to the Romans, Paul gives voice to his own wonder over the love of a God whose Christ died for sinners and the wicked:

> For Christ, while we were still helpless, yet died at the appointed time for the ungodly. Indeed, only with difficulty does one die for a just person, though perhaps for a good person one might even find courage to die. But God proves his love for us in that while we were still sinners Christ died for us. (Romans 5.6-8)

John addresses the self-sacrificial nature of Christian love with the image: "Amen, amen, I say to you, unless the grain of wheat falls to the ground and dies, it remains just a grain of wheat; but if it dies, it produces much fruit" (John 12.24). John makes a similar point: "This is my commandment: love one another as I love you. No one has greater love than this, to lay down one's life for one's friends" (John 15.12-13). The validity of these words rests in the faith conviction that the self-sacrificial love of Jesus meant, in fact, resurrection for Jesus and the gift of the life-giving Spirit to all who believed. Self-sacrificing love triumphed over sin, enmity and violence.

Incarnational pacifism and its scriptural roots describe a way of living--a life orientation. It is not a set of strategies nor a means to achieve peace. In itself this Christian pacifism is the way of peace; it is a response to God's unconditional love inviting sinners to reconciliation. As such pacifism is not something one does or possesses; it is the ongoing process of transforming response to God's love. This transforming response requires the turning of hearts, that is, conversion to the divine way of dealing with human persons. The Christian pacifist not only responds, but is also being transformed into the divine presence who initiates reconciliation, loves unconditionally, heals into wholeness and loves faithfully even through suffering to new life. Conversion means an end to retaliation for injury as well as the end of enemies from the Christian's perspective.

For some this conversion entails a turning away from aggression and hostility; but others must leave behind a victim or doormat mentality. The latter conversion is at least as difficult as the former, for it can be confused incorrectly with pacifism, thereby obscuring the need for conversion. In fact the victim mentality allows hostility and aggression to flourish. The peace which comes from conversion replaces fear with a personal assurance and the nonthreatening presence of the Indwelling Spirit. Such peacemaking presents aggression with another way of approaching life. It breaks the victim's co-dependent relationship with aggressivity. Conversion to pacifism is a core transformation to a new way of living and relating which is both response to the wonder of God's unconditional love and an embodiment of that same loving invitation to others.

Before moving on to the history of pacifism in the Christian tradition, it would be worthwhile to examine some current vocabulary for its connections to these pacifist understandings. Pacifism is a principled nonviolent lifestyle. Christian pacifism is built on the principles of love of enemy and non-retaliation to injury. Nonviolent action may or may not be based on principles and it may or may not be a strategy in contrast to a lifestyle. The expression, nonviolent resistance, refers to the real resistance of evil and violence, but without retaliatory coercion. The expression, active nonviolence, highlights a proactive, initiating stance. The formulation, militant nonviolence, suggests the same sense but the apparent

111

contradiction in terms encourages its quick relegation to oblivion. The term, nonviolent conflict resolution, specifies the use of strategies relative to disputes and discord.

Contemporary word choice makes distinctions within pacifism with regard to its scope. These distinctions, however, could reflect either the separatist or the incarnational pacifist foundations just described. Absolute pacifists choose to refrain from the use of violent or coercive means to force their will or to defend themselves as a matter of principle. Nuclear pacifists object to nuclear instruments of violence on principle. Selective pacifists object to the use of a specific violent or coercive means, for example, war. Conscientious objection is related to but different from pacifism on two accounts. By and large, conscientious objection is connected with participation in war or combatant readiness and with a certain legal status relative to armed services. There can be absolute conscientious objection as well as nuclear or selective conscientious objection.

2. The Christian Pacifist Tradition

One approach to the Christian pacifist tradition maintains that prior to the Roman Emperor Constantine, Christianity was identified with pacifism. After Constantine's recognition of Christianity as an official state religion, the demise of pacifism was connected to privilege, institutional status and the prominence of a just war theory. By implication, Christianity could be true to its pacifist roots only when it was a persecuted minority without institutional structures or privilege. This chapter rejects this approach as simplistic and separatist. In fact, Christians were in the Roman military service prior to Constantine's official recognition of Christianity in 313 and Christian pacifism remained a millennium after Constantine. Secondly, to the extent that Christian pacifism was a separatist pacifism in the early centuries, it was necessary that it be transformed into an incarnational pacifism, capable and desirous of transforming the socio-political and economic structures into the reign of God. This latter transition has not yet been completed.

A complete presentation of the Christian Pacifist tradition is the task of a book in its own right.[1] This chapter section, consequently, serves to introduce significant persons and highlight general trends throughout the centuries.

The ancient Christian writers of the pre-Constantinian era encourage a Christian lifestyle which does not engage in killing and which practices love of enemy within the context of a total Christian lifestyle out of step with the civilization in which it existed. Ignatius of Antioch (+107), Justin Martyr (+165), Clement of Alexandria (+210), Tertullion (+220), Origen (+254), Cyprian (+258), Gregory Thaumaturgus (+270) and Lacantius (@320) all repudiate war and exult peace as the way of Christian living.[2] The incompatibility of love with killing seems the foundation for this consistent teaching.

This consistent teaching of the early Christian writers may not mean the total exclusion of Christians from military service during that same period. There is no evidence that Christians were Roman soldiers by profession prior to 173; nor is there evidence that they were not Roman soldiers. In addition to the prescription against killing, however, other factors suggest the improbability of large numbers of Christian soldiers prior to 173. For example, officers were expected to venerate the emperor as a god; such veneration resulted in the exclusion of Christians from the Eucharist. In addition, the expectation of an immediate return of Jesus caused Christians to disengage

---

[1]R.H.BAINTON, *Christian Attitudes Toward War and peace. A Historical and Critical Re-evaluation*, Nashville-New York, 1960 remains the classic in this field. The more recent work by R.G.MUSTO, *The Catholic Peace Tradition*, Maryknoll, NY, 1986 deserves the place next to Bainton in any Catholic peace library.

[2]BAINTON, *Christian*, 72-78; MUSTO, *Catholic*, 34-38.

themselves from things of this world including political and military concerns. Furthermore, Christian communities were, for the most part, in the cities; and city dwellers were

According to the fourth century Christian historian, Eusebius, Christians were serving in the Twelfth or Thundering Legion under Marcus Aurelius in 173.[1] Fewer than ten inscriptions on tombstones from these first three centuries name the profession of the Christian as soldier; the listing of any profession, however, was not common. The Apostolic Tradition of Hippolytus in the second century forbids converts to enter the army, although it presupposes Christian converts from among those already in the army. This becomes more understandable when one realizes that throughout the Roman Empire during these years of the pax Romana, the Roman army functioned primarily as a police force.

There are also a few Christian soldier martyrs who preferred death to killing or denying their Christian lifestyle in years prior to Constantine. Maximilian is most frequently noted, although Marinus and Marcellus also receive some mention.

---

[1]EUSEBIUS, *Ecclesiastical History*, Book 5, chapter 5. MUSTO, *Catholic*, 42, however, notes Eusebius' apologetic efforts to show longstanding Christian support of the Empire in the years immediately following official recognition by Constantine. TERTULLIAN, *First Apology*, chapter 5, remarks that there are Christian soldiers in the army at the time of Marcus Aurelius. The late addition to JUSTIN MARTYR, *The First Apology*, chapter 71, "A Letter of the emperor Marcus Aurelius Antonius to the people and the Sacred Senate at Rome" does mention numbers of Christians in the army, for whom killing is wrong in conscience, and through whose intercession the emperor won victory from the enemy on the German border. While Musto's critique of Eusebius' account may be valid, the account of Christian soldiers enjoyed a wider audience than Eusebius.

Rome did view Christianity as detrimental to a strong empire. Pliny wrote to the Emperor Trajan about 115 concerning the political and economic threat Christianity posed. Celsus, the critic of Christianity refuted by Origen, wrote @178 that if all Roman citizens were like Christians, then the emperor would be without soldiers. The repetition of these critiques during these centuries occasioned local or imperial persecutions and purges of Christians from the military ranks. The issue behind these persecutions was "being a Christian".[1] Rome recognized the institutional threat of an alternative way of living. This recognition was re-enforced by the death of Christian martyrs who preferred faithfulness to the Christian way, including nonviolent enemy love, even though death was the result.

In 313 Constantine achieved victory in the name of Jesus Christ and gave official recognition to the Christian religion. It is initially noteworthy that the ancient Christian writer Lacantius, who maintained killing was absolutely prohibited for Christians, was both counselor to the Emperor Diocletian and tutor for Emperor Constantine's son. Laçantius was the first of many who struggled to live a pacifist Christianity in the midst of socio-political and economic violence. A pacifist orientation was actively present within Christianity throughout the medieval period until the emergence of the nationalism, individualism and secularism in the fifteenth and sixteenth centuries. Christian thinkers, monks, missionaries and martyrs decried war and the violence of unjust political leaders. Their censure shaped the socio-political order.[2]

---

[1]See, for example JUSTIN MARTYR, *The First Apology*, chapter 4.

[2]In his already cited work MUSTO presents this material chronologically. Although we are relying on his scholarship, we chose to examine the pacifist trends throughout these centuries.

In the post-Constantinian era, Christian intellectuals and theologians continued to recognize the incompatibility of violence with Christianity. Ambrose and Augustine claimed a legitimacy for those wars whose goal was peace. Ambrose, however, maintained that non-violence was the Christian response.[1] Manichaean dualism certainly affected Augustine's approach to peace in *City of God*. There Augustine admits a certain earthly peace of order, but peace in the city of God rests on Christian love.[2] During the barbarian invasions, Augustine and other Christian writers described peace by and large as the result of the relationship of the individual Christian and God.

In the eighth and ninth century Carolingian dynasty, Alcuin of York, Rabanus Maurus and Pope Nicholaus I stretched the understanding of individualist peace to include a social dimension as well as prohibitions against any clerical involvement in killing. Peter Lombard held that military service was sinful in itself. With the rise of humanism, pacifist thinking became characteristic of its adherents such as Thomas More and Erasmus. Through its connection to humanism, however, pacifism moved outside of Christian circles into a secular arena.

The rise of Monasticism has been understood as the response of some Christians to a popularization and the state domestication of Christianity associated with Constantine and the barbarian invasions. The early roots of monasticism were separatist, that is, withdrawal from the world. The hermetic way of living had already begun in the east in the second (cf. Tatian, @160) and third centuries. The desert hermits of the fourth century, like Anthony and Pachomius, founded nonviolent, countercultural communities of followers. Pachomius and his contemporary, Martin of Tours, were

---

[1] MUSTO, *Catholic*, 47.
[2] AUGUSTINE, *City of God*, trans. by G.C. WALSH and D.T. HONAN (The Fathers of the Church, 24), New York, 1954, Book XIX.

soldiers who became peacemakers and critics of violence in social and political order. The monastery of Lerins was established on ideals of peacemaking during the fifth century barbarian invasions.

The tenth century Cluniac monastic reform movement stressed "the conversion of feudal aristocracy to the peaceful service of Christianity".[1] Beginning in the twelfth century in response to the violence experienced with the socio-economic upheaval, various groups banded together in voluntary poverty, associating themselves with the unarmed poor. Francis of Assisi left both a military and business career to preach the gospel message of peaceful co-existence with all persons, events and creatures in this world. Francis forbade arms to his followers and engaged in the conversion of the Islamic peoples by peaceful preaching in contrast to the crusaders' swords.

Peaceful conversion attempts among the invading tribes by missionaries such as Patrick, Columban, and Boniface can be documented in spite of the violence both of the invading tribes and the Holy Roman Empire.[2] We have already noted the later attempts by Francis of Assisi as well as later Franciscans to convert the Saracens peacefully. His contemporary, Clare, is attributed with saving Assisi from the Saracens by her meeting with the leaders of the army while she carried only the

---

[1]AUGUSTINE, *City of God*, trans. by G.C. WALSH and D.T. HONAN (The Fathers of the Church, 24), New York, 1954, Book XIX.

[2]BISHOP DANIEL OF WINCHESTER, *Letter advising Boniface on the Method of Converting the heathen*, 723-724 in BARRY, Readings, 274-276 advises a "calm and moderate" approach which is not "offensive" nor "irritating". See also MUSTO, *Catholic*, 52-56. It can also be noted that some efforts at Christian conversion were violent. See, for example, Christianity in Denmark and Norway, in BARRY, *Readings*, 278-280

Eucharist. Peter the Venerable suggested the study and refutation of the Islamic religion as an alternative to the Crusades. Roger Bacon and Ramon Lull supported the study of languages as an alternative to war in settling disputes and in converting non- Christians. Sixteenth century natives of the Americas knew the peaceful conversion attempts of the mendicant orders especially Bartholomew Las Casas.

Some of these missionaries as well as other prophetic voices endured a martyrdom resulting from their political criticism. Boniface was one of several missionary martyrs whose death at the hands of Germanic tribal leaders witnessed to the nonviolent gospel. In the ninth century a group of Christian intellectuals in Islam- occupied Cordova, Spain, sought an end to social and religious oppression. Their nonviolent public witness to Christianity resulted in martyrdom.[1] There were others, such as Stanislaus of Cracow in the eleventh century and Thomas a Beckett in the twelfth century, whose martyrdom hastened the demise of political oppression and the lessening of injustice.

The fidelity of the intellectuals, monks, missionaries and martyrs to pacifist Christianity did leave its mark in the social life of their day. Ninth century law in the Carolingian Empire decreed the role of government and its leaders to insure peace and justice throughout the realm. Killing was condemned for it meant death to the body of Christ. A similar collection of laws in the same century placed the duty of peace not only with the government, but also with each individual Christian.[2] The

---

[1]MUSTO, *Catholic,* 69-71 notes no apparent change in Islamic policy as a result of the nonviolent witness.

[2]MUSTO, *Catholic,* 65-66 points to the False Capitularies as a direct result of the influence of Nicholaus I, Alcuin and Rabanus Maurus. The Capitularies of 802 do maintain that no citizen can neglect a summons to war or release another from that obligation. The False Decretals sought to protect papal and

eleventh century Peace of God and the Truce of God were the result of popular peace movements and clerical efforts joined together against feudal oppression.[1] The coalition successfully received protection from war for certain social classes and during certain seasons of the year. In the sixteenth century Bartholomew Las Casas' arguments in the Valladolid debates brought legal protection for some basic human rights of the native Americans as well as restricted the conquistador tactics in the New World.[2]

The pacifist tradition during this era also left its mark on church legislation. Severe penances for killing and involvement in soldiering activities appeared on the penitential lists from the fifth through the twelfth centuries. Beginning already in the third century there was a prohibition against ordination of anyone who had killed another. Conciliar decrees condemned war. Canon law prohibited individuals from following a civil authority's command which was contrary to divine or church law. Here specific mention was made of warring activities. In addition, from Gregory the Great in the sixth century to the Avignon papacy in the fourteenth century, the popes played a role in arbitration of political disputes on the European continent.

As the sixteenth century dawned, a new social order was emerging. It was characterized by sovereign national states including the Papal States, by individualism and by secularism. During this period individual rights came to be protected by political systems and rights of nations emerged. These

---

episcopal power with the emphasis on individual Christian's duties of peace and justice.
[1]MUSTO, *Catholic*, 71-75.
[2]BARTHOLOMEW DE LAS CASAS, *Short Report on the Destruction of the Indes*, 1546, in BARRY, *Readings*, 626-631 is pessimistic about the effect of these laws in the new world where power and slavery were more important to the Europeans than these restrictions.

characteristics form the theoretical and practical bases for an 'us' versus 'them' way of viewing other political entities. In addition religious practice came to be viewed as a private matter of conscience, separate from public life and practice. In this period the peace tradition became almost exclusively linked to certain separatist peace traditions such as the Mennonites or Anabaptists.

This historical survey points to three factors shaping the context of contemporary peacemaking. First, nations and cultures which were established on individual rights, national sovereignty and secularism find pacifism countercultural and extraneous to their worldview. As a consequence, pacifism is viewed as a threat to the established socio-political orders.

Second, the privatization of religion and the relegation of pacifism to specific non-mainstream churches work against the possibility that a faith-based pacifism could effect public policy. In fact, church involvement in issues relating to pacifism or non- violence is understood as overstepping the established domain attributed to religion by both Christians and civil leaders.

Third, the general populace is widely unaware of a Christian pacifist tradition prior to the modern state. Cut off from these roots, nonviolent methods are popularly viewed as an expression of the will to power with little or no connection to pacifism or to the Christian lifestyle.

These three factors continue to influence and to hinder Christian peacemaking in the twentieth century. Alongside these remnants from the age of national sovereignty some characteristics typical of the contemporary age are gaining momentum. First, the loss of the papal states in 1870 freed the papacy from the power struggle of politics based on a concept of national sovereignty and the derivative enemy mentality. Since that time loss of membership throughout the Christian churches as well as diminished prestige meant a corresponding loss of privilege and power based on numbers or majority status. The resultant situation allows the pope and Christian churches to address issues without blatant vested interests.

In addition within the Roman Catholic Church there is a growing movement from dualism to incarnationalism. Vatican Council II's pastoral constitution on the *Church in the Modern World* with its call for a scrutiny of the signs of the times became a watershed event highlighting the significance of the world for the church itself. *Justice in the World,* on the ninetieth anniversary of *Rerum novarum,* undergirded this point with an insistence that the concrete practice of justice is a constitutive dimension of the gospel. This truth emerged from the conviction that the incarnation event involved God and the Christian in transforming the world into the reign of God. As such it remains the impetus behind the century-long tradition of Catholic social teaching and gives shape to the task of peacemaking.

Finally, the twentieth century demonstrates the economic and political interdependence of nations and peoples. This solidarity has the potential of transforming political and economic individualism into global cooperation.

This backdrop has allowed a Christian pacifist tradition again to emerge in the twentieth century. These next paragraphs will sketch key people and events within three areas: Roman Catholic papal statements, Christian pacifism in the United States, and wider world Christianity.

The re-entry of papal intervention on behalf of peace began in the area of arbitration. Within the framework of paternalistic and hierarchial thought, Leo XIII understood one function of the pope as supreme arbitrator in international disputes. His actual involvement was limited to two situations. The next pope, Pius X, did offer to mediate the international disputes leading to World War I during the month prior to his death in 1914.

The inaugural encyclical of Benedict XV, *Ad beatissimi* (1914), called for the nations to lay down their arms. Benedict understood himself as the 'father' of Christians on both sides; thus his 1917 three-point peace program was built on impartiality, on an active charity for all those suffering from the war, and on justice as the foundation for a lasting peace. The program was unacceptable to both sides.

Pius XI's controversial concordat policy between the world wars flowed in part from the desire to resolve church-state conflicts through nonviolent recourse to mutual legal agreements. Pius XII's Christmas radio messages called for an end to economic disequilibrium, egoism and distrust in favor of peace based on truth, justice, charity, and the common good. He did, however, maintain the possibility of defensive war.

John XXII approached *Peace on earth,* issued in 1963 after the rapid deterioration in East-West relations, with an appeal for structures of economic justice and protection of basic human rights. Issued in 1965, the *Church in the Modern World* devoted a chapter to peace. Within the context of its discussion on the nature of peace, the document praises those "who renounce the use of violence in the vindication of their rights" (#78). It also calls for "humane provisions" by law for conscientious objectors who serve the human community in some way (#79).

Pope Paul VI is remembered both for his heart-rending plea to the United Nations in 1965, "War no more," and the elaboration of the economic basis of peace in the 1967 encyclical, *Development of Peoples:* "development is a new name for peace". In his 1979 address in New York, John Paul II called on Christians to be bearers of peace and justice in all aspects of human life, for God who is peace and justice dwells in human hearts. While it is clear that the popes of this century have a preference for nonviolent ways of solving conflicts, it is not certain that they are absolute pacifists.

Within the United States, the Quaker pacifist tradition has been a consistent presence from colonial days.[1] The Quaker pacifist tradition combines both non-violence and involvement in the socio- political sphere. One of the more significant Quaker contributions to pacifism in this century was its founding support for the ecumenical Fellowship of Reconciliation organization.

Catholic Worker, a lay Catholic movement begun in 1933 by Dorothy Day and Peter Maurin, was established on a philosophy including pacifism as well as personalism[2] and the works of mercy. Its three pillars, hospitality (houses and soup kitchens), communal farms and clarification of thought (newspaper and round table discussions) give concrete embodiment to the pacifist foundation. Catholic Worker resistance during World War II, the Civil Defense drills in 1950's and the Vietnam War influenced or intersected with virtually every other Christian pacifist movement during these years. Catholic worker Ellen Egan and longtime Catholic pacifist Gordan Zahn[3] provided significant leadership in the reshaping of PAX (1962) into Pax Christi in 1973.[4] Their

------

[1]There has been resistance to every war in which the United States has been involved. See Wm. HEWITT, *History of American Peace Movements*, syllabus at Briar Cliff College, 1987. See also C. DEBENEDETTI, *The Peace Reform in American History*, Bloomington, IN, 1980; L. GARA, *War Resistance in Historical Perspective*, Lebanon, PA, 1970.

[2]Personalism as it is used here reflects the description given in chapter one; it cannot be confused with egoism.

[3]J. FAHEY, *Pax Christi*, in T.A. SHANNON, *War or Peace? The Search for New Answers*, Maryknoll, NY, 1980 describes the founding of Pax Christi. Other persons instrumental in its establishment included C. Dozier, T. Gumbleton, E. Guinan, C. Danielsson and J. Fahey.

[4]Pax Christi International was organized in post World War II France.

priorities include peace education, a just world order, primacy of conscience and alternatives to violence.

The Catholic Peace Fellowship (1964) linked to FOR emerged as the home of more radical Catholic Workers and Christian activists, including the Berrigans, Thomas Merton initially, John Yoder and A.J. Muste. The heart of Thomas Merton's theology of peace was conversion; conversion enabled the nonviolent transformation of the social order to peace. Methods of illegal breakins, destruction of property, and napalm suicides were employed by Cantonsville Nine, Plowshares and other pacifist groups. These methods were not always understood as nonviolent and consequently strained or breached relationships with other Christian peace groups.

Martin Luther King's labors for racial justice through nonviolence were influenced by Ghandi's policy of *satyagraha* as well as the Christian teachings about non-retaliatory love of enemy. With his leadership, American blacks used marches, boycotts and sit-ins to give public voice to their plea for equality in political and economic structures. Although Martin Luther King's focus was racial equality, his nonviolent approach demonstrated an effectiveness in turning public opinion against oppressors. Caesar Chavez employs similar nonviolent methods in seeking economic justice for the farm workers.

The National Conference of Catholic Bishops (NCCB) teachings on peace were initially a response to World War I,[1] when "just war" influence predominated. Developing the emphasis from the *Church in the Modern World* in the midst of the Vietnam era, the NCCB expanded the call for legal

---

[1]NCCB, *In the Name of Peace. Collected Statements of the US Catholic Bishops on War and Peace,* 1919-1980, Washington, DC, 1983 lists a pastoral letter entitled, "Lessons of War" from September 1919. The next documents date from 1942 and 1944.

protection of conscientious objectors to include selective objection.[1] The US bishops officially agreed that conscientious objector status could be based on principles stated in the *Church in the Modern World* and classical moral teachings including just war theory.

The NCCB pastoral letter *Challenge of Peace* presented non-violence and pacifism as legitimate Christian positions rooted in the gospel. Within the US Catholic hierarchy, the pacifist views of bishops Raymond Hunthausen, Leroy Mattieson, and Thomas Gumbleton stand as a witness to peace as well as a challenge to United States Christians today.

There is also a twentieth century Christian pacifist tradition beyond papal teaching and the United States Christian churches. During World War II, the reaction of German churches to National Socialism was so divided that unified action was paralyzed. Much resistance including that of Dietrich Bonhoeffer and *Die Weisse Rose* was not pacifist. Against this backdrop, the story of Franz Jaegerstatter, an Austrian Catholic father opposed to National Socialism, stands out. Against the advice of his pastor, bishop and contemporaries, Jaegerstatter chose fidelity to Christ's command of non-retaliatory love. His conscious refusal to be drafted and fight in the war resulted in death. There were other instances of parishes, villages and religious houses failing to cooperate with National Socialist legislation: Jewish people were hidden, anti-government pamphlets were circulated and critical sermons were preached.

More recently the weekly vigil of the Argentinian Mothers of Plaza de Mayo and the marches of the Irish Peace Women witness to pacifism as an alternative to the violence in these countries.[2] The February 1986 nonviolent transfer of

---

[1] NCCB, *Human Life Today*, Washington, DC, 1968,, #144.
[2] B. BROCK-UTNE, *Educating for Peace. A Feminist Perspective*, NY-Oxford-Toronto-Sidney-Paris-Frankfurt,

government from F. Marcos to C. Aquino in the Phillipines presents yet another example of pacifism in the socio- political arena. The mass demonstrations as well as the protection of the military by crowds of flower-carrying women and children remain an inspiritional vision for twentieth-century pacifists.

In their statement on peace at the 1968 Medellin Conference,[1] Latin American bishops explicitly named the church position in Latin America pacifist. The document highlighted the necessity of just distribution of resources including land, just international economic agreements, and respect of human dignity as the basis of lasting peace (Medellin on *Peace*, #14).

The Christian pacifist tradition is not a twentieth century invention but is a valid Christian stance toward war and violence with a history stretching back to the early centuries. The prevalence of a socio-political concept of national sovereignty served to delegitimate Christian pacifism. The twentieth century resurgence of pacifism attests to an emerging world order based on solidarity rather than nationalism. To this extent, peacemaking is countercultural. To this extent, Christian peacemaking is an incarnational reality.

3. Implications for Christian Peacemakers

This examination of the pacifist tradition in the Scriptures and in practice throughout the centuries suggests some implications for the Christian peacemaker. First, pacifism is a

---

1985, 33-69 tells the story of the peace efforts of these and other women.
[1]SECOND GENERAL CONFERENCE OF LATIN AMERICAN BISHOPS, *Peace*, in D.J. O'BRIEN and T.A. SHANNON, *Renewing the Earth. Catholic Documents on Peace, Justice and Liberation*, New York, 1977, 561-572, here #17

valid Christian way of living. Its roots in the scriptures and the early church, its growth into the medieval era and its resurgence in the twentieth century make it impossible to disregard the pacifist way as a tangent for eccentrics. Pacifism is consistent with Christological statements on the incarnation and the reconciliation of sinners through God's action in Jesus.

In addition a number of moral principles support the choice of a pacifist lifestyle. The pacifist is convinced of the dignity of the human person and the value of life. Pacifism, therefore, aims at the good of the whole human person-in-community considered in all aspects (principle of totality) as well as the good of all humanity (principle of common good). The pacifist lifestyle also is a reminder that a moral actor must always seek to realize as much value as possible (principle of intention) and that the ways chosen to realize the values cannot be incompatible with with the value itself (principle of moral discrimination). In concrete terms, if peace is an intended value, the ways of realizing peace must be peaceful and nonviolent. Pacifism maintains the primacy of the informed conscience, that is, those who have come to believe that the pacifism lifestyle is right for them must follow that way of living. In light of these principles, pacifism cannot be dismissed as folly.

Another implication which the pacifist tradition suggests for peacemakers today is more mundane. Peacemaking results from conversion to God's way of loving; it is not a strategy nor a method. Since any conversion is on-going, one is always in process of becoming a peacemaker. There is no room for the elitism of those who have arrived. Peacemaking is not passivity nor absence of conflict; peacemaking is a proactive way of resolving hostility, which mirrors God's faithful love to us while we were yet sinners. Since peacemaking is a way of living, the choices one makes each day are realizing peace or

127

are options for violence.[1] Peacemaking cannot be a mode we adopt in a crisis situation; it is the way we treat ourselves and others, mindful of God's peacemaking approach with us.

The question remains, however: is pacifism the *only* valid Christian lifestyle? Although the principle of primacy of conscience would question an absolute yes, the accumulated evidence points to pacifism as the normative Christian way. The discussion of deviation from this normative stance will be discussed in the next chapter on the just war tradition. The uniqueness of Christianity rests in God, in God's relationship with us and in the consequent human task in the world.[2] The God of Christianity created peace from chaos and promised peace as the end of fulfilled human existence. God became incarnate in human flesh to reconcile sinners and to show a fearful, hostile people what life lived in peace with God could be. Our relationship to God is one of loving response to the God who is creator and in whose incarnation identifies with our neighbor. Bearing the divine spirit of love in our hearts, we live in oneness with God: we, like Jesus, are the reconciliation of God; in the whole of our living we are peacemakers. The resultant Christian task in the world is to mirror God's approach to enmity. The Christian task is to be an alternative to hostility. This way of loving builds the city of God and hastens the coming reign of God. Such a concrete task in the world requires social change.

---

[1] P. CONNOLLY, *The violence of everyday living,* in *Commonweal* 110 (October 21, 1983) 555-557 points out the routine violence to which we subject ourselves and others.
[2] Cf. G. ZAHN, *Pacifism and the Just War,* in P. MURNION (ed.), *Catholics and Nuclear War. A Commentary on Challenge of Peace. The United States Bishops' Pastoral Letter on War and Peace,* 117-131, here 121-125.

There are objections to pacifism. R. McSorley identifies and refutes the following objections:[1] 1) The gospel cannot be applied to politics. 2) At times war is the lesser evil. 3) Human depravity means war will always exist. 4) Morality is individual, not social. 5) Self-defense is a basic human instinct. 6) Soviet atheism requires eradication. 7) Pacifism is not practical. 8) There are no alternatives to war. 9) Unilateral disarmament is insane. 10) Pacifism opposes the authority of God invested in legitimate leaders. 11) Wars can be just. 12) Loss of spiritual values is worse than war. 13)Only the baptized are children of God anyway.

Such objections do need a personal and collective Christian reflection and response. Any adequate response must be based on an incarnational understanding of pacifism as an alternative or countercultural lifestyle rooted in the response to the God of love.

This fact, however, remains. If God who is love, loved human persons faithfully into conversion from sin to love, then the Christian love of those who name them enemy is the normative life of discipleship.

<pre>
            P
            E
     P E A C E
            C
            E
</pre>

---

[1]R. MCSORLEY, *New Testament Basis of Pacifism*, Washington, DC, 1979, 119-164.

Roman Catholic Church Documents
Official Roman Catholic teaching in the twentieth century has addressed issues in this chapter. The following selections are particularly pertinent.

Challenge of Peace, #111-121
1. Summarize the history of Christian pacifism as it is sketched here.
2. According to this document, what is the significance of The Church in the Modern World?
3. What are the points of convergence between pacifism and just war theory?

Human Life Today, #143-153
1. What is the support in the Christian tradition for conscientious objection?
2. What are the recommendations of the US bishops with regard to selective conscientious objection?

Other suggested readings

BAINTON, R. *Christian attitudes toward war and peace. A historical survey and critical re-evaluation.* Nashville/New York, 1960. See especially chapters 4,5,7, and 10.

BERGANT, D. *Peace in a Universe of Order,* in J.T. PAWLIKOWSKI and D. SENIOR (ed.), *Biblical and Theological Reflections on the Challenge of Peace* (Theology and Life, 10). Wilmington, DL, 1984, 17-29.

CAHILL, L.S. *Nonresistance, defense, violence, and the kingdom in Christian tradition,* in *Interpretation* 38 (1984) 380-397.

FAHEY, J. *Pax Christi,* in T. SHANNON, *War or peace? The search for new answers.* Maryknoll, NY, 1982, 59-74.

FURNISH, V.P. *War and Peace in the New Testament,* in *Interpretation* 38 (October 1984), 363-379.

GUINAN, E. (ed.). *Peace and nonviolence. Basic writings by prophetic voices in the world religions.* New York/Paramus/ Toronto, 1973.

HOLLENBACH, D. *Nuclear Ethics. A Christian Moral Argument.* NY/Ramsey, NJ, 1983. See especially chapter 1: Historical traditions in tension.

KOHN, S.M. *Jailed for peace. The history of American draft law violators, 1658-1985* (Contributions in Military Studies, 49). Westport, CT/London, 1986.

MCGRAW, R. *The Spirituality of Nonviolence,* in *Sisters Today* 58 (April 1987) 459-465.

MCSORLEY, R. *New Testament Basis of Peacemaking,* Washington, DC, 1979. See especially Chapter 6: Answers to objections.

MURNION, P.J. (ed.). *Catholics and Nuclear War. A Commentary on The Challenge of Peace. The U.S.Catholic Bishops' Pastoral Letter on War and Peace.* NY, 1983. See especially Section IV on pacifism and just war.

MUSTO, R. *The Catholic peace tradition.* Maryknoll, NY, 1986.

NCCB. *In the name of peace. Collective Statements of the US Catholic Bishops on war and peace, 1919-1980,* Washington, DC, 1982.

OATES, S.T. *Let the trumpet sound. The life of Martin Luther King, Jr.* New York, 1982.

PIUS XII. *Christmas Eve 1951 radio address,* in *Catholic Mind* 50 (1952) 248-256.

PIUS XII. *Christmas Eve 1957 radio address,* in *Catholic Mind* 56 (1958) 160-179.

SHANNON, T. *War or peace? The search for new answers.* Maryknoll, NY, 1982 especially parts II and III.

SHANNON, T. *What are they saying about peace and war?* New York/Ramsey, 1983. See especially chapter 2 : Survey of Roman Catholic teachings on war and peace.

SHARP, G. *Exploring nonviolent alternatives.* Boston, 1970. See 142-159 for additional bibliography on specific "Cases of nonviolent action"

WADDELL, P. *Pacifism: A Christian option?* in J.T. PAWLIKOWSKI and D. SENIOR (eds.), *Biblical and Theological Reflections on The Challenge of Peace.* Wilmington, DE, 1984, 90-107.

WHALEN, P.A. *A Personal Approah to Peace,* in *Liguorian* 75 (February 1987) 26-28.

Audio-visual Materials

The following are some of the audio-visual materials which are related to the chapter content. The list is not exhaustive, but is intended to give some initial suggestions for previewing.

Active non-violence: a possible alternative to violence for resolving conflict (slide\tape; 27m; Mennonite Central Community; 1983) presents a wide variety of groups throughout history who have used non-violent alternative in responding to conflict.

Nonviolence: toward a peaceful world (slide\tape; 16m) traces the history of nonviolence from world religious traditions to the present age.

Gandhi (film\videotape; 188m; 1982) tells the story of this leader in active nonviolence.

Martin Luther King:from Montgomery to Memphis (film; 27m; PHENIX; 1969) explores active nonviolence in the civil rights movement. A 103m version is also available, entitled King: Mongomery to Memphis.

Are you a Conscientious Objector? **Resisting War in the 80's** (Slides/tape; 17m; Central Committee for Conscientious Objection; 1981) introduces was resistances and the history of conscientious objection.

Every heart beats true (filmstrip; 20m; Packard Manse; 1980) examines military service and the refusal to bear arms from a Christian perspective.

Introductory Activities

The purpose of the introductory activity is to begin discussion on the pacifist tradition as well as to allow students/participants a chance to express what their previous experiences and understandings of pacifism have been.

1. Recall a conflict situation in your life which was handled violently. How could it have been resolved non-violently?
2. What are some ways we do violence to ourselves in our ordinary approach to daily events?

Discussion Questions

The purpose of the discussion questions is to encourage students/participants to integrate the text and/or presented material into their own thinking and living.

133

1. What would you suggest that a friend or family member consider in sorting through a decision regarding conscientous objection?

2. What is the scriptural basis for pacifism in the Christian tradition?

3. What are the historical bases for pacifism in the Christian tradition?

4. What are the attitudes and the life style which a Christian pacifist needs to adopt?

Activities for Application and Integration

The following suggested activities provide opportunities for students/participants to carry the concepts of this chapter beyond the classroom. They are intended to clarify and integrate understandings into lived experience.

1.Read a biography of a pacifist, e.g., Dorothy Day, Martin Luther King, Gandhi, Francis of Assisi and prepare a report on the convictions behind their pacifist efforts.

2. Attend a peace event and do a 2-3 page evaluation and summary.

3. Do a research paper on a pacifist church, e.g. Quakers, Mennonites.

4. Collaborate with at least one other in an introductory presentation on the pacifist history of the Roman Catholic Church to be given to a local church group for adult education.

5. Watch at least ten hours of family or childrens' programming to discover the strategies for resolution of conflict in daily living. What are your conclusion? What are some recommendations?

6. Choose a daily newspaper or a weekly periodical and clip the peace articles which you find in it over a five week period of

time. Conclude with a brief observation evaluating the grass roots mood toward peace.

Spirituality Component

It is one thing to read and study about a theology of peace and quite another to become a person of peace. This spirituality component offers a series of Scripture readings with reflection questions closely aligned with the chapter topic. It is suggested that they be used for prayer and reflection over a series of days. The reader may wish either to find another Christian with whom the prayer and its fruit may be shared on a regular basis or to journal one's growth as a peacemaker.

DAY 1: Matthew 5.38-42
Recall an instance in which I offered no resistance to the threat of injury. What was my motive? What is Jesus' motive for non-resistance?

DAY 2: Matthew 5.43-48
Who are my enemies? What makes them "enemies"? How can I begin to love my enemies?

DAY 3: Luke 23.32-34
Whom do I need to forgive for their unjust violence toward me?

DAY 4: John 15.12-13
For whom or in what situation can I imagine myself laying down my life?

DAY 5: Romans 12.14-21
What do I need to do to live at peace with others in my life?

DAY 6: 1 Corinthians 4.12-13
How have I today actively made peace instead of retaliation?

DAY 7: 1 Peter 3.9-12
How can I be a blessing to those who do me wrong?

CHAPTER 6
THE TRADITION OF THE JUSTIFIABLE
WAR

When I was a child growing up, I hadn't heard about the civilian bombing of Hiroshima and Nagasaki nor the obliteration bombing of Dresden. I did know that my father had been stationed in Alaska and in Europe during World War II, but I had heard almost nothing of those years. There was the story of a building crane sliding off (or at least vanishing) from an Aleutian Island in the dead of night. And there was the time my newly wed mother was able to live with my father in Louisiana for some months. But that was it as far as stories went. There were some uniforms and insignia tucked away in the closet of the guest room, but no one ever explained them or talked about the war. Somehow this mysterious silence led me to suspect that there was a shadow side to Veterans' and Memorial Day festivities. Somehow between the flags and songs about freedom there lurked a secret too dreadful to mention. When I was older, the Vietnam era painfully brought the shadow side of war into the television lights; the unmentionable horror became our daily fare on the evening news. The words and the lights also brought a question into focus: can war ever be just?

* * *

1. The Roots of the Justifiable War Theory in Christian Tradition

The justifiable war theory has long been equated with the Roman Catholic position on war and peace, without much attention given to the roots of the theory. The following section examines the Christian scriptures and the historical evolution of the idea of justifiable war in the Roman Catholic Church.

A look at the Christian scriptures

A number of passages in the Christian scriptures have been advanced as a demonstrative claim to Jesus' support of war. At the onset, however, it needs to be said that just war is neither systematically developed nor even mentioned in the Christian scriptures. At best some passages may seem to address one or another aspect connected to the theory of justifiable war. These apparent links need to be examined more fully.

Before this task it is useful to reconsider the scripture passages mentioned in Chapter four. References to the garb worn by soldiers did not serve to extol military prowess. Rather such references were drawn to function as images for the Christian life. Second, the whip fashioned of cords by Jesus for the cleansing of the temple was hardly a weapon of war. Third, the disciples' turn to swords in the last hours of Jesus' life was yet one more example of their misunderstanding of the nature of the Messiah.

Romans 13, especially verse 4, is used at times in support of those wars called by a competent authority to stop wrongdoing: "for it [authority] is a servant of God for your good. But if you do evil, be afraid, for it does not bear the sword without purpose; it is the servant of God to inflict wrath on the evildoer." The three verses immediately prior to this verse set forth a hierarchical understanding of authority and the consequent obligation of citizens to obey the commands of those in authority. The popular conclusion, according to justifiable war theory, has been that the people's obedience to legitimate authority supersedes the personal task of evaluating the justness of a given war. The resultant inference is: if leaders make war, it must be just. It is not clear that Romans 13 can support these interpretations.

As is true with any scriptural passage, Romans 13.4 must be read in its context. Beginning with chapter 12, Paul addresses the behavioral aspect of the Christian life: how does the Christian act? In the first two verses, Paul sets down two foundational norms: First, "offer your bodies as a living sacrifice, holy and pleasing to God"; second, do not conform yourself to this age but be transformed by the renewal of your mind, ...". After discussing the relationships within the Christian community (12.3-13), Paul begins to expound about the community's relationship to those outside its membership. Chapter 12.14-21 addresses non-retaliatory love of enemy. Immediately, Paul turns to the relationships to civil authority (13.1-7). His time- conditioned understanding of authority describes civil magistrates as sharing in the authority of a God who disciplines wrongdoers. These verses are pointedly concerned with Christians' avoidance of any wrong which would necessitate civil punishment. It is unlikely that Paul was addressing either a civil ruler's right to wage war against an enemy threat or wrongdoing as a just cause for war.

After Paul's exhortation to pay taxes, tolls and respect to those due (13.6-7), he comments, "Owe nothing to anyone, except to love one another;" (v.8). Paul closes off chapter 13 by recalling (cf. Romans 12.2) that Christian conduct is shaped by the end times reality of Christ's second coming any day soon (13.11-14). It is as if Paul reminds the Christians one more time that love and hope in the imminent return of Jesus determine their relationship to authority. In this light an unexamined obedience to military leaders seems a questionable interpretation.

Proponents of the justifiable war theory also point to the favorable evaluations of various Roman centurions in the Christian scriptures. The recorded encounters include the cure of the centurion's servant (Matthew 8.5-13; Luke 7.1-10); the

139

crucifixion comment of a centurion guard (Mark 13.39; Matthew 27.54; Luke 23.47) and Cornelius (Acts 10). Fundamentally all of the accounts are stories of faith. Jesus extols the centurion's faith as previously unseen in Israel. At Jesus' death it is a centurion--a member of a foreign occupation force--who acknowledges Jesus' messianic innocence. It is Cornelius' faith and reception of the Spirit which persuades Peter of the possibility of a Gentile Christianity. The military profession pales to irrelevance in the sight of their faith profession.

Luke 11.21-23 (cf. Matthew 12.22-30) has been used to justify arms for the defense of possessions. The context, however, presents some difficulties with this conclusion. Luke 11.21-22 employs the image of a strong man guarding possessions with arms until he is overcome by one stronger. It is verse 23, however, which provides the scriptural key to the sense of these verses: "Whoever is not with me is against me, and whoever does not gather with me scatters". The interpretive function of this verse fits with the surrounding verses 14-26 which present a series of sayings contrasting Jesus with Beelzebub. Luke is presenting two fundamental approaches to living (cf. fundamental moral option) incarnated in Jesus and Beelzebub. The reign of God incarnate in Jesus ultimately overpowers Beelzebub. Jesus is the stronger (cf. Matthew 3.16)--who incidentally is not mentioned as having arms. Those who are not with Jesus are against Jesus. These verses in their context call for radical Christian conversion and portray the ultimate or eschatological triumph of Jesus.

Yet another passage in the synoptics refers to a certain inevitability of war (Mark 13.7; Matthew 24.6; Luke 21.9). Each of these instances occurs in a discourse which draws on the apocalyptic style of writing and which articulates the clear expectation of Jesus' imminent return (Mark 13.30; Matthew 24.34; Luke 21.32). Since apocalyptic discourse frequently employs the image of a final cosmic battle between good and evil, reference to war and even to its inevitability comes as no surprise. What is significant, however, is the insistence that war does not signal the presence of the second coming of Christ. War and rumors of war are bound to happen but they are not signs of a messianic return. The inevitability of war referred to in the synoptics does not affirm God's plans for humankind, but rather states with resignation the result of human choices. Even while using apocalyptic discourse, which typically draws on battle imagery, the synoptic authors disassociate war from the signs of the second coming of Jesus.

The Letter of James 4.1-6 describes the causes of murder, quarrels and conflicts as envy over what one does not possess. As has been seen from the other passages, this could be an apt comment on warmaking but the context of these verses suggests interpersonal, not international, reality.

The conditions necessary for justifiable warfare are not addressed as a moral issue in the Christian scriptures. Centurians, war, and arms are occasionally mentioned. Their mention, however, is consistently subsumed under central concerns of Christian belief and behavior: love of neighbor, faith in Jesus, and hope in the imminent second coming. The scriptures do not provide a well-devised answer to the questions of warmaking. They do provide, however, some central principles within which warmaking can be evaluated.

First, the preservation and promotion of life is a virtually exceptionless norm which is neither a relative nor an absolute value. There are almost no exceptions to the priority of attitudes and actions which preserve and promote life. The commandments in the Hebrew scriptures and the interpretation given by the Sermon on the Mount illustrate the centrality of the value of life in the Judeo- Christian tradition. Perhaps an exception can be admitted when the life of one person is in direct conflict with the life of another person.

Second, the creating love of God (Genesis 1-2) and the incarnate, reconciling love of Jesus (John 3.16; 2 Corinthians 5.

141

18-20) confirm the essential dignity of each human person, which war routinely disregards and violates.

Third, the whole human family is created by God. All human persons thereby are brothers and sisters of each other (1 Corinthians 12). The almost-certain presence or motivation of nationalism and racism in war consistently violates this principle.

Fourth, the Scriptures uphold peace as a preferred Christian value. (John 20.19-21) We are created in peace for peace. Peace is a constitutive dimension of the vision of life forever at the end of time. Jesus is the peace which reconciles the Christian and God.

Fifth, the Christian disciple is called to love as God loves, that is with a non-retaliatory love of those who name us enemy. (Matthew 5.38-48)

Sixth, suffering undergone with faith in God can occasion risen life as was the case with Jesus. (Philippians 1)

It is such principles rather than the occasional reference to the things of war which are the scriptural legacy to the Christian evaluation of warmaking. This legacy has been obscured, however, through the historical interpretations of the justifiable war theory.

The history of justifiable war theory

At least until the recent past--and perhaps until today--popular opinion has identified the Catholic position on the morality of war with justifiable war theory. This identification is not without difficulties and oversimplifications as the following paragraphs illustrate.

The Greek philosopher and mentor of Thomas Aquinas, Aristotle, first used the term, *just war*. The concept has roots also in the non- Christian thought of Plato and Cicero. It was first brought into the Christian domain by Ambrose (339-397), then developed by Augustine (354-430) during the decline of the Roman Empire. Augustine reasoned, under the influence of Platonic dualism, that true peace belonged to the heavenly realm. Consequently there were circumstances and situations in this world which precluded peacemaking. In other words, there are times when evil is so great that action on behalf of foundational Christian values--life, peace, human solidarity-- is needed to resist that evil. In Augustine's mind the defense of the Roman Empire was one such instance because it was connected with the defense of the Christian faith.

In the minds of others this connection had given rise to the popular and militant tendency to engage in the defense of the empire as if it were a holy war. Augustine's justifiable war theory, therefore, attempted to restrain the excesses of the holy war mentality. To this end Augustine maintained the following necessary constraints on war.

First, the desired end of warmaking must be the restoration of peace. Second, the just cause could be only the avenging of wrongs such as violence, revenge, cruelty or unprovoked attack on innocent victims. Third, a competent, legitimate authority must wage the war in contrast to an individual's decision to retaliate. Fourth, the war must be conducted according to the dictates of justice. Reflecting his Platonic bias Augustine held that one's inward disposition was superior to and could be separated from the acts in which one engaged. In other words love for the enemy's soul could be the motivation for violence waged on the enemy's body. Physical force could be an instrument of love. The use of such force, however, was a lamentable, albeit necessary, state of affairs according to Augustine. His dualistic worldview allowed for an interior intention of love alongside of exterior force and violence.[1]

---

[1]AUGUSTINE, *City of God*, Book XIX, chapter 7. For additional information on the Augustinian foundation for the

143

This initial formulation of the conditions for a justifiable war within the Christian tradition came, therefore, as an attempt to limit the practice of holy war. Its proponents drew on previous non-Christian philosophical thought, especially Platonic dualism.

A second resurgence of a justifiable war theory within the Christian tradition emerged against the backdrop of the Crusades, which were popularly understood as a holy war against the infidel Saracens. Thomas Aquinas added little development to the thought of Aristotle, Augustine, Alexander of Hales and Gratian. He did systematize the criteria within the framework of the common good. As with Augustine, Thomas used rational thought to constrain the notion of holy war. The question under which Thomas discussed the justifiable war illustrated his presumption against war. *Summa theologica* II, II, Q. 40 reads, "Is it always a sin to fight in a war?"

Some three centuries later against the backdrop of religious wars in Europe and the wars of conquest in the new world, a justifiable war theory again came to the fore in an effort to restrain the violence of these wars on behalf of Christianity. Martin Luther applied the 'Two Swords' approach to divide warmaking into two types: the holy war which used spiritual weapons and the just war which used military as well as political means.

A similar division occurred in Spanish scholastic thought of this period. The Spanish conquests in the new world were the catalyst for F. de Vitoria (1485-1546) and F. Suarez (1548-1617) to rethink twelfth century Thomism because the new era had discovered civilizations other than medieval Christianity. In

---

justifiable war, see also D.R. WRIGHT, *War in a Church-historical perspective,* in *Evangelical Quarterly* 57 (April 1985) 133-161, here 150-154. See also BAINTON, *Christian,* chapters 2 and 6.

their effort to contain conquistador aggression, these classic conditions for the justifiable war were set forth: 1)just cause; 2) competent authority; 3)comparative justice; 4)right intention; 5)last resort; 6)probability of success; 7)proportionality. Their thought was picked up by the Dutch lawyer statesman H. Grotius as the basis for international law. The concept of the justifiable war in these centuries passed out of Christian thought into the political, military and legal arenas.

In light of this summary, three factors appear consistently in the history of the justifiable war theory: a specific historical situation, efforts to restrict a holy war mentality and non-Christian philosophical underpinnings. These constant threads raise questions about the potential of justifiable war theory for the nuclear age. Can conditions for a justifiable war in the fifth, thirteenth and sixteenth centuries be used in a historical situation of nuclear warmaking potential? Is nuclear warfare qualitatively different from the so-called conventional warmaking? Can an adequate Christian position relative to war be built on efforts to restrain what is already an error, namely the misunderstanding of the holy war concept? Can there not be some other beginning point, such as core Christian values including peace? Does the return of justifiable war to the secular and political realm signal a collective sigh of relief that the idea has emigrated where it really belongs? Does the centuries- long partnership serve as a reminder that decisions of warmaking are of a moral and religious concern because they involve people? What is the Christian role in this world, when the warmakers regard Christian talk of peace as irrelevant to the real world?

2. Criteria for a Justifiable War

As they have come down to this century, the criteria surrounding justifiable war fall under two major headings: criteria to initiate war and criteria within warfare. This section will examine the classical criteria with an eye to the application of the criteria in twentieth century wars and to the

145

possibility of their use in evaluating current warfare possibilities.

Criteria for initiating a justifiable war

Just intention: The justifiable war theory maintains that the only truly just intentions behind the waging of war are peace, reconciliation, justice and love (Cf. *Challenge of Peace,* #95). Clearly intentions of vengeance and retaliation cannot be called just. Neither does just intention include a demonstration of national superiority or sovereignty. One wonders when was the last time in which a war was fought for a just intention. The identification of intention presupposes a truthfulness and an integrity not easy to come by in the most simple personal decision--to say nothing of those decisions as complex as international warmaking.

This criterion presents a theoretical difficulty for current personalist moral thinking to the extent that it reflects the dualist separation of interior from concrete behavioral choices. When contemporary moral theology speaks of the principle of intention, it includes both the direct intention, e.g., the restoration of peace, and the indirect intention, that is, the intention directing the foreseeable actions and attitudes used to realize that value. In keeping with this more wholistic understanding of the acting moral person, it is difficult to conceive of disembodied and decontextualized just intention desiring peace separated from the intention which informs attitudes and concrete actions employed to restore peace.

There are also some more practical difficulties with the criterion of just intention. For example, if the case in question is an international war, whose intention must be just? Does the intention of the competent authority suffice; or must all participants have a just intention; or the whole nation as a collective body; or each individual member of the nation? In addition the technical and mechanical nature, both of methods in warfare and of the initiation of warfare, obscures the

146

indirect intention through distancing and chain of command. The perpetrator of warring activities can push a button to drop a bomb or unleash a missile from a safe cubicle without ever viewing the target face to face, before or after the attack. The distancing factor makes it easier to disregard or to be ignorant of the foreseeable effects of the intention.[1]

Just cause: The criterion of just cause has traditionally included national self-defense, preservation of innocent life and perhaps the ending of atrocities. The *Challenge of Peace* states that "War is permissible only to confront 'a real and certain danger'" which includes the protection of innocent life, the preservation of conditions necessary for decent human existence and the security of basic human rights (*Challenge of Peace*, #86). War waged for national aggrandizement and probably all offensive wars are excluded by the just cause criterion. This defensive nature of just causes does presume that only one side can be just, while the other side is an unjust aggressor.

---

[1]This fact has also been observed by S.Milgram in *The Perils of Obedience*, in *Harper's Magazine* 247 (December 1973) 62-66 plus 75-77, here 77: "There was a time, perhaps, when people were able to give a fully human response to any situation because they were fully absorbed in it as human beings. But as soon as there was a division of labor things changed. ... A person does not get to see the whole situation but only a small part of it, and is thus unable to act without some kind of overall direction. He yields to authority but in doing so is alienated from his own actions. "Even Eichmann was sickened when he toured the concentration camps, but he had only to sit at a desk and shuffle papers. At the same time the man in the camp who actually dropped Cyclon-b into the gas chambers was able to justify his behavior on the ground that he was only following orders. Thus there is a fragmentation of the total human act; no one is confronted with the consequences of his decision to carry out the evil act. The person who assumes responsibility has evaporated."

147

This criterion is rooted in the conviction that values, even fundamental values, can come into conflict with each other in such a way that both cannot be realized at the same time. For example, peace and the preservation of the conditions necessary for socio-economic and political life may be in radical opposition. At this foundational level, the criterion of just cause thereby admits that the preservation of life and peace are not absolute but virtually exceptionless norms which may be subsumed to other fundamental values. Even though the preservation of life is a virtually exceptionless norm admitting some exemptions, it is not obvious that a leader--or anyone else for that matter--can determine unilaterally whose lives are subordinated to the realization of other fundamental values.

Although the just cause criterion has some ambiguities, it does make a valid contribution to a contemporary evaluation of war in its insistence that not every value can be realized all the time.

Formal declaration by compentent authority: A just war must be declared by competent authority, that is, a person or body which has been invested with the power and offices of governance for the public good through the consent of the governed whether by acclaim, vote or accepted appointment (*Challenge of Peace,* #87). Self-appointed rulers apart from popular consent are not competent authority. The competent authority, with reference to just war criteria, is expected to examine the situation and to decide if, in this instance, other fundamental values take precedence over the fundamental values of peace and life. The decision of the competent authority, however, in no way absolves citizens from their own personal moral responsibility and decision in the situation.

This presumably straightforward criterion has been obscured or ignored in our most recent history by technology and political maneuvers. The Vietnam 'conflict' as well as other military interventions were not initiated with formal declarations of war (Cf. *Challenge of Peace*, #88). It is questionable whether this criterion could call a revolution against unjust but legitimately constituted authority a justifiable war. In revolution it is conceivable that the citizens have transferred their consent to be governed from those in positions of authority to revolutionary leaders (Cf. *Challenge of Peace*, #89).

This criterion takes on additional ambiguity in complex political systems with their necessary systems of checks and balances. The executive and legislative branches of the United States government, for example, each jealously guard their role as competent authority in decisions of warmaking while maintaining that the other branch's exercise of authority jeopardizes national security. These structures and attitudes are far removed from the fifth century political structures and decision-making.

In addition fully automated defense systems open the possibility of an attack or counterattack with little or no immediate decision on the part of competent authority. If such a decision were attempted, the minimal time available between an offensive launch and a defensive counter strike would not allow for the collection of information necessary for the competent authority to make a decision. All of these factors question the applicability or appropriateness of this criterion for the current world situation.

Last resort: In the classical tradition, this criterion placed the decision for war at the end of a series of ultimatums and announcements of the intent to declare war, which were aimed at the resolution of differences as an alternative to warmaking. During the Middle Ages, a thirty day waiting period was proposed between the declared intention and the inauguration of war so that both sides could re-examine the dispute and justify the departure from peace.

149

One major difficulty with this criterion in the twentieth century--as well as from its inception--is the absence of an inter- or better an a-national body to mediate disputes. The absence of an impartial body makes it possible for individual nations to decide when they have reached the end of the search for peaceful alternatives (Cf. *Challenge of Peace*, #96-97). Although the United Nations has the potential and the structures to be such a mediator, member nations have not given the United Nations such authority. The United Nations is thereby reduced to one more body torn by competing vested interest groups.

Another difficulty with the criterion of last resort is connected again to the technological nature of current warring methods. The deterrence arsenal, the possibility of accidental launch and automatic counterattack lessen the likelihood of war coming at the end of ultimatums or the exhaustion of peaceful alternatives. War becomes a reaction and not a regrettable last resort. War without regret would be unthinkable within the classic justifiable war theory.

A reasonable hope of success: War can be justifiable only when there is a reasonable hope that it can realize at least some of the fundamental values which are being threatened (*Challenge of Peace*, #98). Success so understood is less about victory and more about basic human and institutional values. When one looks at the upheaval in social, familial, economic and political values during a time of war, the decision for warmaking must involve some guarantee that fundamental values of personal and institutional life can probably be preserved or achieved through warmaking.

Proportionality between the evil incurred and the evils unleashed: This justification of war requires that war is proportionate both to the evil incurred at enemy hands and to the evils about to be unleashed by warmaking activities (*Challenge of Peace*, #99). First of all the injury experienced must be sufficiently grave to warrant a response of

150

warmaking. One does not dissuade a child's pestering with a sledgehammer. A nation could hardly retaliate with war against restrictions on a luxury-based lifestyle to which it has grown accustomed.

This criterion also demands that more good be done than undone in warmaking. Like the criterion of just cause, proportionality relativizes any absolute claims concerning war. Warmaking does sacrifice some values. The question thereby becomes, what values are so essential to human life in society that the evils unleashed in war are commensurate with these values? Needless to say such an evaluation is difficult, especially when one begins to look further than money spent and lives lost. What is commensurate with an activity like war which re-enforces the expendability of human life within a whole society? What is comparable to fortifying patterns of coercive force and destruction as legitimate means of conflict management? What is proportionate to altering or destroying socio- political and economic interrelationships on a worldwide scale? What can be comparable to the famine, economic dislocation and social fragmentation which results from war?

In theory it could be possible that some fundamental values of personal and institutional life could be proportionate to the evils of war. In practice one becomes less certain.

In the classical theories of justifiable war, all of these criteria need to be met before engaging in warmaking. One becomes hardpressed to name one war so initiated in human history. Yet these criteria are not sufficient. There are three additional criteria concerned with conduct during war.

Criteria for conduct during war

Non-combatant immunity: From its beginning, the theory of justifiable war has insisted on non-combatant immunity. This immunity included monks, clerics, religious, the peasant class, as well as women and children (*Challenge of Peace*, #104). In its origin, the distinction between military, professional warriors and civilians was unambiguous.

In the current era this obvious differentiation has been camouflaged in two ways. First, it is less clear who are non-combatants. For example, are those who produce the weapons of war non-combatants or necessary accomplices? What about those who produce food or provide medical care for combatants? What about those who support warmaking with their rhetoric or their taxes?

Second, the weapons of warmaking have become increasingly indiscriminate with regard to a specific target. A sword or a gun could be directed at a soldier and not at a non-combatant. Submarines and airplanes have much less of that discretionary ability. Chemical, nuclear and germ warfare make no distinction between civilian and belligerent. Even if they initially were able to make the distinction between chemicals, nuclear fallout and germs subsequently effect natural resources and future generations which had no part in original combat.

For the most part, the criterion of non-combatant immunity has been progressively ignored in this century. This may signal the injustice of contemporary warfare or the inapplicability of this criteria to the contemporary situation. In either case, even the modern notion of limited war remains a threat to non-combattants.

Proportionate weapons and strategies: The criterion of proportionality attempts to restrain atrocities and to limit revengeful retaliations through its insistence that evils perpetuated by any weapon or strategy do not outweigh the value achieved (Cf. *Challenge of Peace*, #105). In earlier centuries this was accomplished by limiting war to certain times of year and to certain places. Although the destructive capabilities of our era could not be anticipated in those previous eras, the principle itself offers a valid way of evaluating warmaking practices.

Total war, war of annihilation, and unconditional defeat are excluded by the principle of proportionality. In light of the effects on the biological and environmental chains, especially as they are inherited by future generations, any use of chemical, nuclear or germ warfare is rejected as disproportionate weaponry. Irreversible effects at such a fundamental level cannot be commensurate with the limited objectives of any given war. Proportionality in weapons, tactics and strategies must also examine whether the expenditure for weapons is justifiable when it leaves basic human needs are left unsatisfied. The criterion of proportionality places some definite restrictions on the tactics and actions within war.

Moral discrimination: The criterion of moral discrimination demands that the ways used to realize a value are consistent with that value. In the context of justifiable war the weapons and strategies of warmaking must somehow resonate with a just intention, such as restoration of conditions for peace, reconciliation, just socio- economic and political orders, or love of others, especially the disenfranchised.

This criterion rejects total war (*Challenge of Peace,* #103), unnecessary cruelty and suffering, and inhumane treatment of prisoners of war as inconsistent with love of neighbor. In addition weapons and strategies which constrain enemy forces rather than kill indiscriminately would seem more consistent with reconciliation. The criterion does raise a fundamental question, namely, can warmaking in itself be consistent with an intention of peace, reconciliation, love and justice in the socio-political or political orders?

That question touches on the adequacy of the classical theory of justified war for this century, or for that matter, for any century.[1] In addition to the difficulties addressed with the individual criterion, there are some common problems with the theory of justifiable war. First, there has been a gap between the practice and the theory of justifiable war. The theory was established on the presupposition against killing and warmaking, while allowing that an occasional war might be justifiable owing to exceptional circumstances. In practice, however, the theory became a self-righteous proclamation that war itself was just, a value in itself. Hence the theory became known as the just war theory. In theory the intent behind justifiable war was the restraint of excesses; in practice engagement in warmaking has meant progressive escalation of retaliatory vengeance with little sense of restraint.

Second, the criteria emerged in an era of limited and conventional warfare. Submarines, airplanes, chemical, nuclear and germ warfare have qualitatively changed the nature of warmaking; distinctions between combatants and non-combatants are blurred; irreversible changes in biological and environmental systems themselves threaten not only the present but also future generations. The historically conditioned just war criteria are no longer applicable as a coherent theory.

Third, in this secular and pluralistic era the just war criteria cannot restrain those who have no desire to follow them. This suggests the emergence of a different role for the Christian peacemaker in these times. The role may be that of a Christian prophet denouncing all war as incompatible with a Christian lifestyle. Or the role may be that of an incarnational peacemaker, engaged in dialogue with the realities of this world as part of the process of transformation into the reign of God. In either case, criteria derived from a dualistic philosophy for a monolithic Christian culture are unhelpful.

---

[1]MCSORLEY, *New Testament*, 103 holds that the theory has never worked in practice.

In spite of these fundamental shortcomings, the concept of justifiable war performs a service at least in theory. It reminds those of us in the era between the first and second coming of Jesus Christ that little is absolutely black or clearly white. There are perennial value priorities and value conflicts. Peacemaking, preservation of human life, dignity of the human person and solidarity within the human family are value priorities resonant with the Christian tradition. Although it is not absolute, this same tradition maintains a presumption against killing and coercive force (*Challenge of Peace*, #83). The option for warmaking and coercive force demands justification proportionate to the disvalues which such action unleashes. Furthermore the very presumption against killing and coercive force must determine how the choice for violence is implemented once it is justified. Although the specific criteria of the theory of justifiable war may no longer fit these circumstances, the theory itself suggests the importance of responsible decision- making in the grayness of this intermediary period.

3. Twentieth Century Catholic Church Teaching on Justified War

Two world wars, the arms race, the cold war, as well as the introduction of an arsenal of atomic, bacteriological, chemical, and nuclear weapons have afforded numerous opportunities for re-evaluation and teaching on the justifiable war for the Roman Catholic magisterium.

Benedict XV (1919-1922) conscientiously refused to decide whether the Allies or the Central Powers were justified in their choice to resolve differences through warmaking. Benedict insisted on papal impartiality, for he was the 'spiritual father' of peoples on both sides involved in the World War I. Consequently, he threw his energies unsuccessfully into mediating negotiations for peace. His course of action raised questions about the ability of the justifiable war theory to analyze or to resolve the issues involved.

In the context of the conflict between the Mexican socialist government and the Roman Catholic church, Pius XI (1922-1939) asserted the possibility of a justified insurrection.[1] Pius did nuance this position with the caution that peace was the preferred value; also he cautioned against unjustified revolutions. Pius held, however, defense of persons and nations could provide a just cause for revolution provided that 1) the revolutionary tactics didn't become an end in themselves; 2) the devices used were not intrinsically evil; 3) the strategies were proportionate to the probability of success; and 4) that clergy and Catholic Action laity did not become involved directly in the revolution (*Firmissimam*, #26-28). These comments reflected the justifiable war theory of Thomas Aquinas, but differed from some Thomistic interpretations.

Pius XII (1939-1958) wrote extensively on the emergence of a new world order founded on peace, justice and moral principles out of the ruins of World War II. This beginning point in peace and justice may have signaled the search for new criteria to evaluate warmaking. In these musings, Pius XII connected war to socio-economic and political injustices. In his teachings on war he limited the just causes of war to the defense of the nation or innocent victims against an unjust aggressor.[2] Pius used considerations of proportionality alongside an appeal to divine law to decry total war as well as

---

[1]Pius XI, *Firmissimam constantiam,* in *AAS* XXIX (1937) 189-199.

[2]PIUS XII, *Christmas message, 1948,* in *Catholic Mind* 50 (1952) 248-256, especially 254. *See also Address to Military Doctors* (October 19, 1953), in *AAS* XXXXV (1953) 744-754, here 748 (=*Catholic Mind* 52 [January 1954] 46-54. *In his Address to the eighth Congress of the World Medical Association* (September 30, 1954) in *AAS* XXXXVI (1954) 587-598, here 589 (=*Catholic Mind* 55 [April 1955] 242-252, Pius appears to admit "necessary 'safeguarding' of legitimate possessions" as a just cause as well as defense against injustice.

atomic, bacteriological and chemical warfare.[1] Although Pius held that rulers had a strict obligation to prevent war, to disarm and to deter nations from the war option,[2] he insisted that pacifism was an untenable position for an individual whose duly elected government determined and executed a defensive war.[3] Pius XII, for the most part, addressed war through the criteria of justifiable war, although he appeared to search for a beginning point in the realization of peacemaking values in contrast to these criteria.

John XXIII (1958-1963) seems to have moved away from the justifiable war criteria ever so slightly in the encyclical, Peace on Earth. Issued in April 1963 after an eighteen month escalation of the cold war polarization as reflected in the Kennedy-Khrushchev summit failure, the erection of the Berlin Wall, the Bay of Pigs and the Cuban Missile crisis, the encyclical does not mention a right of self- defense. Instead John XXIII writes, "in an age such as ours which prides itself on its atomic energy, it is contrary to reason to hold that war is now a suitable way to restore rights which have been violated" (#127).[4] The sentence questions the wisdom of warmaking in an age of atomic energy. One wonders, however, whether the encyclical intended to discard the theory of justifiable war.

Some two years later, the *Church in the Modern World* devoted chapter V of its second section to peacemaking. The chapter seem to reflect John XXIII's concerns about the wisdom

---

[1] See PIUS XII, *Military Doctors*, 749.

[2] PIUS XII, *Christmas Message*, *1957*, in *Catholic Mind* 56 (1958) 160-179, especially 179.

[3] PIUS XII, *Christmas Message*, *1956*, in *Catholic Mind* 55 (April 1957) 165-182, here 178.

[4] See J. B. HEHIR, *The Just-War Ethic and Catholic Theology. Dynamics of Change and Continuity*, in NCCB, *In the Name of Peace*, 87-115, here 96 summarizes the ongoing discussion over the meaning of the sentence within the magisterial teaching on the justifiable war.

of war given the existent circumstances. A theory of justifiable war is nowhere named. Although the document admits that "governments cannot be denied the right to legitimate defense once every means of peaceful settlement has been exhausted" (#79), it does so without reference to 'just cause' or 'last resort'. In the following paragraph of the document, total war and obliteration bombing of cities are condemned in the context of "massive and indiscriminate destruction far exceeding the bounds of legitimate defense" (#80). Here again the context resembles the criteria of proportionality and non-combatant immunity without referring to the justifiable war criteria by name. This may reflect the effort by the Council in its own words "to undertake an evaluation of war with an entirely new attitude" (#80).

To an extent, *Church in the Modern World* did articulate at least the beginnings of this new attitude. Chapter V begins with a three paragraph description of peace based on justice and love (#77). This inaugural statement for an evaluation of war includes praise for "those who renounce the use of violence in the vindication of their rights and who resort to methods of defense which are available to weaker parties too" (#78) as well as an appeal for legal provisions in the case of conscientious objectors (#79). It is against this 'new attitude' of recognizing and welcoming the Christian nonviolent tradition that the document evaluates war.

Paul VI (1963-1978) insisted on the irrationality of war, which he saw as caused by social, economic and cultural inequalities (*Development of Peoples*, #30). From his 1965 address at the United Nations ("No more war, war never again") to his final New Year's Message celebrating World Day of Peace in 1977, Paul VI reiterated the absurdity of war in this era: "we denounce the false and dangerous policy of 'recourse to armaments' and to an unadmitted competition between nations for military superiority ... how can we not bemoan the uncalculable expenditure of economic and human energies which is required for each state to maintain its carapace of weapons..." [1] Perhaps mirroring a new attitude toward warmaking, Paul simply dismisses warmaking as absurd and focuses on development which would eradicate the decision for warmaking.

John Paul II has called for Christians to prevent every form of warfare while admitting defense against unjust aggressors as a just cause for warmaking. In addition he has noted that the esential difference between modern, nuclear or bacteriological war and conventional war heightens the urgency of the move toward effective negotiation as a means of resolving conflict.[2]

Papal teaching on war in this century has avoided using the language of the justifiable war theory, while maintaining allegiance to some of the criteria. The criteria which are typically used include proportionality, non-combatant immunity and just cause.

The teaching of the US Catholic bishops reflects papal teaching. In comments on United States involvement in World War I, the US bishops found "freedom and right as the inalienable endowment of all mankind [sic]"[3] provided just cause. In 1942, they asserted that war is a last resort, but that the current world situation was one of those times "when it is impossible to avoid it". The "defense of life and right" had become a duty.[4] The initial NCCB statement relative to US

---

[1]Paul VI, *If you want peace, defend life. Message of Pope Paul VI for World Day of Peace*, 1977 (December 8, 1976), in *The Pope Speaks* 22 (#1) 38-45, here 42.

[2]JOHN PAUL II, *1982 World Day of Peace Message* (December 8, 1981), in *Origins* 11 (January 7, 1982) 473-478, here 478, #12.

[3]*Lessons of war* (1919), in NCCB, *In the Name of Peace*, 3-5, here 4.

[4]*Victory and Peace* (November 14, 1942), in NCCB, *In the Name of Peace*, 7-9, here 7.

involvement in Vietnam held that it was justified.[1] It is noteworthy that the US bishops were less hesitant in judging US warmaking practices as justified than the popes had been. The absence of hesitation can be attributed to either patriotic nearsightedness or to the more specific kind of knowledge about the local situation which enables judgement.

In subsequent statements on United States involvement in Vietnam both in 1968 and in 1971, the moral evaluation centered on questions of proportionality until the following conclusion was reached: "At this point in history, it seems clear to us that whatever good we hope to achieve through continued involvement in this war is now outweighed by the destruction of human life and of moral values which it inflicts."[2]

Five years later, the NCCB treated war within its pastoral letter on the moral life, *To Live in Christ Jesus.* Therein the bishops uphold war as a form of legitimate defense, while raising the question, can modern war as it is actually waged ever be morally justifiable, given indiscriminating weapons and irreversible effects on future generations? Military service is viewed as a viable option for Catholics as long as this form of service does not involve unthinking obedience or violation of moral norms such as non-combatant immunity. Their evaluation of military service stand alongside a call for legal protection of conscientious objectors. These paragraphs call not only for the non-use of nuclear weapons with massive destructive capability, but also for an end to threats of their use. The section ends by acknowledging the need for additional study and reflection on the moral reasons and political

---

[1]*Peace and Vietnam* (November 18, 1966) in NCCB, *In the Name of Peace*, 25-29, here 27-28.
[2]*Resolution on Southeast Asia* (1971), in NCCB, *In the Name of Peace*, 59-62, here 60.

purposes which could justify the use of force in both conventional and nuclear warmaking.[1]

It would seem that the 1983 pastoral letter, *The Challenge of Peace*, is directed toward meeting this need. War is again acknowledged as a legitimate form of defense against aggression (#72) with some additional nuances. First, the context articulates a clear presumption against war (#71). Second, the Christian has an inalienable obligation to defend peace against aggression. Since this obligation does not determine how peace is defended, either nonviolent or coercive methods could be used (#73-74). The pastoral does observe, "We believe work to develop non-violent means of fending off aggression and resolving conflict best reflects the call of Jesus both to love and to justice" (#78). This same paragraph goes on to qualify the above by an acceptance "that force, even deadly force, is sometimes justified". These lines clearly re-enforce the nature of life in these in-between times.

In this light the explicit and detailed treatment of the criteria of just war in *Challenge of Peace,* #86-110, is understandable. On the other hand it has the appearance of an unfortunate regression for two reasons. First, the terminology had been explicitly absent from magisterial teaching for over a generation in preference to "an evaluation of war with an entirely new attitude" (*Church in the Modern World*, #80). Second, some of the criteria had fallen from use in magisterial teaching due to their connection with specific historical contexts far removed from this era. The brevity with which some of the criteria were dealt suggests the discontinuity with this era. The reintroduction of the criteria for a justifiable war in *Challenge of Peace* gives, however, an aura of perennial validity which is not accurate.

---

[1]NCCB, *To Live in Christ Jesus*, Washington, DC 1976, #96-103.

With regard to the nuclear war, *Challenge of Peace* condemns any and all use of "nuclear weapons or other instruments of mass slaughter" directed at population centers or civilian targets in keeping with the principle of civilian immunity (#147-149). No deliberate initiation, even if limited in nature, is morally justified (#150-156). With regard to limited retaliatory use of nuclear weapons *Challenge of Peace* is less definitive, but highly skeptical that such use can remain limited or offer reasonable hope of success (#157-161).

In addition the NCCB calls for reductions of nuclear and conventional forces, prohibition of chemical and biological warfare and an end to arms sales (#210-211).

More than anything else *Challenge of Peace* performs the same service as the concept of justifiable war, namely the reminder that responsible decision-making in the grayness of this time before the end times involves value conflicts and sometimes justifiable departures from the values of peacemaking, preservation of human life, dignity of the human person and solidarity of the human family in order to realize other, equally foundational human values. Although it does provide this service, the theory of justifiable war as a coherent unit is not an adequate tool for making a responsible decision in the area of contemporary warmaking.

4. Implications for Christian Peacemakers

Justifiable war has had a long history within the Christian tradition, although its roots are more clearly in pre-Christian philosophy than in the Hebrew and Christian scriptures. Christian writers and thinkers turned to the theory of justifiable war, when specific historical situations required some means to restrain the practiced excess in civil or religious warmaking. In spite of its shortcomings, throughout history the justifiable war theories were an attempt to interface Christian and rational principles with socio- political realities.

Although nuclear and chemical capabilities have radically transformed contemporary warmaking, Christian peacemakers can not disengage themselves from these changes and this historical situation. The history of justifiable war compels peacemakers to enter into ongoing dialogue in an effort to unearth and articulate those principles and values which can direct Christian response to warmaking in these days. The earlier analysis of this chapter illustrates the time-conditioned nature of justifiable war theories and the subsequent, urgent need for a current moral framework within which to assess warmaking. The incarnation calls the Christian peacemaker to transform the existent world. Withdrawal from the fray does not suffice, although there is no guarantee that the Christian assessment of warmaking--even within a contemporary moral framework--will permeate the socio-political world.

In developing this moral approach, the Christian peacemaker cannot ignore this fact: justifiable war theory sought to restrain the practical excesses in warmaking. The Christian peacemaker must demand that any armed conflict today be confined and limited by human dignity and basic Christian values. There is no place for unrestrained excesses in international conflict. This ceaseless appeal to restraint is already a countercultural position in today's world.

In addition the Christian peacemaker must act on a presumption against warmaking. The presumption against war has been repeated time and again in the twentieth century magisterial teaching. War is not one more neutral option among other equally valid alternatives to the resolution of conflict, with each option having a slate of positive and negative consequences. Warmaking is replete with disvalue. At its best warmaking is a failure of reconciliation and peacemaking. The avoidance of war is a moral norm to which there is virtually no exception. In theory it is conceivable to maintain the possibility that a specific war may be the best of disvalue-laiden options. Given the destructive nature of current warmaking, however, it is questionable whether any war in actuality could realize values proportionate to the disvalues unleashed. Again the presumption against war appears to be a countercultural position in practice.

Although the appeal to restraint and the presumption against war do not represent the practiced mainstream view of warmaking, they are hardly sufficient for the Christian peacemaker. The Hebrew and Christian scriptures invite the peacemaker to incarnate those values in their lives which make warmaking obsolete. The values of life, dignity of the human person, solidarity of all persons, justice, and non-retaliatory love of enemy are such foundational values.

The above discussion of war in the Christian scriptures associates warmaking with human effort at self-justification. This fact challenges Christian peacemakers to examine their tendencies toengage in personal warmaking from the perspective of salvation. Is not our insistence on imposing our ways and means on others as well asour trust only on our efforts a simple rejection of the God who creates, justifies and lives within and among us. Is God incarnate-with-us or are we the gods alone? Are national and international wars collective efforts at self-justification? When we call a war justifiable, what do we mean from this perspective of salvation?

Roman Catholic Church Documents

Official Roman Catholic teaching in the twentieth century has addressed issues in this chapter. The following selections are particularly pertinent.

Peace on Earth, #126-129
This was written in 1963. What needs to be changed so that it can be an accurate assessment of the world situation today?

Challenge of Peace, #71-110
1.What is the binding Christian presupposition underlying the justifiable war theory?
 2. Under what circumstances did Augustine see the possibility of a just war?
3. What are the presumptions today with regard to justifiable war theory according to paragraph 83?
4. Explain the criteria which a war must meet in order to be justifiable?
5. What are the moral principles which must be applied to the conduct of war?

Challenge of peace, #142-161
What is the US bishops' teaching with regard to
    a)nuclear warfare against civilian population
    b)the initiation of nuclear war
    c)limited nuclear war

Church in the Modern World, #79-80 and 82
1. To what extent does Vatican Council II refer to the just war tradition in its assessment of war today?
2. What are the considerations necessary in evaluating modern warfare?

Other Suggested Readings

BAINTON, R. *Christian attitudes toward war and peace. A historical survey and critical re-evaluation.* Nashville/ NewYork, 1960, especially chapters 2,6, and 8.

CHILDRESS, J.F.   *Just-war Theories,* in *Theological Studies* 39 (1978) 427-445.

FINN, J.   *Pacifism and just war: Either or neither,* in P.J. MURNION (ed.), *Catholics and Nuclear War. A Commentary on The Challenge of Peace. The U.S.Catholic Bishops' Pastoral Letter on War and Peace.* NY, 1983, 132-145.

FURNISH, V.P.   *War and Peace in the New Testament,* in *Interpretation* 38 (October 1984), 363-379.

HANNIGAN, J.P.   *War and peace: Christian choices,* in *Religion Teachers Journal* 17 (November/December 1983) 21-24.

HEHIR, J.B.   *The Just-War ethic and Catholic theology: Dynamics of Change and Continuity,* in USCC, *In the name of peace.   Collective Statements of the US Catholic Bishops on war and peace, 1919-1980* Washington, DC, 1982, 87-115.

HOLLENBACH, D.   *Nuclear Ethics. A Christian Moral Argument.*   New York/Ramsey, NJ, 1983. See especially chapter 4: Criteria for policy evaluation.

JOHNSON, J.T.   *Just War Tradition and the Restraint of War. A Moral and Historical Inquiry.*   Princeton, 1981.

MACGREGOR, G.H.C.   *The New Testament Basis of Pacifism.* Nyack, NY, revised ed., 1954.   See especially chapter 2: New Testament texts used for war.

MURNION, P.J. (ed.).   *Catholics and Nuclear War. A Commentary on The Challenge of Peace. The U.S.Catholic Bishops' Pastoral Letter on War and Peace.*   NY, 1983. See especially Section IV on pacifism and just war.

NAIRN, T.A. *The peace pastoral: A product of the just war tradition,* in J.T. PAWLIKOWSKI and D. SENIOR (eds.), *Biblical and Theological Reflections on The Challenge of Peace.* Wilmington, DE, 1984, 108-120.

NCCB, *In the name of peace. Collective Statements of the US Catholic Bishops on war and peace, 1919-1980.* Washington, DC, 1982.

SCHNEIDERS, S.M. *New Testament Reflections on Peace and Nuclear Arms,* in P.J. MURNION (ed.), *Catholics and Nuclear War. A Commentary on The Challenge of Peace. The U.S. Catholic Bishops' Pastoral Letter on War and Peace.* New York, 1983, 91-105.

SHANNON, T. *War or peace? The search for new answers.* Maryknoll, NY, 1982. See especially part I.

SHANNON, T. *What are they saying about peace and war?* New York/Ramsey, 1983. See especially chapter 1 : The development of the just war tradition.

WEIGEL, G. *Tranquillitas ordinis. The Present Failure and Future Promise of American Catholic Thought on War and Peace,* Oxford, 1987. Weigel differs from this chapter in his assessment of the just war position and contemporary Catholic thought. For a review of Weigel's theological position, see P. STEINFELS, *The heritage abandoned II,* in *Commonweal* 114 (September 25, 1987) 530-534.

WRIGHT, D.F. *War in a Church-historical perspective,* in *Evangelical Quarterly* 57 (April 1985) 133-161.

Audio-visual Materials

The following are some of the audio-visual materials which are related to the chapter content. The list is not exhaustive, but is intended to give some initial suggestions for previewing.

Arming the earth (video; 28m; Beyond WarII; 1984) illustrates the development of the weapons of war in this century: machine gun, submarine, airplane and atomic bomb.

Booom (film; 10m; Journal Films; 1979) takes a humorous look at the history of aggression and the theory that might makes right.

The last slideshow (filmstrip; 20m; 1977) traces military history to the present nuclear arms race.

War and the Christian conscience II (filmstrip; 20m; Klise) reviews the just war theory and its inapplicability to the current situation.

Introductory Activities

The purpose of the introductory activity is to begin discussion on the just war tradition as well as to allow students/participants a chance to express what their previous experiences and understandings of the justifiable war have been.

1. Describe a just war of the twentieth century. What made it justifiable?
2. Is a just war the same concept as a justifiable war?

Discussion Questions

The purpose of the discussion questions is to encourage students/participants to integrate the text and/or presented material into their own thinking and living.

1. What has changed about twentieth century warmaking in comparison with previous centuries?

2. Evaluate the scriptural bases for a justifiable war.

3. Evaluate the criteria for a justifiable war. Can they be met today?

4.Describe how a justifiable war would be initiated and waged. Does it seem possible today?

5.Is there any role for a theory of justifiable war today given the socio-political and economic situations? What is the role of Christian peacemakers today?

Activities for Application and Integration
The following suggested activities provide opportunities for students/participants to carry the concepts of this chapter beyond the classroom. They are intended to clarify and integrate understandings into lived experience.

1. Watch a war movie for the presuppositions about either the initiating or the waging of war. How do they compare with the justifiable war criteria?

2. Choose a daily newspaper or a weekly periodical and clip the articles about war which you find in it over a four week period of time. How would you describe that paper/periodical's philosophy of warmaking?

3. Interview a veteran of a war about her/his understanding of when one should/must fight for one's country.

4. Research contemporary positions with regard to the applicability of justifiable war theory today. Evaluate these positions in a research paper.

5. Prepare an adult education session on the history of the justifiable war in the Roman Catholic tradition.

Spirituality Component
It is one thing to read and study about a theology of peace and quite another to become a person of peace. This spirituality component offers a series of Scripture readings with reflection questions which are closely aligned with the chapter topic. It is

169

suggested that they be used for prayer and reflection over a series of days. The reader may wish either to find another Christian with whom the prayer and its fruit may be shared on a regular basis or to journal one's growth as a peacemaker.

DAY 1: James 4.1-3
James suggests the source of conflict is inner cravings, desires and envy. What have I experienced as the source of conflict?

DAY 2: Mark 13.7-13
Often this passage is used to support the position that war is simply one of the givens of life. Does this mean that war is from God or from human decisions? What wars am I waging in my life at the moment?

DAY 3: Matthew 8.5-13
In this passage Jesus heals a military leader's child. What was the condition for the healing--the military position or faith? Do I look to positions of power or faith in my own living?

DAY 4: Luke 11.21-23
What armaments do I store as protections against the power of Jesus?

DAY 5: Romans 13.1-7
How do I understand law and authority in my life?

DAY 6: Matthew 27.54
The soldier recognizes that Jesus is of God. What does this faith conviction mean to me?

DAY 7: Acts 10. 30-48
The story of the conversion of Cornelius is a story of faith. What in my life needs conversion if I am to become a peacemaker?

CHAPTER 7
PEACE IS MORE THAN THE ABSENCE OF WAR

I was ten in November of 1956 when Soviet tanks and forces rolled into Hungary to redirect the political powers along a course more in keeping with Eastern Bloc Communism. Our family had gotten its first television set sometime before that, so the news clips of the Russian reaction to the Hungarian uprising provided a graphic, visual introduction to war for me. Evidently the media portrayal affected me profoundly. I remember my disbelief as I saw classmates and peers shooting one another with their imaginary guns at recess: didn't they understand what war meant? Out of my ten year old understanding of this uprising somehow rose a definite aversion to the song we sang in church choir, "Faith of our fathers, living still in spite of dungeon, fire and sword...how blest would be their children's fate if we, like they, could die for thee." Dungeon, fire, sword brought back memories of what I had seen on television and that did not seem to be 'blest', no matter what the reason.

As I look back on that experience, there seems to be a connection with this chapter. Neither I nor my family nor my country was involved in war. Yet the knowledge that an uprising in Hungary had been ended by military force and that children played war games and that our church sang songs which glorified violent death disrupted the idyllic existence of one rural Iowa farm girl. In my young heart, I was to some extent experiencing that peace was not merely the absence of war. Today neither I nor my family nor my country is involved

171

in a declared war. Yet I am haunted with the knowledge of terrorist attacks, domestic violence and the popularity of war toys for children. Still I experience that peace must be more than the absence of declared war.

* * *

1. Peace and the Absence of War

The secular Greek word for peace, *eirene,* and the *pax Romana* both equated peace with the absence of war. The *pax Romana* came about through a strong military whose presence was facilitated by the Roman network of roads. J. Carter Swain suggests that this was hardly peace but a "semblance of tranquillity" which rested on a broad-based federation without self-determination for individual members, personal subjugation to the emperor and slavery for many.[1] In many ways, such an understanding of peace has a certain popular appeal, for it places the task of peacemaking on military and political personnel.

Paul and the other first century Greek Christian writers did use the Greek equivalent of this concept of peace, but filled up the word with the Hebrew sense of the word *shalom.* In both the Hebrew and Christian scriptures, the source of peace is not the absence of war. Peace results rather from God's covenant with the people (Isaiah 54.10), from the teachings of God (Isaiah 54.13), and from the Spirit (Galatians 5.22).

The prophet Jeremiah particularly insists that when the covenant is broken (Jeremiah 14.19-21) and the law is ignored, peace slips away (Jeremiah 8.10-12) and a punishing war threatens (Jeremiah 12.7-13; Jeremiah 8.14-16). According to

---

[1] J.C. SWAIM, *War, Peace and the Bible,* Maryknoll, NY, 1982, 46 adds mention of the leisure activities of a few which made sport of human life and death in games related to warmaking activities.

172

Jeremiah, peace does not emerge from armed conflict. Rather combat occurs when human decisions have reversed the peace of the beginning and at the heart of human life. Such an approach suggests first, that peace is more than the absence of war and second, that peacemaking is a proactive commitment. Peacemaking is more about creating conditions conducive to lives lived in peace than it is about preventing war. Effective efforts toward peace require a clear vision of peace, a deep understanding of personal and collective beginnings as well as the vibrant hope that peace has already been realized for this world in Jesus Christ.

Vatican Council II in its document, *Church in the Modern World,* approaches the fifth chapter on the topic of peace from a similar perspective. Already the chapter title, *The Fostering of Peace and the Promotion of a Community of Nations,* suggests that peace entails the creation of a world in which peace can dwell and not merely the prevention of war. This inference becomes a point blank statement within the chapter itself: "Peace is not merely the absence of war. Nor can it be reduced solely to the maintenance of a balance of power between enemies. Nor is it brought about by dictatorship" (#78). This negative description of peace goes on to name the sources of peace as love and the beginning created harmony actualized in the contemporary situation. Since situations change, the realization of peace is a continuous project. The listed conditions necessary for peace include recognizing human dignity, personal respect, and values; the mutual contribution of talents and resources to the common good; practiced love of neighbor; mutual trust; nonviolent redress of grievances; and daily effort on behalf of peace. The positive promotion of these qualities of social life result in peace.

As a matter of fact a good proportion of 'peacemaking' today starts with the presupposition that peace derives from negotiations or the cessation and avoidance of conflict. In the context of the Christian tradition such a concept of peace appears limited in scope. Since it is, however, the socio-political environment of this world today, the examination of peacemaking efforts through negotiations and avoidance of war seems fitting.

2. Deterrence

Deterrence is the current American nuclear weapons policy. The non-military, dictionary descriptions define deterrence as the discouragement or prevention of an action through fear of its consequences. In specific nuclear nomenclature, "Deterrence is a condition resulting from the creation of a state of mind brought about by the existence of a credible threat of unacceptable counteraction in response to a contemplated attack on an adversary thereby inhibiting the temptation to initiate such an attack."[1] Nuclear deterrence is further divided into counterforce deterrence (tactical) and countervalue deterrence (strategic). Counterforce strategy aims at the destruction of enemy nuclear and military resources. Credibility is dependent on a large number of highly accurate nuclear weapons. Countervalue strategy aims at the destruction of enemy population and industrial centers. It is more compatible with less accurate and more powerful nuclear weapons.

Present American nuclear weapons policy historically has aimed at the existence of a nuclear weapons system which is capable of surviving a nuclear attack (first strike) and of launching a counterattack (second strike) against the instigator. In the recent years there is the growing conviction that unless the available nuclear weapons system is perceived by the adversary as capable of a first strike, it would lack a deterrent capability. At this point, the United States has not

---

[1]C.W.KEGLEY, Jr. and E.R.WITTKOPF (eds.), *Nuclear Nomenclature. A selective dictionary of terms*, in KEGLEY and WITTKOPF, *The Nuclear Reader. Strategy, Weapons and War*, NY, 1985, xiii. The selective listing provides a valuable introduction to nuclear jargon.

committed itself to a 'no first strike policy.[1] Intertwined with the policy of deterrence are the issues of arms buildup and disarmament.

In addition to the above clarification of the field which nuclear deterrence covers, there are some general principles from the justified war discussion which moral theology has turned to in the discussion of deterrence.[2] The principle of intent examines the motivation behind the policy of nuclear deterrence. The morality of deterrence systems is dependent, for example, on whether the intention is to use nuclear weapons or to avoid nuclear war. The principle thereby questions the morality of a deterrent policy which includes an option for a retaliatory as well as a first strike attack.

The just war principle which grants immunity to non-combatants in this context would condemn countervalue attacks. Given the complex operative socio-economic systems in place in today's world, there is ambiguity with regard to whom non-combatant status can apply. This principle also calls into question the place of powerful nuclear warheads with imprecise targeting ability as well as strategic (in contrast to tactical) weapons systems.

---

[1]C.W.WEINBERGER, *A rational approach to nuclear disarmament*, in J.P.STERBA, *The Ethics of War and Nuclear Deterrence*, Belmont, CA, 1985, 116-121 argues that the current world situation precludes an official policy statement of 'no first strike'. The article first appeared in *Defense* of August, 1982. The article stands in an interesting juxtaposition to footnote 81 in the *Challange of Peace* which gives an official assurance that the United States did not have a 'first strike' policy.
[2]M. MAHON, *Nuclear Morality: A Primer for the Perplexed*, in *National Jesuit News* 12 (special supplement to #2, November 1982) 1-7 suggests that the central principles are 1)proportionality, 2)civilian immunity, and 3)war as the last resort.

The principle of multiple effects, presupposing that most human actions have both good and bad consequences, holds that an actor must intend the good and have proportionally grave reasons for allowing evil side effects. This principle asks whether a policy of deterrence is a tolerable side effect of a good, for example the avoidance of nuclear war, or are the risks involved morally unacceptable? Those maintaining that nuclear deterrence is disproportionate to the possible good achieved list the dubious control of nuclear weapons systems, potential for escalation, possibility of accidental launch as well as the disproportionate amount of resources tied up in the management, research and production of deterrence systems.

The moral discussion of the issues related to deterrence, by and large, centers on application of these principles to the issue. Obviously it is impossible to present the argumentation of all who have addressed this concern; however, a selection of documents and theological arguments could be a helpful beginning point in evaluating the relationship of deterrence to a theology of peace.

Against the backdrop of Hiroshima and Nagasaki, the post-World War II years saw a buildup of arms including atomic and nuclear weapons. The initial response of Pius XII called for the "simultaneous and reciprocal reduction of armaments" while acknowledging that true peace required the abolition of hate, greed and desire for power.[1] Six years later, Pius XII again called for armament reduction under a system of effective inspection. The appeal for reduction was based on the need for

---

[1]PIUS XII, *Christmas Eve 1951 radio address*, in Catholic Mind 50 (1952) 248-256, here 254. *Challenge of Peace*, #167-177 provides a summary of the moral assessment of deterrence from 1945-1983.

"breathing space" and a world order based on friendship not competitive rivalry.[1]

John XXIII called the unchecked armaments race an obstacle to peace without the glimpse of a solution.[2] A similar hopelessness appeared about the same time in a document by the forerunner of the National Conference of Catholic Bishops (NCCB). While warning against communism, the bishops encouraged government leaders to continue "their often disheartening quest for peace, reductions in armaments".[3] These first references to disarmament were intuitive insights that armaments were not the way to peace.

In John XXIII's encyclical *Peace on Earth*, disarmament is developed as a topic in its own right and the use of weapons as deterrents is specifically addressed. John XXIII urges that the arms race cease, that simultaneous and equal stockpiled reductions occur, that nuclear weapons be banned and that mutual negotiations achieve progressive disarmament with control (#112). John's argumentation is based on the principle of multiple effects. The passage acknowledges that "present-day conditions of peace" claim to require a balance of arms which in turn "allegedly justifies" continued arms production. The disproportionate outlay of intellectual and economic resources, the possibility of deliberate or accidental war as well as the consequences of nuclear testing for life on earth are listed as effects which question the morality of nuclear weapons as deterrents (#109-111). Instead of a peace bought by the balance of arms, John XXIII calls for a true peace founded on mutual trust (#113). Such a peace is required by

---

[1]PIUS XII, *Christmas Eve 1957 radio address*, in *Catholic Mind* 56 (1958) 160-179, here 179.

[2]JOHN XXIII, *Christmas Eve 1959 radio address*, in *The Pope Speaks* 6 (1959-1960) 200-207, here 203.

[3]NCCB, *Freedom and Peace* (November 19, 1959), in NCCB, *In the Name of Peace*, 17-23, here 19.

reason (#114), is a value in itself (#115), and is a value for individuals, families and the family of nations (#116).

The *Church in the Modern World* addresses disarmament and deterrence within the context of Chapter Five: *The Fostering of Peace and a Community of Nations.* Within this context, the explicit distinction between weapons for war and weapons for deterrence (#81) illustrates at least an acknowledgement that intention plays a significant role in moral decision making. The underlying question which the document asks, however, is this: to what extent does the amassing of weapons as a deterrence to enemy attack bring about genuine peace? Consequently the argumentation does not proceed along the lines of the principle of multiple effects. Rather the vision of genuine peace is the beginning point and the measuring stick of current efforts toward peace. The peace based on deterrence is called a "peace of a sort" (#80), which is distinguished from a "steady", a "sure and authentic" peace. The "peace of a sort" aggravates the possibility of war because weapons systems deflect more money from humanitarian needs and because it allows disagreements to fester.

Authentic peace challenges human persons to find ways of resolving conflicts which are worthy of the human person, to pursue means which encourage a common international security, and to foster mutual trust. Each of these requires an end to the arms race and a beginning of multilateral disarmament (*Church in the Modern World,* #81). In this document, therefore, it is the nature of peace itself which demands a change from the policy of nuclear deterrence.

In the period between the *Church in the Modern World* and the *Challenge of Peace* in 1983, the popes and the US bishops reiterated and advanced these basic arguments. Progressive, mutual, verifiable arms reduction continues to be requested. Second, a policy of arms for deterrence is a contradiction to a

Christian vision of peace.[1] On one occasion, John Paul II questions whether the intention behind the spiraling arms race in the name of deterrence is the service of world peace or nuclear and military superiority.[2] More positively the documents continue to encourage structures and understandings which will promote a genuine peace built on mutual trust[3] as well as a new world order.[4] This world order at times sounds similiar to the eschatological reign of God. Ever since Jesus has come, the world has experienced "a transforming dynamism, a hope which is no longer unlikely, a new and effective progress, a future and longed-for history which can make itself present and real."[5] On another occasion Paul VI refers to a "prophetic vision open to the hopes of the future" which he cautions must be "solidly based upon the hard and concrete reality of the present."[6] *Justice in the World*, the document produced by the 1971 Synod of Bishops, perhaps is defining this concrete reality when it calls for a new order based on the rights and dignity of the human person (#64).

There is, however, evidence of some development in the positions. *Justice in the World* sees the arms race as a threat not only to the Christian vision of peace but also to basic human values, such as life, economic justice and self-determination

---

[1]For example, PAUL VI, *Address to the General Assembly of the United Nations* (October 4, 1965), in R. HEYER (ed.), *Nuclear Disarmament. Key Statements of Popes, Bishops, Councils and Churches,* NY/Ramsey, NJ, 1982, 24. See also NCCB, *To Live in Christ Jesus,* #100.

[2]JOHN PAUL XXIII, *Address to the XXXIV General Assembly of the U.N.* (October 2, 1979), in HEYER, *Statements,* 46.

[3]See for example PAUL VI, *Message to the General Assembly of the U.N. for its Session on Disarmament* (May 24, 1978), in HEYER, *Statements,* 38.

[4]See for example PAUL VI, *Annual Message for Day of Peace* (January 1, 1976), in HEYER, *Statements,* 29

[5]PAUL VI, *Day of Peace,* 29.

[6]PAUL VI, *U.N. Disarmament,* 38

(#9). Already in 1968, the NCCB wondered if the United States' deterrence policy could even maintain the "peace of a sort" as it claimed. In their estimation, the policy was built not on balance but on nuclear superiority which requires each side to escalate with every new advance.[1] In the next decade, the NCCB expanded the principle of immunity to non-combatants by maintaining that "it is also wrong to threaten to attack them (civilian populations) as part of a strategy of deterrence."[2]

Three years later in his testimony to the SALT II hearings, Cardinal John Krol speaking on behalf of the NCCB explained the above statement. He said that both the use and the declared intent to use strategic nuclear weapons as part of the United States deterrence policy are morally wrong. He did, however, hold that

> Catholic moral teaching is willing, while negotiations proceed, to tolerate possession of nuclear weapons for deterrence as the lesser of two evils. If that hope were to disappear, the moral attitude of the Catholic Conference would most certainly have to shift to one of uncompromising condemnation of both the use and the possession of such nuclear weapons.[3]

According to Krol in 1979, it is wrong to use or to threaten to use strategic nuclear weapons. Possession without the threat of use, however, remains morally tolerable as long as negotiations aimed at the reduction and eventual phase-out of nuclear weapons are proceeding.

In John Paul II's message to the UN Special Session on Disarmament in 1982, he seems to have taken a slightly more positive--or less discriminating--position: "Under present

---

[1]NCCB, *Human Life in Our Day*, Washington, DC, 1968, #107-113.
[2]NCCB, *To Live in Christ Jesus*, #100.
[3]J. KROL, SALT II. *A Statement of Support*, in NCCB, *In the Name of Peace*, 73-82, here 77.

conditions, dissuasion based on equilibrium--certainly not as an end in itself but as a stage on the way to progressive disarmament--can still be judged morally acceptable."[1] John Paul II's remarks appear to be general and not to distinguish between use, declared intent to use and possession. In addition, "morally acceptable" appears to have a more positive tone than the terminology "tolerable consequence" used by Cardinal Krol.

John Paul II's statement to the UN came in the drafting process of the NCCB's May 1983 document *The Challenge of Peace. God's Promise and Our Response,* which did quote John Paul II's position on deterrence (#173). *Challenge of Peace,* however, coming from the hierarchy of a major nuclear power, develops at length the moral argumentation behind their position on deterrence. Their conclusion is "strictly conditioned moral acceptance of nuclear deterrence" (#186), based on a just war analysis.[2]

The document reaffirms the immorality of any intention to kill noncombatants, that is countervalence targeting (#178). Given the potential of indirect casualties coming from the targeting of military installations within civilian population centers, the bishops maintain that it is not enough to refrain from intending to kill noncombatants (#188). Such deterrence policies must also be evaluated according to the principle of proportionality. Using this principle, *Challenge of Peace* holds that "the 'indirect effects' of initiating nuclear war are sufficient to make it an unjustifiable moral risk in any form" (#194). The bishops also maintain "profound skepticism" that any use of nuclear weapons would be acceptable according to

---

[1]JOHN PAUL II, *The Necessary Strategy for Peace,* in *Origins* 12 (June 24, 1982) 81-87, here 85, #8
[2]B. RUSSETT, *The Doctrine of Deterrence,* in P. MURNION (ed.), *Catholics and Nuclear War. A Commentary on The Challenge of Peace. The US Catholic Bishops' Pastoral on War and Peace,* NY, 1983, 149-167, here 157, concurs.

this principle (#193). Yet a third just war principle considered is reasonable probability of success of a deterrent policy to prevent the use of nuclear weapons (#184). This principle questions means of deterrence which destabilize or which extend deterrence beyond its limited objective.

The "strictly conditioned moral acceptance of nuclear deterrence", consequently, is dependent on criteria flowing from the application of just war principles to nuclear deterrence. The limited objective of nuclear deterrence cannot extend beyond dissuasion from the use of nuclear weapons by others. Deterrence proposals involving repeated nuclear strikes, counterstrike or winning a nuclear war are beyond this limited objective (#188). Proposals for superiority instead of balance are rejected (#188). Any change in current deterrence policy must be evaluated in terms of its ability to move toward progressive disarmament (#188). The development of weapons systems which destabilize the balance of arms include automatic launch on warning systems and the proliferation of nuclear weapons among the nations do not meet these criteria. Also excluded from deterrence policies are weapons suitable for first strike use, strategies for fighting limited nuclear war and proposals which blur the distinction between nuclear and conventional weapons (#189-190).

In November 1985, the National Conference of Catholic Bishops announced the formation of an ad hoc committee "to assess whether the conditions of the pastoral letter are being met" with regard to nuclear deterrence.[1] The episcopal request for a committee to study the criteria necessary for continued support of "strictly conditioned moral acceptance of nuclear deterrence" was based on evidence that the current deterrence policy goes beyond minimum deterrence and is not seeking

---

[1]See *Origins* 15 (November 28, 1985), 400 for the text of the announcement.

progressive disarmament.[1] In March of 1985 the president and speaker of the NCCB, Bishop J. Malone, urged congressional members to vote against the MX missile. The argument was based on the potentially destabilizing impact of this weapons system according to norms established in *Challenge of Peace* and on disproportionate use of resources for deterrence in the US and abroad.

Other American theologians, grappling with possession of nuclear weapons for deterrence are uncomfortable with even "strictly conditional moral acceptance" and prefer the terminology of conditioned tolerance. Richard McCormick gives due consideration to the current "sinful situation", which should not exist in the first place. But it does exist and many options connected with existent deterrence are simply regrettable. Within this framework, he concludes:

> We have been able to arrive at only the following clarities. 1)The possession of nuclear weapons is at the very best morally ambiguous, and therefore at best only tolerable. It may not even be that. 2)Such possession is tolerable only for the present and under certain conditions. 3) These conditions are: a firm resolve never to use nuclear weapons and a firm resolve to work immediately to assure their abolition, in law and in fact. 4) While unilateral disarmament may not be a clear moral mandate, unilateral steps toward multilateral disarmament certainly are.[2]

David Hollenbach speaks about the moral tolerance of concrete, nuclear strategic options, rather than possession in general. He, too, gives due consideration to the historical situation, for he believes any moral conclusion must be derived

---

[1]NCCB, *Nuclear Deterrence: Are the Conditions Being Met?* in *Origins* 15 (November 28, 1985) 399-400.

[2]R.A.MCCORMICK, *Nuclear Deterrence and the Problem of Intention: A Review of the Positions*, in MURNION, *Catholics*, 168-182, here 180.

from prudent politics as well as moral norms. Hollenbach holds that possession of nuclear weapons is evil due to the accompanying risks. It is, however, a given of life in this era. The moral rightness or wrongness of possession is dependent on how human agents respond to or work with this given so that values are maximized and disvalues are minimized. The intention of deterrence proposals must be directed to the prevention of nuclear war as well as to the promotion of arms reduction. A proposal must demonstrate a positive contribution to arms reduction and prevention of nuclear war.[1]

Writing in a more popular vein, Richard McSorley simplistically denounces possession of nuclear weapons for deterrence. He maintains that the existent situation is not deterrence but overkill. A policy of massive retaliation even against a first strike is contrary to the scriptural injunction to love one's enemies. McSorley also calls the resources used for nuclear deterrence disproportionate given the current humanitarian needs. Finally McSorley argues that since it is wrong to use nuclear weapons, it is wrong to intend to use them as well. Possession of weapons which cannot be used are proximate occasion of sin and therefore morally wrong.[2]

Although thought-provoking, McSorley's presentation can be critiqued on two counts. First, he presumes that the intent behind deterrence is to use nuclear weapons. It is possible that the intent is to prevent nuclear war or even that the intent varies according to the concrete tactic or system. Second, a certain ahistorical idealism prevades the article. Such an approach is inspirational or even prophetic, but its solutions are disjunctive from the hard work of redeeming the existent situation.

---

[1]D. HOLLENBACH, *Nuclear Ethics. A Christian Moral Argument*, New York/Ramsey, NJ, 1983, 73-76.
[2]R.T. MCSORLEY, *It's a sin to build a nuclear weapon*, in *US Catholic* 41 (October 1976) 12-13.

3. Implications for Christian Peacemakers

After having examined some of the issues connected with deterrence, the just war principles traditionally applied, theological commentaries, papal and joint US episcopal statements, it is appropriate to draw this thought into dialogue with the theological framework for a theology of peace which has been previously set forth.

It has been illustrated that peace is the created origin of human persons, that the final vision is ahead of them, and that the peace which is Jesus has been handed over to the Christian community. This framework suggests a reversal of what is a typical approach. The peacemaker begins with a vision of peace and then seeks to promote structures and attitudes which realize peace.[1] Peace is the beginning point and not the result of armed conflict or negotiations. This approach suggests that the avoidance of nuclear war is not a sufficient intention for deterrence. Rather deterrence and any aspect of the deterrence policy needs to be evaluated in terms of its potential as a structure for embodying peace. Such a beginning point demands the establishment of socio-economic and political structures which support and make peace a reality. Efforts must be put into peacemaking instead of preparation for war.

A second thread has been the essential nature of the concrete, historical givens for a theology of peace. One simply cannot disregard the existent situation of escalating arms buildup and proliferation of nuclear weapons in favor of either a return to pre- nuclear weapons state or withdrawal into a millenial community. The incarnational nature of Christianity demands that the peacemaker enter into this concrete set of circumstances seeking to transform it into peace.

---

[1] T. SHANNON, *What are they saying about war and peace?* New York/Ramsey, NJ, 1983, 112 suggests the vision of peace as the premise as well.

The incarnation of the divine began in Jesus and awaits its completion in humanity. The reconciliation of God was made present first in Jesus and now in all who live in the Spirit of Jesus. The fulfillment of God's reconciling activity in Jesus is dependent on the disciples who come after Jesus. The present world is incomplete and on the way to the full establishment of the reign of peace. The peacemaker, imbued with the vision of this reign, knows the continuing effort which concretely realizes in mundane structures and attitudes what is present in inception and promise.

The work of realizing the reign of peace in the concrete, historical givens including nuclear deterrence can benefit from the clarity given through moral principles. It seems misleading to evaluate nuclear deterrent policies by just war principles for two reasons. First, it suggests that nuclear war could at least conceivably be just. Second, it presupposes a continuity of historical context from Augustine through the present. It is not clear that either of these ia a valid consideration. The introduction of nuclear weapons has qualitatively changed the nature of warfare. It seems, therefore, that the nuclear era is a radically different historical context in which principles derived for just war in another context cannot apply. Other principles, however, can be of assistance.

The principle of intention calls for the realization of as much value as possible and the minimization of as much disvalue as possible. It includes what the actor directly wills to accomplish as well as foreseen consequences of the action. This understanding of the principle of intention, then, can not be used, for example, to justify nuclear strikes on military targets in which the foreseen results (massive loss of life and disruption of socio-economic structures for present and future) are simply disregarded because they are not 'directly' intended. Accordingly, the principle of multiple effects cited earlier works hand in hand with the principle of intention. The whole act inclusive of the expected side-effects is material for moral evaluation. When the whole act is considered, these principles

186

could not admit an intention to use either countervalue or counterforce weapons. Even more fundamentally the principle of intention calls for the promotion of peace as the value seeking to be realized as completely as possible.

The principle of moral discrimination holds that there can be no contradiction between the actor's intention and the action or non- action used to realize that intention. There can be no contradiction, then, between the intention of peace and deterrent methods seeking to realize that intention. This principle would judge any proposals for a destabilization of present deterrent policy as contradicting the intention of peace. The same is true for systems aiming at nuclear superiority. The principle would also caution against systems which include the possibility of an accidental launch or launch on warning, since such systems enhance the probability that a use of the system was not the intention. More fundamentally this principle questions whether a deterrent policy based on fear of retaliation is compatible with peacemaking. Since the promotion of fear is the nature of a deterrence policy, this principle alone cannot justify possession of nuclear weapons systems. Rather the principle of moral discrimination encourages actions which actively promote peace. On the international level this would include progressive multilateral disarmament as well as conversion to mutual trust.

When a situation involves value conflicts, moral principles oblige the realization of the more fundamental value, the more institutional value, the more urgent value and the long-term value. In the situation of deterrence, the value of peace is in conflict with other values such as national security, ideological superiority and the avoidance of war. According to Maslow's hierarchy of needs, life is more fundamental than safety/security needs. It follows that peace which is supportive of life is more fundamental than peace which is supportive of national security or ideological superiority. In fact national and personal security come to consciousness after one's basic human needs have been met. Peace proposals which ignore basic human life needs in favor of security needs would seem doomed to failure. Consequently the use of nuclear weapons destructive of present and future life is inadmissable. Instead the energies of the peacemakers must seek to establish a peace which first of all is supportive of life.

An institutional value is one without which social life would be impossible. Peace is a quality of harmonious relationships between persons and groups of persons. As such the continuation of social life is more dependent on peace than on ideological superiority or the mere avoidance of war. If one looks only at the potential destruction which a nuclear catastrophe could unleash, a peace which would enable nuclear disarmament appears to be a most urgent value. The Christian vision of the final reign of peace illustrates the necessity to promote this value now in preference to other more immediate values.

The use of these principles in an effort to realize the reign of peace in this concrete, historical situation first of all indicates that the promotion of peace--and not the mere avoidance of war--must be the central concern. A peacemaker is proactive on behalf of the reign of peace. At best systems of deterrence are a given evil of the existent situation with which the peacemaker must deal so that God's reign becomes an incarnate reality. Deterrence which plays on fear must be systematically dismantled by bonds of trust and reconciliation. It is not enough to be against war or nuclear deterrence.

One's energies, talents and resources must be engaged in peacemaking. The peacemaker can replace defensive and retaliatory behavior with reconciling methods of conflict management. One can put one's energies into education on the issues of peace and peacemaking. Peace groups and activities need that support of time, talent and monetary resources. The peacemaker can actively support legislation and legislators in promotion of peace. One can refuse to pay federal telephone tax which goes to support the military or one can refuse to pay that portion of federal income tax which goes to the military budget. These monies could be rechanneled to support peace or the proposed federal Academy of Peace. Lastly, peacemakers can nurture peace in their personal lives by putting aside deterrent behavior, by encouraging conversion to the vision of peace through prayer or reflection and by practicing the incarnation of peace in the routine of daily life.

```
        P
        E
P E A C E
        C
        E
```

Roman Catholic Church Documents

Official Roman Catholic teaching in the twentieth century has addressed issues in this chapter. The following selections are particularly pertinent.

Church in the Modern World, #77-78 and #81
1. If peace is not the absence of war, what are the foundations for real peace?
2. What is the position given with regard to the arms race?

Peace on Earth, #109-119 1. What do these paragraphs suggest is necessary for peace?
2. How does the arms race and even disarmament militate against peace?

Human Life Today, #110-116
1. What is the position of the US bishops on destabilizing weapons systems?
2. What is the position of the US bishops with regard to nuclear superiority?

Challenge of Peace, #178-194
1. What are the two poles in the moral dilemma regarding deterrence?
2. What are the criteria of the US bishops regarding nuclear deterrence?

Other Suggested Readings

HEYER (ed.), R. *Nuclear Disarmament. Key Statements of Popes, Bishops, Councils and Churches.* New York/Ramsey, NJ, 1982.

HOLLENBACH, D. *Nuclear Ethics. A Christian Moral Argument.* New York/Ramsey, NJ, 1983.

JOHN PAUL II. *The Necessary Strategy for Peace*, in *Origins* 12 (June 24 1985) 81-87.

MURNION (ed.), P.J. *Catholics and Nuclear War. A Commentary on The Challenge of Peace. The U.S.Catholic Bishops' Pastoral Letter on War and Peace*. NY, 1983. See especially Section V: Nuclear War and Deterrence.

NCCB. *In the Name of Peace. Collective Statements of the United States Catholic Bishops on War and Peace, 1919-1980*. Washington, DC, 1983.

PIUS XII. *Christmas Eve 1951 radio address*, in *Catholic Mind* 50 (1952) 248-256.

PIUS XII. *Christmas Eve 1957 radio address*, in *Catholic Mind* 56 (1958) 160-179.

SPAETH, R.L. *No Easy Answers. Christians Debate Nuclear Arms*. Minneapolis, 1983. See especially Part Two: Moral Issues.

STERBA (ed.), J.P. *The Ethics of War and Nuclear Deterrence*. Belmont, CA, 1985. See especially Part IV: Moral Assessments of Nuclear War and Nuclear Deterrence.

SWAIM, J.C. *War, Peace, and the Bible*. Maryknoll, NY, 1982. See especially Chapter 4: The Prince of Peace.

Audio-visual Materials

The following are some of the audio-visual materials which are related to the chapter content. The list is not exhaustive, but is intended to give some initial suggestions for previewing.

War without winners I and II (films; 28 and 30m; Films, INC.; 1979 and 1984). American and Russian people express their fears, thoughts and hopes about the future in an age of nuclear weapons.

The Time has come (color film; 27m; NARMIC; 1982). A documentary on the 750,000 people who marched for peace in New York on June 12, 1982 and on the worldwide disarmament movement.

Inevitability (color videotape; 7m; Beyond War; 1985). An illustrated lecture on the probability of nuclear war given the situation of armed defense. The conclusion is that a third possibility, namely a situation of "beyond war" must be created.

Introductory Activities
The purpose of the introductory activity is to begin discussion on an understanding of peace as well as to allow students/participants a chance to express what their previous experiences and understandings of peace have been.

1. The October 1976 issue of **US Catholic** contained an article by Richard T. McSorley entitled *It's a sin to build a nuclear weapon*. In connection with the article were ten statements asking the readers to agree or disagree (pp 13-14). Poll the group with these or adapted questions and compare the responses with those 1976 respondents.

2. Initiate a discussion based on previously conducted interviews, using this question: We are not "at war". Are we "at peace" in our lives? in our community? in our world?

Discussion Questions
The purpose of the discussion questions is to encourage students/participants to integrate the text and/or presented material into their own thinking and living.

1. What is needed to bring about world peace? What conditions are needed in addition to an absence of war?

2. Evaluate the suitability of just war principles in analyzing the morality of nuclear deterrence.

3. Can the possession of nuclear arms for deterrence ever be morally acceptable? Justify your response by reference to specific moral principles.

4. What are the major moral difficulties with the buildup of arms?

5. Discuss the values in conflict when deterrence is the issue. How does one go about choosing which values to protect and support?

Activities for Application and Integration
The following suggested activities provide opportunities for students/participants to carry the concepts of this chapter beyond the classroom. They are intended to clarify and integrate understandings into lived experience.

1. Read and critique an article or a chapter from a book on nuclear deterrence on the basis of principles presented in this chapter. See **Other Suggested Readings** for some initial suggestions.

2. Research a deterrent system currently in use. When the information has been gathered and the method of deterrence understood, evaluate it according to the moral principles presented in this chapter.

3. Create your own scenario of the year 2020 based on your projection of what the human race and the nuclear powers have done with deterrent weapon systems and arms reduction.

4. Be part of a team to plan and carry out an information session on Catholic Church teaching since World War II on nuclear arms.

5. Collect official government documentation on the current thinking behind nuclear deterrence systems. Try to find answers to the following questions. a) Is the current policy a "no first strike" policy? b) Is the current policy interested in equity or superiority of nuclear deterrent systems? c) Is the current policy countervalue or counterforce? d) What is current policy with regard to targeting military installations in civilian population centers? e) In the event of a major first strike, what is given as the value of a retaliatory strike?

Spirituality Component

It is one thing to read and study about a theology of peace and quite another to become a person of peace. This spirituality component offers a series of Scripture readings with reflection questions which are closely aligned with the chapter topic. It is suggested that they be used for prayer and reflection over a series of days. The reader may wish either to find another Christian with whom the prayer and its fruit may be shared regularly or to journal one's growth as a peacemaker.

DAY 1: Galatians 5:22-23
Paul claims peace comes from the Spirit, not the absence of war. Has the Spirit born the fruit of peace in my life?

DAY 2: Isaiah 54.9-12
Here God's love brings about a covenant of peace, not the absence of war. How is God loving me today? Does this love bring me peace?

DAY 3: Isaiah 54.13-14
Here peace comes from having God as a teacher, not the absence of war. What does God wish to teach me?

DAY 4: Jeremiah 8.9-12
On what foundations do I seek to establish peace?

DAY 5: Jeremiah 8.14-16
Here the absence of peace is linked to sin and illness. How am I
sinful and sick? Where is my peace?

DAY 6: Jeremiah 12.7-13
The absence of peace for all is connected to violence, hunger
and exhaustion. For what am I hungry? How have I exhausted
myself?

DAY 7: Jeremiah 14.19-21
Here the absence of peace is connected to breaking the
covenant. What is God's covenant with me? How has my
unfaithfulness to it resulted in lack of peace in my life?

CHAPTER 8
IF WE WANT PEACE, WE MUST WORK FOR JUSTICE

The first time I went to serve at the Sioux City soup kitchen, I arrived some five minutes after the meal had begun. As I walked in, the silence of some eighty people intent on eating overwhelmed me. Never before had I experienced so many so silent when food was the reason for their coming together. My experience of meal gatherings that size consisted of family reunions, weddings or banquets celebrating a milestone event. There conversation and the delight of being together resounded. In what seems to be the luxury of bounty, I had come to know the security that a meal would always be there for me. With that fundamental knowledge, food itself was not an all- encompassing focus. It became a way of drawing us from our diverse schedules into a shared life. Food has always symbolized and nourished human community. But without that sure access to food, the richness of that symbol of shared nourishment is lost to a preoccupation with survival, that silent, purposeful ingesting. There must be something wrong, something unjust when mere survival monopolizes the life energies of whole groups of people. Human life should be about more than mere survival. Justice demands that human persons have what is required to live human lives. Our Christian scriptures and the recent magisterial teachings make the further claim that peace is dependent on at least this minimal understanding of justice.

* * *

1. The Nature of Justice

Justice in the Hebrew and Christian scriptures

Sedekah, in the Hebrew scriptures, came to be translated as *justitia* in Latin and justice or righteousness in English. The concept behind *sedekah* is not, however, identical with the popular notion of justice today.

Yahweh, the God of the Israelites, was the source of *sedekah.* This justice was the saving power of Yahweh's covenant with the people. The central event of the Israelite history and the foundational event of their faith was the Exodus event. Yahweh had seen the injustice done against the Israelites in Egypt and had heard their lamentation (Exodus 3.7-8). Yahweh liberated the people from their oppression and brought them into the land of promise. Yahweh made the order of things right again. The Exodus was Yahweh's judgement on oppression and injustice in the social order. Through the covenant with Yahweh the Israelites were saved, were justified and were made righteous.

It is God's justification which is the foundation of all Christian justice. The Judeo-Christian faith asserts that justice mirrors to others God's own justice toward the believer. Justice, therefore, mirrors God's justifying action; it is not dependent on the reaction or the worthiness of those to whom justice is done.

In actuality covenant justice resembles faithful and unconditional love more than rigid adherence to the law or to what the other deserves. In spite of their repeated unfaithfulness, Yahweh remained steadfast in loving concern for this people. The Israelites, in turn, were to mirror Yahweh's deeds of liberation and faithfulness through deeds of faithfulness and justice. Their justice was dependent on Yahweh's faithful and unconditional love of them, not on the reactions of others. The Law with its Ten Commandments did

198

have a place in Israelite life. It was not, however, the means to Yahweh's justification; it rather delineated some fundamental ways in which the Israelites could mirror the fidelity and justice of Yahweh to the larger human community.

In part through the Law, the justice of Yahweh into which the Israelites were introduced was also Yahweh's judgement or indictment of sin. Sin was unfaithfulness to the covenant or to the community as well as injustice to Yahweh or to others.

The measure of the community's justice was their treatment of the powerless, those unable to demand that justice be done to them. Most typically this included the widow, the orphan, the poor and the alien (Deuteronomy 14.29-15.7). The reason behind the demand of justice for the disenfranchised was connected to the oppression of Israel in Egypt. When Israel was powerless in Egypt, Yahweh saw that justice was done. Now Israel must do the same for the defenseless in their society (Exodus 22.21-26; Deuteronomy 5.14-15). Doing justice to others mirrored what Yahweh had done for the believer. Doing justice to others was a sign that one was truly justified, that is, made just by God. Doing justice distributed God's just love to the larger community of humankind. Justice was not an abstract concept; one did justice in concrete, specific actions. The justification which came from the covenant was not a state of being but a way of acting.

At its heart *sedekah* described Yahweh's relationship with the Israelites as well as their relationship as a people with Yahweh and with each other. The framework for this network of relationships was a blend of religious, social, moral and legal dimensions which overlapped and meshed into each other. Yahweh's saving action through the Exodus was the formative event of Judaism. This same Yahweh made a covenant with the twelve tribes of Israel which shaped them into one people. The covenant with Yahweh modeled a certain way of living, namely a holy life of one people who remembered it was Yahweh who first did justice to them, who first righted the

199

injustice of oppression in Egypt and who taught them what just living included. The Law described in detail the just response to this intervention on their behalf.

Although the Law bound the whole people, in time a special convergence of responsibility for justice was attributed to kings. The logic of this association rested not only in the socio-political leadership provided by the king, but also in the theological understanding that the ruler was the representative of Yahweh, the Just One. The classical prophets of this era consistently describe the ideal king as the one who does justice (Isaiah 9.5-6 and 11.4-8; Jeremiah 22.3-4; Psalm 72.1-7). When the king ruled with justice, peace was the result.

As the unfaithfulness of the king and the whole nation continued to repeat itself, the reign marked by justice and peace became an eschatological hope. When the historical inability of the kings to bring about justice became apparent, Judaism turned to Yahweh as the one who would establish justice definitively (Isaiah 45.23-24 and 60.21-22).

During this late period yet another aspect of justice emerged. Almsgiving came to be viewed as a work of justice. In the Book of Tobit, the giving of alms was presented as a means (14.10-11; 12.8-19; 4.7-11) and as an expression of one's justification (1.3). The Pauline collections referred to in 2 Corinthians 8-9 and Galatians 2.10 illustrate a similar notion.[1]

With the incarnation the justice of God was revealed in a person, Jesus (1 Corinthians 1.30). In Jesus all are undeservedly justified (Romans 3.21-26). The response to this gift of God is faith (Romans 3.28-30). Acceptance of the salvation which God offered in Jesus re-establishes the right order of things. The

---

[1]J.R.DONAHUE, *Biblical Perspective on Justice*, in J.C.HAUGHEY (ed.), *The Faith that Does Justice. Examining the Christian Sources for Social Change*, NY/Ramsey, NJ/Toronto, 1977, 68-112, here 82-85.

believer does not earn justification by personal effort nor by following the law (Galatians 3.11-13) nor by esoteric knowledge (1 Corinthians 2.1-5) nor by blood and family ties (Mark 3.31-35). Justification is God's action based on divine righteousness; faith is the believer's response.

Faith in God's saving action in Jesus can not remain content in passive receptivity. In the Christian scriptures faith expresses itself in action. It is God's saving love distributed. In Pauline language justification by faith means incorporation into a new social structure, the body of Christ (1 Corinthians 12.27; Romans 12.5). In both Corinthians and Romans, the fact of inclusion in the one body of Christ means gifts for the building up of the Christian community (Romans 12.6-8; 1 Corinthians 12.28) and a way of life together which includes love, hope, perseverance, generosity and peace (Romans 12.9-21; 1 Corinthians 13). Through this new social structure Paul urges concern for the weak (1 Corinthians 8.9-13), for the poor (1 Corinthians 11.20-22; 2 Corinthians 8.13-15), and for that which promotes communal peace (1 Corinthians 6.1-11; 1 Corinthians 11.26-32). This scriptural image, the body of Christ, obviously has implications for Christian justice, namely justice is about the structures of social life. Ever since the covenant formation of the Hebrews into God's own people, the scriptural understanding of justice has a social and structural context. Efforts on behalf of justice today dare not lose their social and structural dimensions nor their biblical roots.

The letter of James insists that the faith which does not respond to bodily needs is powerless to justify (James 2.14-17). The last judgement parable in the gospel of Matthew calls just those who met the bodily and human needs of others (Matthew 25.31-40). These needy in Matthew's parable recall to mind the widow, the poor, and the orphan, that is, those powerless to demand that justice be done to them from the tradition of the Hebrew scriptures.

201

Christian justice, then, has its source in God's justification or saving love. Christians, in turn, do justice to others because of their own experience of justification and unconditional love, not on the basis of response or worthiness. Christian action on behalf of justice mirrors and distributes God's justice and love. In addition this Christian justice has radical social and structural implications which extend beyond the Christian community. In fact the responsibility for promoting justice which the Hebrew scriptures attributed to their rulers has been given to the body of Christ, that is, the whole Christian community. The establishment of justice, therefore, is no longer a hope in a future activity of God. In Jesus the reign of justice has dawned; through the body of Christ today justice seeks to burst into the full light of day.

The scholastic understanding of justice

The *Summa Theologica* of Thomas Aquinas synthesizes the classical understanding of justice. The scholastic concept of justice was a product of the worldview of its thirteenth century times. Thomas and his contemporaries viewed all reality as static and unchanging; as governed by pre-established and universal principles; and as structured hierarchically from God down to the lowly feudal peasant. Consequently there was a clear and right order of things.

Thomas treats justice within the framework of the moral virtues, which he situates after the theological virtues and prior to the charisms of the Holy Spirit in his presentation of a moral theology. In contrast to the other moral virtues which are dependent on the intention of the agent, justice is concerned with the action itself. The object of justice is the 'what is right' in a relationship of equity. There are three focal points in this understanding: 1) a specific action external to the agent; 2) the creation or establishment of the right in a situation; and 3) a relationship of equity between the agent and another person. Justice, then, is realized in concrete, exterior actions which give what is due to another according to a certain commensuration.

Classical justice attempted to determine the 'what is right' according to three different equitable relationships. Commutative or contractual justice was concerned with 'what is due' in one-to-one relationships. Justice was met when two persons fulfilled the terms of the agreement or contract which they had made, hence its name. Contractual justice did not attempt to determine if the contract itself was exploitative of one member or particularly advantageous to another. If an agreement had been made, justice demanded that its terms--no matter what they were--be fulfilled.

Distributive justice regulated the relationship between the whole and its individual parts. In justice society had certain responsibilities to provide for its members that which they as individuals were not able to provide. Traditionally education, police protection and public service have been included under distributive justice. In its classical sense, distributive justice did not address the responsibility of one social class to another, that is, one collective part of the social order to another collective part.

General or legal justice measured the relationship of the individual member to the whole. Individual members were obliged in justice to contribute time, abilities or money for the good of the whole society. Military service, participation in governance and taxes have traditionally been viewed as fulfilling the dictates of general justice. Legal justice did not, however, examine the social structures which may have hindered or made impossible an individual's ability to contribute to the common good.

Classical justice, like justice in the scriptures, was concerned with the ability of concrete actions to embody what was the right order of things in context of relational life. It is less clear that justice was understood either as a response to the God

203

who first justified or as the embodiment of God's justification to others. In addition the framework of equitable relationships ignored for the most part the 'poor, the widow and the orphan', that is, for all those who could not lay claim to equity in relationships. Rather than lamenting the inadequacy of the classical notion of justice for the medieval ages, these observations address the inapplicability of the concept for later historical periods.

Social justice

It was not until the last decades of the nineteenth century that a post-Industrial Revolution concept of justice began to be articulated by moral theologians. By the 1930's the term social justice was used in the official teaching of the Roman Catholic Church, including the encyclicals of Pius XI. Social justice focused on the common good of a whole society including individual members, collective groups and the structures which ordered the whole. The concern of social justice was both the structures of the social order and the interaction of all its aspects for the common good.

The structural dimension of social justice seems to be a new insight arising particularly from the socio-economic changes after the Industrial Revolution. Just structures provide reasonable access to the fulfillment of legitimate human needs for individuals and groups. Social justice, for example, is not content with the fulfillment of salary contracts, but goes on to require that the contract provide adequately for the legitimate human need of the persons involved. Social justice does not rest easy when a society provides police protection and education, but requires that the education or protective structures are accessible to all persons and groups. To the extent that those unable to demand justice for themselves are the ones against whom the structures discriminate, social justice urges advocacy on behalf of the disenfranchised.

The interactive emphasis in social justice does not deny the classical divisions of justice, but seeks both to integrate them into the whole in service of the common good and to insist on their communal context. This social context probably was presupposed in the original medieval articulation, but the individualism of subsequent centuries blurred that framework. Social justice, therefore, explicated that communal context.

The equitable relationship in society derives from a common shared humanness. Social justice is concerned with the provision of what is legitimately necessary for the development both of the person and the whole society. The provision is dependent on the interactive relationships of groups of people (for example, the First World and the Third World) and on the means which expedite the distribution of resources. The distribution of resources necessary for human development becomes a dictate of justice, not of charity. Social justice measures the 'what is due' according to the human person in the fundamental, that is, the God-given reality. It is the dignity of the human person which demands that justice be done. Social justice recognizes that attitudinal and institutional structures as well as expected behavior patterns create or hinder the possibility of doing 'what is right'.

This understanding of social justice is not far from the Pauline concept of incorporation into the body of Christ or the formation of Israel through God's saving action and covenant. Each attempts to set forth a specific social order in which the right is done. The scriptural images specifically link justice to God's just and liberating action in the Exodus and in Jesus Christ. The scriptural context calls the Judeo-Christian to do justice to others as a mirror image of God's justification and recalls the identification of God with neighbor. The promotion of the common good according to the dictates of social justice requires human response to God's contemporary revelation through human persons and historical situations. This incarnational revelation demands a response of just action particularly to those unable to claim justice for themselves.

205

2. The Relationship of Peace and Justice

With the above introduction to justice, attention can now be given to the relationship of peace to justice as it appears in the scriptures and some documents from the Roman Catholic Church. This connection hinges on two foci, namely that peace results from the establishment of a just order on earth and that the eradication of injustice is a prerequisite for peace.

Peace requires a just social order

The tradition which views peace as the fruit of God's justice present in the world is as old as the Hebrew scriptures themselves. Neither justice nor peace were conceived in purely spiritual or interior categories. Peace and justice walk hand in hand when the messianic ruler of righteousness reigns (Psalm 72.1-7; Psalm 85.9-14). The messianic king of Davidic lineage was endowed with God's own spirit and therefore did the justice which brought peace (Isaiah 9.1-6; Isaiah 11.1-9). Justice was God's right order for the whole of creation and was the special responsibility of the leaders. Peace typically referred to a general well-being including interpersonal, social and religious relationships.

Paul VI describes peace in a similar vein: "peace is something that is built up day after day in pursuit of an order intended by God, which implies a more perfect form of justice among men" (*Development of Peoples*, #76). The *Church in the Modern World* adds: "Peace results from that harmony built into human society by its divine Founder, and actualized by men [sic] as they thirst after ever greater justice" (#78). Both of these quotations recognize the origin of peace in God, the human task to realize peace ever more fully, and the necessity of a present just order. The nature of a just order is described by John XXIII as "founded on truth, built according to justice, vivified and integrated by charity, and put into practice in freedom" (*Peace on Earth*, #167). The Medellin Conference of

Latin American bishops in 1968 translated the above virtues into the personalist and socio- political vocabulary of their situation:

> It [Peace] presupposes and requires the establishment of a just order in which men [sic] can fulfill themselves as men [sic], where their dignity is respected, their legitimate aspirations satisfied, their access to truth recognized, their personal freedom guaranteed; an order where man [sic] is not an object, but an agent of his own history (Medellin on *Peace*, #14).

Recognizing that peace is more than the absence of war, the document continues with a strong rejection of oppressive regimes, even those which may be able to prevent conflict and violence. Order maintained without freedom and justice, they proclaim, is preparation for inevitable revolution (Medellin on *Peace*, #14). Peace comes from a just social order, not merely the disappearance of war.

Peace requires an end to injustice

The prophets in the Hebrew scriptures saw war as a result of injustice (Amos 5.7-21; Isaiah 59.8-9). Therefore, they called for a conversion to justice. The *Church in the Modern World* continued this urgent call to conversion: "If peace is to be established, the primary requisite is to eradicate the causes of dissension between men [sic]. Wars thrive on these, especially injustice" (#83).

Two categories of injustices emerge in the magisterial teachings on peace and justice. The first category is **unequal distribution of resources** both within and among nations. Statistics do change according to the year and the point to be made; however, statistics do agree that the rich of a nation or of the world control an amount of resources disproportionate to their small number. Some 20% of the people control 70%-80% of the world's resources, leaving some 80% of humanity with access to the remainder. 'Resources' refers not only to natural but also economic, political, educational and cultural resources. Although the amount of resources may change, they do comprise a given and limited pool from which all peoples draw.

Classical justice by definition requires that each person receives 'what is due' in a relationship of equity. Modern socio-political thought has come to call this 'what is due' a 'right'. Rights flow from the unique and great potential of each person and the conviction that no person inherently deserves superiority over another. As a consequence certain basic human rights, socio-political rights and socio-economic rights deserve protection. Official church teaching maintains that the basis of the equity in a relationship is the dignity of each human person from creation and the human task in the world, namely the completion of God's reign on earth.[1] Because of their human dignity and their task, each human person has certain legitimate human needs. Social justice requires that each person and the whole of humanity have access to what is necessary to fulfill legitimate human needs. One has a right to what is necessary to satisfy basic human needs.

Churches and the United Nations have set forth basic human rights in an attempt to frame the general lines of what justice requires. In a report on the international year of peace in 1986, the Secretary- General of the United Nations lists food, shelter, health care, education, labor and a beneficial environment among the basic requirements of peace in the contemporary world.[2] The Universal Declaration of Human Rights (1948) passed by the United Nations has a more complete listing of personal, socio-political and socio-economic rights.

---

[1]PIUS XI, *Divini Redemptoris*, in *AAS* 29 (1937), 65-106, here 77-78, #25.
[2]UNITED NATIONS GENERAL ASSEMBLY, *Report of the Secretary-General: International year of Peace* (September 26, 1985), 11.

The first Roman Catholic listing of rights flowing from human dignity and the human task appeared in a 1937 encyclical by Pius XI. There Pius XI noted "the rights of life and bodily integrity, the right of striving toward what is necessary, rights of directing oneself toward the final end in the way and path proposed by God, rights of joining together in society, rights of possessing goods privately and enjoying their use." [1]

Probably the most complete magisterial listing of human rights appeared in John XXIII's encyclical *Peace on Earth.* Within the context of setting forth the order of the universe established by God, John XXIII addressed the just order of relationships between human persons. He treated of this order under the headings of rights, duties and the contemporary historical context. The rights can be divided into seven major groups of rights. Under rights to life, bodily integrity and the means necessary for proper development of life, John XXIII included the same kinds of rights mentioned in the 1986 report of the United Nations Secretary-General on the International Year of Peace. Other groupings of rights are personal, moral and cultural rights (respect, truth, freedom and access to culture), the right to worship according to conscience, marriage and family rights, economic rights (opportunity to work, safe conditions, private property), rights to assemble and to form associations, political rights (participation and juridical protection), and the rights to emigrate and immigrate (#14-27).

The *Church in the Modern World* focused on the relationship of economic rights and world peace. Chapter III on socio-economic life initiated the discussion with reference to the economic disparity within the nations and among nations. As a consequence to this growing contrast, "the very peace of the world can be jeopardized" (#63). The chapter recalls that "the right to have a share of earthly goods sufficient for oneself and one's family belongs to everyone" (#69). Satisfaction of this

---

[1]PIUS XI, *Divini* , 78, #27. Translation is my own.

right requires the distribution of resources such that both individuals and the whole community have adequate provision for human needs, that present needs and the needs of future generations be taken into account, and that those who are unable to demand their rights are given their due (#70). Recognition of these rights and norms "can make a great contribution to the prosperity of mankind [sic] and the peace of the world" (#72).

John Paul II underscored the connection between peace and human rights in a 1982 message for World Day of Peace: "Unconditional and effective respect for each one's unprescriptable and inalienable rights is the necessary condition that peace may reign in a society" (#9).

These attempts by ecclesial and international authorities do give a direction with regard to the distribution of resources. Justice requires that human persons have access or the right to those resources necessary to fulfill their basic human needs.

These norms question the justice of huge expenditures on weapons for war while the basic human needs of the majority of the world's population are not being met.[1] Dwight Eisenhower is quoted as having said already in the 1950's that every bomb is theft from the poor. This same point is repeated in the papal and magisterial statements of the last decades. Vatican council II maintained that the poor suffer intolerable injury because of expenditures for the arms race (*Church in the Modern World*, #81). Paul VI called the arms race a scandal in the face of widespread destitution, ignorance, disease and homelessness (*Development of Peoples*, #53). John XXIII

---

[1] For current information on the monetary resources spent on weapons in comparison to basic human needs, see R.L.SIVARD, *World Military and Social Expenditures 1985*, Washington, D.C., 1985. World Priorities, Inc. publishes an annual report. Another source of current information is SANE, 711 G Street SE, Washington, D.C., 20003.

called attention to the absorption of intellectual as well as economic resources in technologically advanced countries which deprived other countries of those very resources which would aid their economic and social growth (*Peace on Earth*, #109).

Both civil and church leaders do recognize that the economic and intellectual resources tied up in weapons research and production are diverting resources which could meet basic human needs. Justice requires that all and each have access to the resources necessary to meet legitimate human needs. Therefore, to the the extent that budgets for weapons are absorbing the resources which belong to other people, they are unjust. In a strange paradox, disproportionate expenditures for weapons are actually decreasing the possibility for the peace they purport to preserve by increasing the unjust distribution of resources. True peace must be established on justice or, more specifically, a just distribution of the earth's resources.

A second category of injustice which must end if peace is to reign is **structural injustice.** Unjust social structures, be they political ideologies, economic institutions, or cultural attitudes and behaviors, cause strife as well as an inadequate foundation for authentic peace.

When socio-political systems exclude people from participation in government on the basis of racial, sexual, economic or religious reasons, injustice is done. A literacy requirement when education is unavailable or the prohibitive financial outlay for public office campaigns restricts participation in governance. When the excluded groups begin to object to the injustice, public unrest mounts.

Presently Western tastes have cultivated an international economic system which encourages the production of non-food (tea, coffee, sugar, cocoa, tobacco) or export crops (pineapples, bananas, peanuts) in developing countries. This system does

211

provide cash income but monopolizes and sometimes depletes the agricultural land to the extent that the indigenous peoples are under- or malnourished. One can cite the growers of pineapples in the Philippines, sugar in the Caribbean nations and peanuts in the Subsahara.

Western countries also rely on developing countries for raw natural resources, which do provide a source of export income. The developed nations, however, process the raw material and sell it back to the developing nations. The West promotes these product markets in the developing nations, while they jealously guard the technological skills which would enable the processing of the raw material by Third World countries. Tax breaks lure conglomerates to developing countries which seek employment and products for their inhabitants. These same tax breaks, however, lower the ability of the local governments to provide social services for their own people.

All these factors increase economic inequality between the technologically advanced nations and developing nations. The current economic system is further vitiated through corporate monopolies of specific production areas (*Development of Peoples*, # 56-61; Medellin on *Peace*, #9) or through transnational corporate structures which elude national controls. Within some nations, there are economic structures which allow tax evasion and the flow of money outside of the country in which it was garnered into other countries with more favorable taxation or investment possibilities (Medellin on *Peace*, #9).

When socio-cultural behaviors or attitudes allow some to exclude others from the cultural mainstream and from access to the satisfaction of basic human needs, injustice is done. Relegation to marginal existence, class inequality, concentration of power in the hands of a few and the exodus of the intellectually or technically skilled to other cultures are specifically mentioned by the Medellin Conference bishops as structures in Latin American countries which are disruptive of peace (Medellin on *Peace* #2, 3, 5, and 9).

Yet these structural injustices have become such an integral part of international relationships that they become difficult to change. Great difficulty, however, does not exempt a person from movement toward justice. Rather, it challenges persons to creative expertise based on sound knowledge and Christian conviction. The creation of just social structures is required from a double perspective.

First, unjust structures are part of the cycle of violence. Structures can systematically thwart persons and groups of persons in their drive for self-determination, for their share of the goods of the earth and for participation in the human task. The *Challenge of Peace* recalls the many faces of structural violence: "oppression of the poor, deprivation of basic human rights, economic exploitation" (#285). Growing awareness and frustration at such violence can escalate to open conflict. A typiical reaction from the dominant power consists in reprisals and additional restrictive measures aimed at repressing the uprising. The cycle of violence begins anew. The cycle can be broken when structures of violence are replaced with just institutions, attitudes and behavior patterns. Only then can there be the minimum foundation for peace.

More positively, the eradication of unjust structures is required so that a just world order may be established. Authentic peace is the result of justice.

3. Implications for Christian Peacemakers

The Hebrew and Christian Scriptures as well as the twentieth century church documents insist that there can be no peace which is not founded on justice. This too has implications for peacemakers.

The link between justice and peace challenges the peacemaker to justice formation as well as information. It is not clear that the Christian community as a whole is well informed either on its peace and justice tradition. It, therefore, becomes of paramount importance that the Christian teachings on peace and justice become widely disseminated. In addition to the principles and values set forth in Judeo-Christian thought, it is crucial to stay informed on current socio-economic and political facts. Efforts toward a just world order must begin in this historical context. Good will without facts and expertise is insufficient in today's technological and global family.

Besides staying current with information, the peacemaker needs to become formed in justice and peace through reflective consideration of Christian sources, personal and communal prayer. Formation in justice realizes itself in action which is at the heart of the Christian message:

> Action on behalf of justice and participation in the transformation of the world fully appear to us as a constitutive dimension of the preaching of the Gospel, or, in other words, of the Church's mission for the redemption of the human race and its liberation from every oppressive situation. (*Justice in the World,* Introduction)

Action on behalf of justice is not an optional Christian activity. Through the Exodus and the incarnate activity of Jesus, God has made statements about the nature of divine action. Liberation and the action of justification are formative of Christianity. Because of this, it is not enough for a Christian to do justice using superfluous resources (*Church in the Modern World,* #69), but "As was the ancient custom in the Church, they should meet this obligation out of the substance of their goods, and not only out of what is superfluous" (*Church in the Modern World,* #88). Like the widow who gave from her poverty, the peacemaker is called to do with less that others may have access to what is theirs in justice.

On the basis of the information gathered and the formation adopted, the Christian peacemaker can avoid the purchase of products and services from transnational or local companies which have violated the standards of justice and peace as well as disregarded the human dignity of their employees. Companies need to be informed of such conscience choices, whether it is a personal, familial or group action. If Christian peacemakers are shareholders, active involvement on behalf of justice and peace has potential for education and change within corporations. The corporations may or may not incorporate more just practices leading to greater peace, but the Christian peacemaker will have acted on informed personal values.

The Christian peacemaker can go without a meal and donate the money involved to food research or distribution programs. Christians can serve and share the fare of the poor as it is available in a soup kitchen. Peacemakers can lobby for higher taxes so public authorities would have monetary resources to increase public services, or they can contribute a self-imposed tax to private programs which seek to meet basic human needs.

Anyone can begin by establishing just structures in personal behaviors and attitudes. What attitudes keep us from giving others what is rightfully theirs: affirmation of their worth, recognition of their talents or access to education and self-determination? As we remove the unjust personal structures in our own lives, we are taking a preferential option for peace established on justice.

Each person has been given abilities and inner resources for the service of the whole human family. Justice encourages persons to develop their personal talents in a way which contributes to the common good. Justice also challenges persons to make career choices or to develop skills which provide for the basic human needs of others, for example careers in agricultural, business or health services with an eye

215

to advocacy for those unable to demand what is their due. In addition justice invites each peacemaker to consider the possibility of service with the Peace Corps or a Christian volunteer program among people who have limited access to education, health care and economic self-determination. The obligation to do justice out of the substance of our resources applies to time and abilities as well as material goods.

Peace is more than the absence of war. Peace is built upon justice. The presence of the reign of peace is dependent on justice in personal, socio-economic and political relationships. Christian peacemakers must work for justice in their personal and social lives because God has justified us.

```
            P
            E
    P E A C E
            C
            E
```

Roman Catholic Church Documents
Official Roman Catholic teaching in the twentieth century has addressed issues in this chapter. The following selections are particularly pertinent.

Church in the Modern World, #83
What is the articulated connection between injustice and war?

Medellin Conference on Peace, #14 and 16
1. What does it mean to say that peace is, above all, a work of justice?
2. What are some of the examples of institutionalized violence? How do they militate against peace?

Challenge of Peace, #68-70 1. How are truth, justice, freedom and love central human values on which to build peace?
2. How is respect for basic human rights a necessary condition for peace?

Peace on Earth, #14-27
How would a world order based on these rights change your lifestyle? your attitudes?

Other Suggested Readings

CATE, W.B. *Ecumenical action for justice and peace*, in *Ecumenical Trends* 15 (November 1986) 160-161.

DONAHUE, J.R. *Biblical Perspectives on Justice*, in J. HAUGHEY (ed.), *The Faith That Does Justice. Examining the Christian Sources for Social Change*. New York/Ramsey, NJ/ Toronto, 1977, 68-112.

HAMMER, P.L. *The Gift of Shalom*. Philadelphia, 1976. See especially chapter 5.

HOLLENBACH, D. *Modern Catholic Teachings Concerning Justice*, in J. HAUGHEY (ed.), *The Faith That Does Justice.*

Examining the Christian Sources for Social Change. New York/Ramsey, NJ/ Toronto, 1977, 207-231.

SPRAGUE, R.L. *A Sense of Injustice,* in E.A. POWERS, *Signs of Shalom.* Philadelphia, 1973, 125-132.

THOMPSON, W.C. *Christology of Love, Justice and Peace,* in *The Ecumenist* 23 (March-April 1985) 33-38.

Audio-visual Materials

The following are some of the audio-visual materials which are related to the chapter content. The list is not exhaustive, but is intended to give some initial suggestions for previewing.

Guess who's coming to Breakfast (slides or filmstrip; 18m; Maryknoll; 1978) is a documentary on the policies of a multinational firm, Gulf and Western, which owns and exploits rich agricultural holdings in the Dominican Republic.

Sharing Global Resources (slides; 40m; NARMIC; 1978) depicts the struggle of Third World nations to have a more equitable share in global resources through the efforts to establish a New International Economic Order.

Taking Charge (slides; 27m; NARMIC; 1983) introduces the issues and institutions that affect economic justice in the Third World and here at home. Looks at the Phillipines, Chile, Kenya, Appalachia and Philadelphia where people are challenging their legacy of poverty and oppression.

Hamburger,U.S.A. (slides; 30m; AFSC; 1980) looks at U.S. agri-business production and marketing practices and suggests ways consumers can play a more active role in food distribution.

Who's in Charge here? (film; 15m; UN, Institute for World Order and the International Assoc. of Machinists; 1980) follows a group of defense workers discussing the economic problems related to military spending and national defense.

Whose budget is it anyway? (slides; 20m; NARMIC; 1982) compares and contrasts decreased spending for domestic programs and unlimited military spending.

The Business of Hunger (film; 28m; Maryknoll; 1984) examines typical implications of transnational pressure to plant non-food and export crops on developing countries' economic systems and nutrition. It purposes just distribution of the earth's resources.

Introductory Activities
The purpose of the introductory activity is to begin discussion on peacemaking as well as to allow students/participants a chance to express what their previous experience and understandings of peacemaking have been.

1. Drawing on St. Augustine Paul VI has said, "If you want peace, work for justice". Discuss what Paul VI means by that statement.

2. To some extent Amelia Marcos' shoes juxtapositioned next to the Managua slums has become an international symbol of injustice. What were the injustices which led to unrest in the Phillipines? In other trouble spots in the world?

3. Sometimes there are situations in our own experience in which injustice hinders peace. Susan received much pressure NOT TO HIRE an excellent person for an opening in her department because the person had a reputation of advocacy for other employees whose rights were violated. Timothy finds himself in an escalating situation which he initiated by harassing a slower inept co-worker. Now other employees have followed suit and expect Timothy to set the pace. Neither Susan nor Timothy are comfortable with the expectations placed on them. What can they do to see that justice is done and

219

peace returned to their workplace? Have you ever been in a situation in which injustices have led to unrest? What did you do? What else could you have done?

Discussion Questions

The purpose of the discussion questions is to encourage students/participants to integrate the text and/or presented material into their own thinking and living.

1. In the face of world poverty/hunger, should there be a percentage ceiling on the amount of money spent on armaments? What reasoning leads you to your conclusion?

2. A colleague of mine from the social sciences once said that given the amount of resources an American baby uses in its lifetime, the world can't afford a high birth rate in the United States. Do American parents have an obligation in justice to limit family size so other peoples have a portion of the resources which they need?

3. What is the relationship between the distribution of the earth's resources and violence?

4. What are the unjust structures in your community? How do they hinder peaceful living here? What can we do?

5. How do these ideas/insights impact on your life's experiences?

Activities for Application and Integration

The following suggested activities provide opportunities for students/participants to carry the concepts of this chapter beyond the classroom. They are intended to clarify and integrate understandings into lived experience.

1. Compare the defense and human services budgets (basic human needs, education, social services) for a number of recent years. What does the information tell you? What is the

relationship of the defense budget and the current crisis in agriculture?

2. Find out how many calories you need for a well-balanced diet in a week. Keep track of the total calories you consume. Evaluate the source of your calories (junk food, sweets, high calorie/low nutrition). Study the food advertised on television for a four hour period of time. Evaluate the calories and the potential for nutrition in the foods advertised. Visit five vending machines. Evaluate the calories and the potential for nutrition in the products available. What connections between justice for peace and American eating habits can be made?

3. Put together a list of a variety of groceries. Go to a supermarket in a poorer section of town. Compare prices to those in your usual supermarket. Do the same for a suburban store. What conclusions can you draw? What might be the reasons behind the price differences? What is necessary to bring about change?

4. Analyze your own eating habits or clothing habits as to their impact on promoting/discouraging world peace. To what extent are you willing to pay the kind of prices for imported food/clothing which would allow just wages for Third World laborers? How does one's support of multinational corporations instead of local producers impact on peace?

5. Write a letter to your congressional representative urging passage of legislation which seeks to establish peace on justice. What is your representative's record on such legislation?

Spirituality Component

It is one thing to read and study about a theology of peace and quite another to become a person of peace. This spirituality component offers a series of Scripture readings with reflection questions which are closely aligned with the chapter topic. It is suggested that they be used for prayer and reflection over a series of days. The reader may wish either to find another

221

Christian with whom the prayer and its fruits way be shared regularly or to journal one's growth as a peacemaker.

DAY 1: Psalm 72.1-7
This psalm describes a politico-religious leader. As a member of the Christian community, what do I do that justice and peace flower in my days?

DAY 2: Psalm 85.9-14
How do I experience the unity of justice and peace in my life?

DAY 3: Isaiah 26.1-3
The strength of the nation is associated with a national policy of peace and justice. What is my contribution to national strength on the basis of this criteria?

DAY 4: Isaiah 9.1-9
This passage also describes a politico-religious leader as one who does justice that peace may reign. As one in charge of my own life, how just am I to the marginal and poor in my life?

DAY 5: Isaiah 11.2-9
What unjust practices do I need to root out of my life that peace may dwell there?

DAY 6: Isaiah 32. 15b-19
How can justice bring about peace in my communal living?

DAY 7: James 3.13-18
Given my life, do I "cultivate peace"? Do I "harvest justice"?

CHAPTER 9
DEVELOPMENT IS A NEW NAME FOR PEACE

Sarah is a Christian, a nurse, wife and mother of five teenagers. For the last five years, she has spent several weeks after Christmas in Haiti as part of a health care team, which provided care for the Haitian people and additional training for the local health care personnel. One evening last summer, when I visited the family, Sarah showed me a slide lecture she had put together on her work in Haiti. The undernourished children and related health problems, open sewers and minimal housing I had expected. But I am still haunted by one slide: three or four children of ages 10 to 12 studying at night under a street light because it is the only electric light in the village. Perhaps it is the educator in me which is so deeply moved. I don't know if I am awed by the children's determination to receive an education or appalled by the obstacles to that education.

The slide presents such a sharp contrast to my own educational experience. Dedicated teachers, parents who valued education and a home filled with reading materials were givens for me. Eagerness and not necessity kept me reading late into the night with inadequate lighting. In short I was given a multiplicity of opportunities- -health care, education, communal and familial values--through which my native aptitudes and qualities might be developed. My world encouraged my desire to transcend limitations and difficulties that I might become all I could be. The good of the whole human person and of all human persons is the development

Paul VI called "a new name for peace". While justice, in some respect, focuses on the essential requirements for the survival of peace, development focuses on the optimum environment for peace.

* * *

1. Describing the Development Which Means Peace

As a term development is currently enjoying a popularity which can spell a word's decline into empty slogans and jargon. Fund raising is called institutional development and the transformation of agricultural ground into malls is now land development. A rather neutral description--but one approaching its use here--is: "Development is the process through which societies gain access to and utilize the earth's physical and human resources."[1] The strengths of this definition are the notion of process, the social nature of humanity and the inclusion of human resources.

Development of Peoples

The most complete description of development in the Christian tradition occurs in the *Development of Peoples*.[2] Christian development is concerned with wholeness and with the good understood in its personal, Christian and social dimensions. Personal good is the maturation of God-given abilities and qualities into full personhood (#15). For those baptized into Christ, development is also the process of giving concrete expression to those Christian values which Paul II

---

[1]K. COOPER, M. MCWHORTER, and C. GAMON, *Ethics of Development in a Global Environment,* in *Peace and World Order Studies. A Curriculuum Guide,* NY, 3rd ed., 1981, 216-222, here 220

[2]PAUL VI, *On the Development of Peoples,* Washington, DC, 1967, #14.

calls "transcendent humanism" (#16). The values of love, friendship, prayer and contemplation are specifically mentioned (#20). Since persons by their nature are social beings, Christian and personal development is intimately intertwined with the good of other persons and peoples (#17). Much of this good has been inherited from past generations. The human response to this bequest is to continue the transformation from less human to more human conditions for peoples today and for future generations. *Development of Peoples* describes more human conditions as follows:

> Conditions that are more human: the passage from misery towards the possession of necessities, victory over social scourges, the growth of knowledge, the acquisition of culture. Additional conditions that are more human: increased esteem for the dignity of others, the turning toward the spirit of poverty, cooperation for the common good, the will and desire for peace. Conditions that are still more human: the acknowledgement by man [sic] of supreme values, and of God their source and their finality. Conditions that, finally and above all, are more human: faith, a gift of God accepted by the good will of man, [sic] and unity in the charity of Christ (#21).

Such a concept of development presupposes a rich sense of wholeness. Personal development does not happen in isolation from others. Each generation stands on the shoulders of those who have gone on before, whether they are our emigrating ancestors, the Christian mystics or musical geniuses. In this world more than ever before, each person rubs shoulders with the banana packer in Honduras, the computer chip technician in Japan, the seamstress in Malaysia, and the theologian in Kenya. Temporal and spatial interdependence in the global village is a reality.

Recurring themes in development

Development is a new name for peace. As such, it emphasizes five threads. Development is, first of all, a particular **vision** of peace which is able to inspire, to empower and to measure peacemaking efforts. As a contemporary vision of peace, development is rooted in basic human needs and human dignity (*Justice in the World,* proposition #1) as well as in those common human bonds such as experience, faith and aspirations. The vision of a common future which celebrates human dignity and rejoices in the actualization of human potential can inspire its adherents to hasten that future. The vision actually can empower its disciples to realize peace through its charge to participation and self-determination. Like any vision of peace, this contemporary image evaluates efforts to effect development in a personal, socio-economic or political sphere. This vision of peace relies both on conversion of heart and on social structures to strengthen and support that which binds peoples into one family (*Challenge of Peace,* #236). Development entrusts the actualization of peace to women and men who make up the one human family, to those men and women whose living shapes and determines the future. Understood in this way, development is a vision compatible in method, approach, and content with contemporary insight.

Closely connected is a second recurring thread which links peace with development, namely the development which leads to peace is marked by **positive action.** Peace is not an absence of war nor a refraining from the injustice which breeds violence and dissension. Rather development has a clear sense of the vision seeking enfleshment; the vision requires a definite commitment to positive action on behalf of peace.

Quest for Peace, sponsored by the Quixote Center, is one graphic example of positive action. In June 1985 the U.S. Congress appropriated $27 million in so-called humanitarian aid to the contras in Nicaragua. At that time Quest for Peace pledged to match and subsequently did match this amount in medical supplies, basic educational supplies, food and clothing delivered to the poor through the Red Cross and the Institute of John XXIII. Quest for Peace again matched the $100 million congressional aid to the Contras in 1987 and continues to repeat the campaign. Quest for Peace views itself as a "nonviolent, positive campaign" contributing to the establishment of a U.S. foreign policy based on peace and friendship.

Positive action of this kind is subversive in actuality. Marches, demonstrations and protests in essence recognize that the opposition has the power. In some ways the positive action of development ignores and subverts the existent power base by the creation of grass roots alternatives. On an interpersonal level, when the only alternative in an abusive domestic setting is remaining in the situation, the power rests with the abuser. Positive action, such as offering alternative living situations, the acquisition of skills or the enhancement of self-esteem, subverts that previous power base. Positive action has unleashed a personal development which is capable of resisting oppression. Positive action toward international development has similar subversive capabilities.

Positive action on behalf of peace is modeled on Jesus, the reconciliation of God made flesh. Jesus' life was the embodiment of this reconciliation in its most concrete form: Jesus announced the indwelling Spirit of God; Jesus healed persons into wholeness; Jesus freed people from servitude and brought life from death. These positive actions flowed from Jesus' vision of the unity of humanity with God; they were not reactions to religious or political oppression in and of itself. This remains true for the Christian today. Development entails positive action which flows from the vision of one common future for the one human family created by God, living by the one Spirit in the one body of Christ.

227

When U.S. Apollo astronaut Russell Schweickart viewed the earth from the space capsule, he noted the absence of boundary lines dividing countries. From that far away, earth was one whole. Such a **sense of wholeness** is the third characteristic of peace as development. Partisan boundary lines, such as nationalism, racism, and individualism, are overlooked,so that interdependence may become more visible. This is not easily done, especially by those for whom the boundary lines have given the advantage. Wholeness of the human person, of the human race, and of the whole world is a fact often awaiting conscious realization. Peacemakers can in fact provide an environment for one another and for future generations. Our choices can facilitate the move from a begrudging acceptance of the fact of interdependence to a warm welcoming of this solidarity.

For Christians solidarity is, in addition, a faith conviction: the one Spirit of Jesus enlivens the one body of Christ. Christians remember Jesus who was a human person with them; they recall the one God who creates all. For the Christian human solidarity has taken on the Christian vocabulary of creation, redemption, and Pentecost. We are all creatures of the one creator. We are all brothers and sisters of the one Jesus whose love to death saved us all. We all live by the one Spirit in the one body of Christ. In emphasizing the good of the whole person and of all persons in the whole world, development seeks to make apparent the bonds of cooperation in daily lived reality until war or dissension loses all attractiveness as an option to settle grievances.

The fourth emphasis in development as a contemporary image of peace is its **preferential option for the poor.** One can view this emphasis as a pragmatic realization that a great threat to peace is the exclusion of the poor from development. As long as the poor have little access to human, socio-political and economic resources, they have little to lose from violent demands of access to resources. The pragmatist may logically conclude the poor's access to development means peace.

On another level the defense of the widow, the orphan and the poor is a mandate in both Hebrew and Christian Scriptures. One origin of the mandate rests in the re-enactment of God's saving activity toward the Israelites when they were enslaved in Egypt (Deuteronomy 15.15). Another origin recognizes that those without resources are often ready to receive justification from God while those more richly endowed often prefer self-justification (Luke 1.48-53). Both Hebrew and Christian scriptures attest that powerlessness can be an attitude conducive to acceptance of salvation.

From this perspective advocacy for the marginal embodies a value system based on human dignity, human solidarity and a positive commitment to actualize the vision of peace. It is the commitment to human dignity which seeks the actualization of the gifts and talents of all--even those enslaved by fear, ignorance or malnutrition. It is an embodiment of human solidarity to act on the belief that the development of another person's or of another people's aptitudes enhances one's own personal or cultural development. It is the enfleshment of a Christian value system which puts people ahead of profit, the poor on the same level as the powerful, and persons before systems. By their existence the marginal folk challenge value systems which are built on a hierarchical distribution of power and on a disregard for that which does not fit the predetermined system. Development accepts the challenge of the marginal and seeks to involve them in the determination of a common human future. Wherever inclusion takes precedence over disregard and exclusivity, development promotes peace. To the extent that development of this nature succeeds, the status quo and hierarchical systems are endangered.

Finally, the development which makes for peace is not another social program, an increased GNP or one more long-range plan. Rather, it is **a way of living**. Beliefs and attitudes thread themselves together in an approach to life. A belief that development is the form peace takes in today's world reveals itself in a constellation of behavioral and attitudinal choices.

Trust is the focal point of the constellation. Usually the passage of time proves people or things trustworthy. The understanding of development which is described in this chapter requires a more proactive understanding of trust. Essential is the conviction that persons are worthy of trust before that quality has been proven. The proactive person, therefore, creates situations in which trust can be practiced, so that this fundamental way of living can become more widespread. The proactive trustmaker nourishes trust in relationships by sharing responsibilities, decision-making and faith with colleagues as well as friends.

Another attitudinal choice is an understanding which transcends differences to reach a deeper commonality, that is, the search for what is 'standing-under' the apparent event, reaction, or demeanor. Such an understanding fashions strong interpersonal links. On a community or international level, however, understanding connects the socio-economic and political events to the people. What did the introduction of large-scale beef operations mean for the majority of Mexican people? In spite of well-meaning intentions to increase sources of protein, in fact, it meant an increase in price for a poorer quality of corn tortilla which is a main source of protein in the Mexican diet: only a few are now able to buy the more expensive beef protein.

As the news media recounts natural disasters and world unemployment, it takes a concerted struggle to tie the media report to families like those in the neighborhood or among one's personal acquaintances. Is it possible to understand the joy or sorrow of others joined to us 'only' by a shared humanness with its common human experiences?

There are also concrete behavioral choices reflective of the conviction that development is the form peace takes in today's world. The options for collaboration, dialogue and nonviolent resolution of conflict are some of the more significant choices. Collaboration on the personal, social, and global levels is a concrete choice to encourage skills formative of cooperation, wholeness and participation. Churches and religious orders as well as transnational corporations can play a key role, because a network of structures which link persons and institutions is already in place. What remains is the consistent decision to practice those collaborative methods which facilitate peace. Educational and health care systems provide another existent network based on common concerns. This mutual interest could result in cooperative exchange programs as well as in this provision of expertise and development for peace.

The choice for dialogue promotes development and peace. Since dialogue requires an acceptance of other persons and the thoughtful consideration of their convictions, its practice demonstrates a belief in human dignity and solidarity. The openness to change which is constitutive of dialogue suggests the readiness for the conversion of heart so necessary to bring about peace. Dialogue also implies an expanded base of participation in the formation of ongoing consensus. Skills and attitudes essential to dialogue are essential to development and peace.

The option for nonviolent conflict resolution such as mediation, confrontation, or non-cooperation contributes to the development of full humanness and peace. The decision to disavow violence as a more obvious reactive option invites creativity and an expanded range of human response. The choice of a proactive response to conflict, instead of a reaction, promotes self-determination and integrity in character formation. If it is the sense of the human heart that persons were created in peace for peace, then personal integrity would

231

prefer peaceful resolution of conflict. If the vision of peace beckons toward its fulfillment, then peaceful responses in conflict resolution accelerate its completion.

The above attitudes and behavior which advance development could be a description of unconditional love. Unconditional love is pro- active and does not require love in return. Unconditional love focuses on the person under trappings which at times can obscure human dignity. Unconditional love seeks what is best for the beloved, not from a paternalistic perspective, but from the perspective of human needs, dignity, solidarity and self-determination. Unconditional love is a way of living which transcends categories and distinctions, thereby uniting all in all.

2. Specific Applications of Development

This understanding of development as a contemporary vision of peace, like any vision, seeks embodiment in the world today. Since Jesus passed on the Spirit to those who were disciples, the vision of peace is already present but awaits its completion by the hands of the body of Christ today. Two orders which can be intimately entwined with this understanding of development are the socio-political and the socio-economic orders.

Socio-economic order

The *Challenge of Peace* states that the danger of world war is a direct result from the following socio-economic tensions: "worldwide inflation, trade and payments deficits, competition over scarce resources, hunger, widespread unemployment, global environmental dangers, the growing power of transnational corporations, and the threat of international financial collapse" (#242). A similar connection is reiterated frequently in the regional seminar reports during the UN International Year of Peace. The African nations cite deteriorating socio-economic conditions, an inequitable world economic order and the international economic environment as major threats to peace.[1] Their stated desire to move from situations of economic dependence to an "economic community capable of achieving accelerated, self-sustaining and self-reliant socio-economic development in the interest of the human masses" (#24). After noting the debilitating effect of external debts and interest which consumes one-third of their combined export income, the Latin American and Caribbean nations call for dialogue as well as a regional and international co-operation to ensure peace, stability and cooperation (#33-34). The European participants acknowledged that "more effective forms of international economic cooperation are essential for all efforts made towards the achievement of international peace and security" (#44).

If religious and civil leaders alike can so readily recognize the interrelationships of peace with economic development, the question remains: Why has so little been done? Without appearing simplistic, four suggestions are possible. The magnitude of the tensions suggested in the *Challenge of Peace* are staggering, for example, worldwide inflation and international financial collapse. The difficulties are further increased because structural systems are retarding development.

Second, a kind of near-sightedness tends to allow a preoccupation with personal ability to earn and to consume. As long as personal income tax remains stable, there is little thought given national or global socio-economic structures.

Third, the more successful one is by virtue of the operative socio-economic order, the less interest there is in furthering an

---

[1]UN SECRETARY-GENERAL, *Contribution of the regional seminars in promoting the objectives of the International Year of Peace*, New York, 1986, #21 and 25.

alternative system. The risk of loss runs too high. It is impossible that the earth's resources could support the lifestyle which is typical of the economically successful for all people. Rather the more affluent must expect a less advantageous position so that others may have what is necessary for full human development.

Last, self-depreciation proves to be a ready response to the magnitude of the task: namely, what could I as one person possibly do to stem the tide of events? Each of these four hinders the advance of the kind of development which is peace by turning in on oneself and away from the needs of others. In religious vocabulary this is sin.

There are at least three areas to which economic development can turn in order to expedite the vision of peace. Maximization of profits as a presupposition behind socio-economic systems must be converted to the promotion of social and human values. The promotion of human dignity, basic human rights, solidarity of peoples, participation, and self-determination need to become the warp and woof of the economic structures. Then mutual trust, cooperation, dialogue and nonviolent conflict resolution can become the managerial style. Such a shift in presuppositions necessitates positive action to realize the vision of peace. Whenever the socio-economic order can be urged or compelled to act on behalf of social and human values or to employ methods and structures supportive of development, then peace is becoming a here-and-now reality.

Secondly, the promotion of peace requires that socio-economic systems divert the personal and financial resources currently expended for weapons and related military purposes to the process of development. This has been repeatedly stated by Catholic magisterial teaching (*Development of Peoples*, #58; *Human Life Today*, #126; *Challenge of Peace*, #271) and civil leaders alike (*UN Regional Seminars on Peace*, #44 and

51). There are a number of reasons supporting this change in the socio-economic structures. The most obvious reason is the incongruence between building weapons which are destructive of human life and work while claiming that peace for all is the reason behind the policy. Such destructive capabilities undermine the vision of peace described as the development of all persons into their full humanity.

Another reason touches on the unemployment issue. It is granted that the weapons and defense industries provide jobs. The kinds of jobs required in these industries, however, require primarily skilled and professional persons while unemployment is highest among production and semi-skilled workers. Military spending does not provide a solution to thereal issues of unemployment. In addition military spending creates fewer jobs for an equal amount of money than would civilian spending in a human services area.[1]

Of crucial importance to development is funding. Seventy per cent of the federal funding for research and development in the United States goes to the military. Besides the monies involved this policy siphons off intellectual resources which could be hastening peace built on development. The transition from weapons and military industries to human and social services could mean more jobs and the release of personnel, talents and intellectual resources for development. Such a transition not only promotes peace, but also represents positive action encouraging trust among nations.

A final area in which the socio-economic system needs reform, if it is to promote development, is global awareness. The economic systems must move from methods and

---

[1]SANE, *Economic Benefits of the Freeze*, Washington, DC, 1984 gives the following statistics. For one billion dollars, military spending = 21,000 jobs; mass transit = 40,000 jobs; hospitals = 54,000 jobs; education = 72,000 jobs.

presuppositions which support corporate or personal individualism. The world is a whole and its economic systems are interconnected. A kind of economic growth which depends on exploitation of member economies will boomerang back to the exploiting economies. The sense of global, economic interdependence consequently requires that dependent economies be nurtured into self- reliance. Interpersonal collaboration needs the interaction of mature persons to be effective. It would consequently seem that economic collaboration also needs self-reliant parties. It is, therefore, beneficial to the whole, that each and all local economies be healthy and self-sufficient. The international consequences of Black Monday, 1929 demonstrated the interconnectedness of economies after World War I. Today the ties binding economic systems together are even more intertwined.

Socio-political order

The socio-political order can scarcely be separated from the socio-economic system. This fact illustrates the actual interconnectedness of the world and its people in all phases of their living. There are, however, socio-political tensions which make the warm welcome of a world without boundary lines a formidable choice. The United Nations does exist as a structure of international regulation, yet member nations resist United Nations' attempts to exercise a formative role in a transition to a governmental institution for the common good of all.

The socio-political transition to sovereign nation-states was not without trauma; the transition to a socio-political structure of global interdependence can not expect to be easier. In spite of its contemporary inappropriateness a nationalism which calls for policies and attitudes to exert dominance over--rather than equity with--other nation-states holds sway. The interdependent realities of this late twentieth century world make vying for superiority an antiquated remnant. International socio-political structures which facilitate self-management and collaboration of states for the common good of all will usher in an era of peace. Internationalism does not necessarily spell the demise of distinct nations and cultures, but it does challenge practices of domination.

Magisterial documents have repeatedly questioned nationalism's adequacy in this interrelated world (*Church in the Modern World*, #82 and 90; *Peace on Earth*, #62 and 65; *Challenge of Peace*, #242). In the language of Christian faith, internationalism can be considered a socio-political expression which reflects the conviction that God is the creator of all peoples who, then, are brothers and sisters to each other.

Another socio-political tension which delays the emergence of peace is the propensity to turn to military solutions of conflicts. The proliferation of resources for war and a lack of trust among nations favor the choice for war. Given the potential for nuclear disaster, the interconnectedness of nations, and the incongruence of using war to enforce peace, the option to wage war is no longer a viable choice. Rather nation-states must begin to choose the more demanding path of negotiation for the sake of the common good. In a realistic statement of Christian hope, the U.S. bishops urge that the United States-Soviet relationship dismiss war as an option. Their statement, however, has a validity beyond that specific relationship:

> To believe we are condemned in the future only to what has been the past of U.S.-Soviet relations is to underestimate both our human potential for creative diplomacy and God's action in our midst which can open the way to changes we could barely imagine. We do not intend to foster illusory ideas that the road ahead in superpower relations will be devoid of tension or that peace will be easily achieved. But we do warn against the "hardness of heart" which can close us or others to the changes needed to make the future different from the past(*Challenge of Peace*, #258).

237

Like the socio-economic sphere, current tensions in the socio-political order can also be opportunities to hasten the completion of the reign of peace begun in peace. It is the vision of peace and the reality of life in the one Spirit of Jesus which is Christian hope.

3. Implications for Christian Peacemakers

An understanding of peace as development points the peacemaker to a vision of wholeness, of completeness personally, socially and globally. Development, the new name for peace, can be pictured as a grid in which the recurring themes of this chapter--basic human needs and dignity, solidarity of peoples, participation and self- determination, action incarnating the vision, preferential option for the marginal, and wholeness--intersect with the personal, social and global spheres. The values and methods which further peace in the personal sphere are the same values and methods which further peace on the global level. The stress, therefore, is on making conscious choices in all aspects of living which are supportive of peace and development.

In light of the link of peace with development, peacemaking means a proactive commitment to wholeness. Personal, social and global wholeness shows its priority position when time, abilities and finances support it. When as many personal and material resources are employed in the promotion of peace as are engaged in armaments, then peace will have a chance to become a reality. This equalization can be done on a personal as well as a national level. For example, if a person is unable or unwilling to divert the federal telephone or income tax used for military buildup, one could contribute that same amount for peacemaking.

Not everyone and not every group is able to be whole all the time. Environmental stresses, personal limitations and crises tear away at wholeness. Christian peacemaking requires, however, that peacemakers seek to reduce unhealthy stress for others as well as for themselves and to resolve those areas of personal unwholeness. Neither continued coexistence nor peace at any price reduces stress or resolves brokenness. These are rather resolved through the acquisition of skills and knowledge at the risk of personal change.

There are also needs for persons who are skilled in healing brokenness, who are able to mediate through conflict to a resolution, who can counsel and encourage emerging maturation into full human development. Trained personnel are needed for personal, industrial and international mediation. The local or human community which is committed to wholeness can support persons through their training programs and then trust their expertise enough to call on them in difficult situations.

A proactive commitment to wholeness entails inclusivity. There is no place for language, attitudes or behavior which exclude on the basis of ideological persuasion, religion, sex or race. Distinction is not necessarily excluding, but it can be used to exclude. Inclusivity promotes the dialogue and understanding which leads to wholeness.

Peace is not a value or a state into which one falls by chance. Peace is a incarnational process, ratified by daily choices to abstain from violence and to make peace with ourselves, our colleagues, our family and acquaintances.

Another implication for peacemaking is an awareness of and openness to other cultures, other peoples and other ways of doing things. Foreign pen pals provide a person-to-person introduction to another culture. Domestic and foreign exchange programs which expose persons to another cultural experience are often in need of host families. The study of a foreign language breaks down the attitude that there is only one way of saying or doing something. Experimenting with the foods of other peoples can open up one's sensitivity to other customs. Most newspapers and news magazines do have international news somewhere on an inside page. Reading the articles can give a sense of what is happening globally, although the perspective is often western. Larger communities have ethnic communities or sponsor arts programs and cultural exhibits from other peoples. Even in smaller communities, there are opportunities for travelogs, slide lectures or even an ethnic church dinner. For the above possibilities, one needs only to develop an awareness of the possibilities and an openness to the opportunities.

Such beginnings hopefully lead to additional research, appreciation or involvement with other cultures. Human development work in domestic or foreign cultures needs persons skilled in education, agriculture, medical and social services. In whatever profession or career, there are opportunities to advance global awareness of colleagues, clients or students. Educators teach units or courses which introduce other cultures. A teacher who is sensitive to the values and worth of other cultures teachs such units differently from a teacher who sees differences as odd aberrations from the American way.

Civic and business leaders can sponsor cultural exchange programs or events. When the emphasis is on meeting people rather than seeing sights, such programs enhance cultural exchange. Co-workers and colleagues need to be reminded that ethnic and cultural slurs are derogatory. Church groups already have an international network in place which offers opportunities to contact and to learn about other cultures through speakers, financial support of volunteers or through personal service.

Finally, this understanding of development asks the peacemaker to make connections between personal choices and development. The choice to buy the cheaper and foreign-made products supports a transnational corporation which often is more concerned with profit than human development. A refusal to buy the foreign-made products of transnationals could lessen the little income some Third World families have. There are some alternatives. For example, one could purchase products from Third World cooperatives or exert stockholder influence to direct transnational concern for human development and world peace. Whatever the decision the consumer must see the connection between their personal choices and development.

The choice of pre-packaged convenience foods and fast food chains is linked to a multiplication of human and natural resources in their preparation for the consumer. The consumption of foods with little nutritional value usually entails the necessity to consume other food with nutritional value or to suffer from malnutrition. In all of these instances, personal choice devours more than our share of resources. To change such eating habits requires conversion of life- style and the conviction that personal choise changes at least the Christian peacemaker.

The choice of a career only on the basis of its material advantages is joined to a disregard for personal as well as global development. The constant choice to amass possessions bespeaks a lack of interest in the development of moral, religious or intellectual values. For the Christian peacemaker, service and sufficency must replace status and superfluity.

Routine choices do impinge on personal, social and global development. Awareness of the connection allows persons to make choices consistent with their vision of peace and development. A lifestyle, which seeks to develop all of one's personal resources in service of the common good while utilizing only the necessary natural and material resources, would seem in keeping with the understanding of development as a new name for peace. Peter Maurin says it this way:

The world would be better off
if people tried to become better.
And people would become better
if they stopped trying to become better off.
For when everybody tries to become
better off,
nobody is better off.
But when everybody tries to become better,
everybody is better off.
Everybody would be rich
if nobody tried to become richer.
And nobody would be poor
if everybody tried to be the poorest.
And everybody would be what he ought
to be
if everybody tried to be
what he wants the other fellow to be.[1]

Let us seek to become better.

```
        P
        E
P   E   A   C   E
        C
        E
```

---

[1]P. MAURIN, *The Case for Utopia*, in *The Green Revolution. Easy Essays on Catholic Radicalism*, Cambridge, MA, 2nd ed., 1961, 37.

Roman Catholic Church Documents

Official Roman Catholic teaching in the twentieth century has addressed issues in this chapter. The following selections are particularly pertinent.

Church in the Modern World, #83-86
Evaluate the useful norms in terms of their ability to foster socio- economic and political development.

Development of peoples, #14-21 and #76-87 1.
Describe three elements of the "Christian vision of development".
2. What does Paul VI mean when he says development is a new name for peace? How can peace become a reality?

Challenge of Peace, #234-244 and #259-273
1. Describe those elements which the U.S. Catholic bishops consider essential in Catholic teachings on world order.
2. What guidelines do the U.S. bishops suggest in the realization of interdependence?

Other Suggested Readings

FELLER, G., SCHWENNINGER, S.R., SINGERMAN, D. *Peace and World Order Studies. A Curriculum Guide.* New York, 3rd ed., 1981, 216-225.

JOHN PAUL II. *1985 World Day of Peace Message,* in *Origins* 14 (January 10, 1985) 491-496.

SHANNON, T. *What are the saying about peace and war?* New York/Ramsey, NJ, 1983. See especially chapter 5: Peace and War...The State of the Question.

Audio-visual Materials
The following are some of the audio-visual materials which are related to the chapter content. The list is not exhaustive, but is intended to give some initial suggestions for previewing.

No frames, no boundaries (film; 21m; Creative Initiatives; 1983) Explores the "frames" of reference and the artificial "boundaries" which exist between nations.

The Beyond War Spacebridge (Video; 60m; Beyond War; 1985) is a vivid and hopeful statement of "we are one" with an inspirational example of U.S. and Soviets working together to build a world beyond war.

The Choice is Clear: Jobs with Peace (slides; 15m; Jobs with Peace; 1985) shows a positive vision of how the US economy could be revitalized by investing in the civilian sector and by converting military industries to peaceful production.

Toward a Human World Order (4 filmstrips; 10-12m; Global Educational Associates) includes the following titles: The whole earth community; The National Security Straightjacket; World order alternatives; Strategies for World Order.

Kentanza--Kenya, Tanzania, Zambia and Zaire (4 filmstrips; 22m; United Church of Canada; 1985) look at the effects of international systems on people of that region. These systems--monetary, political, military, foreign aid--and the church as a system supporting, changing and challenging the others in Kentanza are explored.

Let Them Eat Missles (slide/tape; 23m; AFSC; 1985) explores the links between underdevelopment and the arms race. It offers approaches to change.

244

Introductory Activities

The purpose of the introductory activity is to begin discussion on peacemaking as well as to allow students/participants a chance to express what their previous experiences and understandings of peacemaking have been.

1. Ask the participants to prepare for this session by asking five to ten other people what keeps them from being whole persons. Discuss the results of the interviews.

2. The last number of years have been marked by an increase in terrorist attacks. From which countries do the terrorists often come? Against which countries are the attack often directed? What is the socio-economic and political situation of the "terrorist" countries? Some people hold that improvement in the economic situations of these countries could cause an decrease in terrorism. What is the logic behind such thinking?

Discussion Questions

The purpose of the discussion questions is to encourage students/participants to integrate the text and/or presented materials into their own thinking and living.

1.If the modern historical sequence of political systems has been: pre-colonial, colonial, dependence, interdependence, transnational, where are we now as a world? How do we move beyond that phase?

2.What would a developed world look like? What are the major constraints in achieving that worldview? Where do we begin to work toward it?

3. What are development values? How can I integrate these into my life today?

245

4. What are development strategies? How can I incorporate these into my life situation?

5. What part does God play in the development which is peace?

Activities for Application and Integration

The following suggested activities provide opportunities for students/participants to carry the concepts of this chapter beyond the classroom. They are intended to clarify and integrate understandings into lived experience.

1. Research and report on the United Nations efforts on behalf of world peace. What contributes to its effectiveness or ineffectiveness?

2. Spend at least a day on a farm working in the fields, caring for the animals or picking and hoeing in the garden. Talk about your experience in terms of wholeness and interrelatedness.

3. Plan and organize an international meal with dishes from developing countries. If possible invite members of these countries to tell you about their diet and their culture.

4. Find out about volunteer programs serving in domestic and foreign cultures. What are the qualifications asked of applicants? Which professions and skills do they prefer?

5. Write a 2 to 3 page reflection-strategy paper on the topic: How can I be a peacemaker in my career/profession/state of life?

6. Interview someone who has lived or worked in another culture about their experiences. What are the difficulties and the pleasures of living in another culture? How did they come to that opportunity?

Spirituality Component

It is one thing to read and study about a theology of peace and quite another to become a person of peace. This spirituality component offers a series of Scripture readings with reflection questions wich are closely aligned with the chapter topic. It is suggested that they be used for prayer and reflection over a series of days. The reader may wish either to find another Christian with whom the prayer and its fruit may be shared regularly or to journal one's growth as a peacemaker.

DAY 1: Mark 5.25-34
Here physical wholeness is associated with peace. How can I bring peace to those in need of healing?

DAY 2: Luke 7.36-50
Here peace is connected with forgiveness. Which relationships in my life presently are dismembered and need forgiveness to become whole?

DAY 3: Luke 24.36-41
Here Jesus offers peace to the frightened disciples. How does fear keep me from being whole?

DAY 4: Psalm 122.6-8
Have I known peace in my life apart from physical and material well- being?

DAY 5: James 2.14-17
Is it enough to wish there was peace in the world? Where can I begin?

DAY 6: Jeremiah 6.13-15
Jeremiah abhors words of peace when the social network is filled with greed, fraud, and injury. What can I do to bring about wholeness in society?

DAY 7: Isaiah 48.18-19
How can I be a peacemaker in my current situation?

CHAPTER 10
CHRISTIAN PEACEMAKING

Nearly eight years ago this time of year, I taught a course in social justice to theology majors. In conjunction with the course some of the students wanted to attend a workshop on pacifism sponsored by a nearby univeristy. I went along, more from a sense of duty than anything else. That was the first time I met a pacifist. His name is buried in my memory somewhere under years of living. I recall, however, that he was a Notre Dame educated, Irish Catholic lawyer and father for whom pacifism was a gradual conversion to a way of living. At some point, a participant asked him about his involvement in the anti-war demonstrations of the Vietnam era. The speaker responded that he may have been at a demonstration once, but in those years his pacifist tendencies had not yet matured to the point where he trusted himself to respond to the probable violence in a pacifist way. For him pacifism was not a strategy or a method, but a way of living which permeated the whole of life from parenting to promoting international disarmament. To me such an approach sounds remarkably similar to the early descriptions of Christianity as 'the Way'.

* * *

In their watershed document, *Challenge of Peace*, the National Conference of Catholic Bishops describes peace as a "gift and a task". Peace is both God's gift to us and our task in the world today. This portrayal of peace is more than a clever combination of words in its insistence that peace involves both divine and human persons. This understanding of peace brings us to the heart of a Christian peacemaking located at the

249

intersection of divinity and humanity. It is in the context of the incarnation of Jesus that the bishop's comments and Christian peacemaking make sense.

1. The incarnation is the context for Christian peacemaking

Perhaps as Christians we have grown accustomed to the Christmas story. In that familiarity it is possible for us to lose sight of the uniqueness of Christianity, namely that the Creator God became one of us in Jesus. Jesus is fully human and fully divine. Jesus is not divinity which took on a mere human shell for a few years. Nor is Jesus essentially a human person although an outstanding one. Since the time of the evangelists, Christians have grappled with this mystery. Both Matthew and Luke include an elaborate record of Jesus' human ancestry, while they attribute Jesus' conception to the Holy Spirit. The mystery of the incarnation is a mystery of the oneness of God and humanity. Jesus--the literal embodiment of that unity--is peace. The foundation of Christian peacemaking is not in Jesus' words about peace but in the person of Jesus--fully human and fully divine.

The incarnation so understood provides a framework for Christian peacemaking. Jesus, the incarnate one who is our peace, proclaims the inseparable unity of the divine and the human in peacemaking. Thus Christian peacemaking resists the notion that God at some point of time will intervene in the human course of events and establish the end times reign of peace. Such a notion can appear attractive because it removes the task of peacemaking from human shoulders and places it squarely in God's realm. It allows believers to be passive and disengaged from the affairs of the world. This attitude misses the point of the incarnation, namely the unity of divinity or humanity. No longer are some things God's job and other things the human task. No, rather God and Christians work hand in hand in this world as it is to give flesh to the reign of peace. Perhaps the end times reign will arrive only when

250

God's labors for peace become incarnate not only in Jesus but in the whole human family.

The inseparable unity of divinity and humanity in Jesus provides some challenges for us, the body of Christ now. We cannot ignore the reality that Jesus lived, ministered and died in a specific historical time and place. When this is forgotten, it becomes easy to spiritualize peace and to diminish the significance of flesh and blood action in this world. Peace is not only interior feelings or inner harmony. Peace requires a living and tangible enfleshment in the specific circumstances of human life: our families torn by generations of hurtful behavior; our colleagues at work divided by jealousies and competitive insecurities; our parish and religious communities split by theological and practical differences; our church embittered by unexplained changes or rigid clinging to the past; our world separated by political and economic ideologies; our own selves alienated by personal neglect and frenzied activity. Both the mundane realities of daily discord as well as the threat of war urge us to peacemaking today.

The inseparable unity of divinity and humanity in the incarnation challenges the body of Christ to give at least as much attention to the divine dimension of Christian living as to the human dimension. How does one do this? Maybe it is less *doing* something than *recognizing*--and naming--God's presence one-with-us as we move through our days. We can expect to meet God at the traditional places of encounter: prayer, Scripture, Eucharist, the mystical writings. We can tell the stories of peaceful resolution of conflict and God's unexpected presence there. We can continue to forgive even though we've been hurt. We can take the first step toward reconciliation in faith without the clear assurance of the outcome. We can replace fear with trust. We can allow room for the divine dimension to emerge. We can recognize insight as a gift of God and we can name the unanticipated outcome grace. All of these try to nurture in the Christian peacemaker a sense of being--like Jesus--a unity of what seems radically different dimensions, namely the divine and the human. The peace which the incarnation of Jesus proclaims is continued in the body of Christ. This peace is the foundational context of Christian peacemaking.

2. Peace has been God's gift to humanity from its creation beginnings

The Hebrew and Christian Scriptures link God's gift of peace with the beauty and order of creation in the beginning. The accounts in Genesis 1 and 2 depict the spirit of God hovering over the primordial chaos and the watery abyss. Then God's creation brought ordered harmony out of the chaos. The man and the woman walked with God in the cool of the evening. The garden took care of their needs and the animals came to them for names. Harmonious relationships and rhythmic beauty abounded.

When the prophets described the new creation, these same elements occurred. Ezekial 36-37 speaks of new spirit and a desert transformation into cropland. It is the Spirit which brings the dry bones to life. Isaiah 9 and 11 describe the child as new life for the dying stump of Jesse. The Spirit of Yahweh inspires Israel's leaders and brings a peace which re-creates harmonious relationships between human persons, animals and their environment.

The resurrection accounts are built on these same elements. Jesus' Easter greeting is "Peace be with you". The Easter gift of the Risen Jesus is the Spirit. The birthing waters of baptism usher the believer into the new creation of risen life in Jesus. From the beginning peaceful, harmonious relationships made possible by the Spirit consistently characterize God's creation. I suggest that our own heartfelt longings for peace affirm this age old tradition: in the beginning we were created for peace in peace. The depths of our heart know this truth. Peacemaking is participation in ongoing creation.

252

3. Peace is envisioned as an integral part of life at the end of time

In the Biblical visions of the way things will be, there will be peace: God and we people are next door neighbors; the poor and oppressed will live in harmony within the community; the blind and the captives are liberated; the sorrowing are consoled; the poor are heirs; joy and delight ring out in the streets; and nations will live in unity together. The scriptural authors name the vision of end times life the new city Jerusalem and the reign of God. It is noteworthy that these images come from the socio-political world. The use of socio-political images reminds us that God's gift of peace is neither individual nor private, but rather communal and public. Peace marks the quality of relationships within a community or a people. Peace cares about the structures and attitudes of a society which threaten or enhance the possibility of peace. These biblical visions of peace urge that the social and public dimensions of the gift of peace be recognized.

The notion of a vision of peace provides a beginning point of reference for peacemaking. Sometimes it appears that conflict along with mediation or negotiation results in a 'peace of sorts'. The peace which is God's gift is more like the star by which we chart our course than the harbor emerging from storm-threatened navigation. As a star, peace dazzles and inspires; it lights an uncharted path. It remains ahead and beyond us but provides a true standard to measure the direction we are headed.

4. The peace of God is undeserved gift from God's own initiative.

The incarnation already reminds us that God's saving activity is peacemaking. Jesus is the unity of God-with-us. Jesus is the reconciliation of God; Jesus is the justification of God; Jesus is our peace.

God has initiated the peacemaking activity. In the Hebrew scriptures God comes to a hesitant Moses and initiates the introductions: I AM Yahweh, I AM for you or I AM on your behalf. God's personal name Yahweh denotes a gracious, intervening presence on behalf of the oppressed Israel. In addition God promises to be an active, initiating presence in the liberation of the people, if only Moses will respond in faith and trust. In Jesus God comes to sinners who have broken faith with God. As Paul reminds us in Romans, "... while we were still sinners Christ died for us." (Romans 5.6-8). This peace should make it difficult for the Christian peacemaker to sit around waiting for someone else to make the first move.

The reconciliation, justification and peacemaking of God does not depend on human worthiness or merit but on God's love. The human choice to go it alone without God has introduced an immense wall of estrangement. Although the resultant strain on the relationship is of our doing, God takes the initiative to make peace with us in Jesus. Reconciliation and justification are God's ways of making peace with people throughout the ages. God's peacemaking has not been brought about by adherence to every law, nor by membership in the right tribe or religion, nor by religious practices and rituals. This way of making peace should make the Christian peacemaker hesitant to judge whether others are deserving of reconciling activity.

Peacemaking cannot be separated from action on behalf of justice. Often the word justification is used with little regard to its connection with justice. Perhaps this disregard saves us from recognizing how poorly our human justice imitates God's justice. God takes the initiative to justify us, to 'make us right' or righteous. God's justice dissolves the barriers to intimacy which we have erected; it recreates the harmonious relationships and the peace of the primal times; and it prepares us to participate in the peaceful reign at the end of time. God's justice toward us is peacemaking. Any human peacemaking

254

efforts apart from considerations of justice cannot reflect the approach of God.

5. God's peace is the pledge of the indwelling Spirit of Jesus.

According to John's gospel, Jesus "handed over the spirit" at his death, thereby passing on that Spirit to the community of disciples as he had promised before the crucifixion. After the resurrection, the Risen Jesus connected peace with the gift of the Spirit. Paul names peace one of the fruits of the Spirit (Galatians 5.22). Jesus, who is our peace and reconciliation (Ephesians 2.13-19), handed over the Spirit of peace to the new body of Christ. Peace is not some external, sought- after thing. God's peace emanates from the personal, indwelling self gift of God. Peace is not some flakey, bandwagon fad for eccentrics; proceeding from God's own Spirit, peace is an aspect of God's very essence or being.

We are the incarnation now, that is, we give flesh to God's Spirit in the world. In this one Spirit of the Risen Jesus, we are inspired and enabled to do what Jesus did, namely to be God's reconciling activity in the world. Paul reminds us in 2 Corinthians that God was in Christ reconciling the world to Godself; but now God has enlisted us in the ministry of reconciliation and entrusted us with the message of reconciliation (2 Corinthians 5.18-21). The presence of God's peacemaking Spirit is not an idle existence. Rather the Spirit enables us both to welcome the divine overtures to peacemaking and to embody peace in the events of our lives. God's peace does not stop with personal contentment or peace of mind. Like all God's gifts, peace is a ministry given to build up the Christian community and to hasten the reign of God.

The mention of ministry brings us to the point of addressing the human task, that is, our role in Christian peacemaking.

255

6. The task of Christian peacemaking is both a response to God's gift of peace and a ministry to others.

Since God has already made peace with us, our task is to respond to the invitation of reconciling forgiveness. We respond by mirroring God's way of peacemaking to others. The Christian scriptures are insistent that what we do to others, we do to God: "Should you not have had pity on your fellow servant, as I had pity on you?" (Matthew 18.33); "Amen, I say to you, whatever you did for one of these leas brothers [sic] of mine, you did for me" (Matthew 25.40). We have pity, reconcile, do justice to the little ones and make peace because God has first had pity on us, reconciled us, justified us and made peace with us through the blood of the Lamb.

The task of Christian peacemaking challenges us to take the initiative in making peace. Peacemaking is not passivity; it is rather the active, enfleshed re-presentation of divine peacemaking in the circumstances of our lives.

Peace for the Christian rests on God's forgiving love, not the human response from those to whom we mirror God's way of relating. Christians make peace not because it is convenient or in season or to win over enemies and influence world leaders. Christians are peacemakers in response to their God who made peace first with them.

7. Christian peacemaking is a way of living rooted in conversion.

Peacemaking is an approach to life, a way of living which affects personal, social and international relationships. Peacemaking is not strategics or methods; in fact it is less what one does than who one is. It is an ongoing process of transformation from the inside out.

The beginning point of this lifestyle is conversion, a turning toward God's way of peacemaking. This conversion seeks the truth which can reconcile conflict; it seeks a way for all to 'win'; and it trusts the peaceful spirit in other members of the human and Christian community. Such conversion entails turning away from protection of my interests, from an I win-you lose approach to life, from a self- righteous insistence on my point of view or my way. It is the task of the Christian peacemaker to undergo conversion to peace, believing that my subsequent approach to life will never be quite the same. An initial conversion to peacemaking is ratified in daily decisions to promote harmony, to mediate tensions nonviolently and to build trust whether in the home, in the workplace or in the National Security Council.

8. The task of Christian peacemaking is to infuse the peace of God into the concrete structures and institutions of contemporary society.

The vision of peace is God's gift, but it is our Christian task to give flesh and blood to that vision. The hard labor of discovering the structures appropriate to the vision and shaping institutions into faithful embodiment of the vision of peace belongs to the peacemaker.

We know that in Jesus the peace of God has already broken into this world, but it is not yet completely present. We can proclaim the Pauline insight that God has been already reconciling us to God in Jesus; therefore we complete the reconciliation begun by allowing ourselves to become reconciled to God. The reign of peace is already begun and yet it awaits completion not only in Christian hearts but also in the whole of creation. The continuing responsibility for the transformation of this world into peace belongs to the Christian peacemaker. God will not intervene like a bolt out of the blue to establish a reign of peace disjunctive from the existent state of affairs. The vision of peace is God's already present gift to us; the human institutions and structures which promote and actualize peace are our human task.

257

The Christian peacemaker lives at that intersection of the already and the not yet where divine gift and human task become one effort. There is always the temptation to spiritualize peacemaking completely into God's gift to the believer. And there is always the temptation to reject God's role in peacemaking. The Christian peacemaker avoids these temptations with a consistent affirmation both of God's role in peacemaking efforts and the human task at the same time. It is not either God or human effort but both God's gift and human task. Peacemaking at that intersection is the unique contribution of Christianity.

At our college, there is much talk about being at the cutting edge of an academic discipline. Living at the crossroads of the already-not yet is the ultimate cutting edge. But as one colleague noted, the cutting edge cannot be a comfortable position. She is right! The crossroads or the cutting edge means discomfort and suffering. Suffering emerges from interior resistance to disarming personal lives as well as from external resistance, fears and misunderstanding. Yet suffering in itself sends us to the center of the crossroads where the passion and death of Jesus became the post-resurrection greeting of peace, where the profoundly human experience of dying undergone in faith occasioned reconciliation. From human suffering, including daily dying to routine disharmony and discord, the peace of God is possible.

9. Because the locus of Christian peacemaking is the world, peacemaking is political activity.

Politics has a dirty reputation. The Greek root word, *polis,* means city. It is concerned with the overall quality of public life in the city: the patterns of attitudes and social relationships as well as the organization provided through government, economic institutions and public services.

Shalom in the Hebrew scriptures carries a similar, wholistic sense of personal, social, cosmic and religious well-being. The heart of shalom is the covenant relationship with God. When Israel walked with Yahweh in right relationship, the people enjoyed long life, health, prosperity and descendants (Isaiah 65).

Shalom had socio-political implications as well. Justice done to poor, the widow and the orphan were the test cases of socio-political peacemaking. Leaders had a signficant responsibility in the promotion of peace (Isaiah 9 and 11). Zechariah 9 linked peace to meekness and to the animals of commerce and agriculture, not to violent domination and to animals of war.

Shalom even brought about a cosmic well-being: the land cooperated with the Israelites in bringing forth the harvest; the heavens offered rain; and animals laid down their predatory natures. The whole world knew peace.

This wholistic notion of peace appears to be the backdrop for Paul VI's statement in *Development of Peoples*, describing development as the new name for peace. Development, as it is used by Paul VI and subsequent documents, seeks the concrete realization of a vision of wholeness: one common life for the whole human family in interdependence with the earth and cosmos. The realization of this vision requires commitment to positive action on behalf of peace and particular attention and concern for the powerless and the voiceless. Like shalom, development, entails socio-political action.

The link between peace and politics was severed with the privatization and secularization of modern western Christianity. As a result, peacemaking became either the tactic of governments promoting absolute national sovereignty or a quality of individual conscience before God. A nationalistic political system, however, must give way to organizations and structures which promote internationalism and total cosmic wholeness. The wholistic scope of peace both as shalom or development provide an age old framework within which to reclaim peacemaking as a public religious activity.

To the extent that the task of Christian peacemaking is about actualizing God's gift of peace in the people, events and social structures of this world, it is political activity. To the extent that the task of Christian peacemaking is about nonviolent, non-retaliatory love of enemies, it publicly confronts other political ideologies. To the extent that the task of Christian peacemaking is about hastening the final end times reign of peace through establishing structures and patterns of action which promote peace, it is concerned with socio- political structures. To the extent that the task of Christian peacemaking is about an alternative way of living, it calls into question the socio-political organization of national sovereign states. Thus, peacemaking is political activity even if we never leave our homes nor march in a downtown peace rally. To the extent that peacemaking is not the fabric of our public structures and institutions, daily decisions to prefer the way of peace are not only public, that is political activity, they are countercultural and even subversive.

10. Nonviolent and non-retaliatory love of enemies is the method of Christian peacemaking.

The God of Jesus responded to the violence and injustice of the crucifixion with resurrection peace and the self-gift of the Spirit. Jesus responded to the passion and crucifixion with truth and forgiveness.

In the writings of the early Christian communities, non-retailatory love of enemies was a persistent and central theme. For example, Matthew places love of enemy and non-retaliation in the Sermon on the Mount, Jesus' inaugural statement on Christian discipleship. Paul exhorts the Thessalonians, the Corinthians and the Romans to non-retaliatory love (1 Thessalonians 5.14; 1 Corinthians 4.12-13; Romans 12.14-20). The context of the Romans statement reveals the central place of the teaching for Paul. Paul begins his ethical exhortation in chapter 12 with two significant

260

ground rules: First, "offer your bodies as a living sacrifice", that is, enflesh the good news you have heard; and second, "do not conform yourselves to this age, but be transformed by the renewal of your mind", that is, Christianity is a countercultural lifestyle based on conversion. Paul is telling the Romans: don't expect to fit in with the social order! With this framework in place, Paul then addresses ministries within the Christian community, before he turns to the community's external relationships. The heart of the Christian community's ministry to the society within which it dwells is love of enemy, blessing persecutors and non-retaliation.

In the ensuing centuries, Christian folk, martyrs, monks, missionaries and scholars kept alive this teaching and practice. Non- retaliatory love of enemies remained a living tradition in the church until the rise of secularism and the national sovereign state in the sixteenth century. In the post-World War II era, as internationalism struggles to replace nationalism, non-retaliatory love of those who name us enemy has again emerged as a legitimate way of Christian peacemaking. Further, the magisterium has recognized this way of peacemaking. *The Church in the Modern World* praised those who renounce the use of violence and the vindication of their rights (#78). The *Challenge of Peace* stressed its support of nonviolence as rooted in the Christian theological tradition (#111-121).

In addition there is a certain moral logic involved in the nonviolent way of peacemaking. The principle of moral discrimination maintains that the ways used to achieve an intended value may not contradict or be inconsistent with that intended value. Peacemaking, therefore, must logically employ nonviolent, non-retaliatory, loving actions; for violent, spiteful, retaliatory efforts are inconsistent and contradictory.

In light of God's way of peacemaking, the witness of the scriptures, the centuries-long nonviolent traditions, and the principle of moral discrimination, non-retaliatory love of enemy is the normative method of Christian peacemaking. Any other approach must be justified as a deviation from this norm. The theory of justifiable war, for example, has attempted to do this in its historical origins. Justification may be possible on basis of moral principles associated with conflict of values. It is less clear, however, that such a justification could find support within the framework described here, namely a peace-loving God incarnate in Jesus and the response-embodiment nature of Christian peacemaking.

11. The motivation for Christian peacemaking is finally a question of personal integrity.

At some point intellectual conviction and interior belief alone, apart from expression or action, become insufficent. If prayer occasions an inspiration to which I give expression neither in a journal nor in my life, it is gone, lost. So too with peacemaking. As I come to know that God has made peace with me before I even cared about peace, and as I come to believe that the lifestyle of a peacemaker is the appropriate response to God's reconciliation, I need to do something about that in my life. In *A Man for all Seasons*, Thomas More attempts to explain his resignation as chancellor. He comments, "But what matters to me is not whether it's true or not but that I believe it to be true, or rather, not that I believe it, but that I believe it".[1] It is that I, the self-aware, knowing and willing subject whose self- identity cries out for a correspondence between interior convictions and bodily expression. Not to act on convictions is a threat to personal identity and integrity.

I recall once walking with a friend when we were accosted by a gypsy begging for money. I was surprised that my friend gave her money, but I was moved by the explanation: "I didn't give her money because I judged her deserving of it, but

---

[1] R. BOLT, *A Man for All Season. A Play in Two Acts.* New York, 1960, 91.

because I need to do generosity, if I want to call myself a generous person." Maybe ultimately we make peace because we need to do peacemaking, if we want to call ourselves Christian. We need to do who we are, that is, undeservedly reconciled to our God and commissioned to a ministry of reconciliation.

Peace is God's gift and our task.

```
        P
        E
P  E  A  C  E
        C
        E
```

Roman Catholic Church Documents

Official Roman Catholic teaching in the twentieth century has addressed issues in this chapter. The following selections are particularly pertinent.

Challenge of Peace, #200-273

1. The *Challenge of Peace* lists six specific steps to reduce the danger of war. Evaluate their suggestions.
2. The *Challenge of Peace* lists three areas to consider in shaping a peaceful world. Evaluate the strengths and weaknesses of their comments.

Other Suggested Readings

COX, G. *The ways of peace. A philosophy of peace as action.* New York/Mahwah, 1986.

FAGAN, H. *Pastoral Possibilities: Conscience Formation, Education and Conflict Resolution,* in P.J.MURNION (ed.), *Catholics and Nuclear War. A Commentary on The Challenge of Peace. The U.S.Catholic Bishops' Pastoral Letter on War and Peace.* New York, 1983, 229-244.

HAUGHEY, J. *Disarmament of the heart,* in P.J.MURNION (ed.), *Catholics and Nuclear War. A Commentary on The Challenge of Peace. The U.S.Catholic Bishops' Pastoral Letter on War and Peace.* New York, 1983, 217-243.

JEGEN, M.E. *How you can be a peacemaker. Catholic teachings and practical suggestions.* Liguori, MO, 1985.

KLASSEN, P. *Love of Enemies.* Philadelphia, PA, 1984. See especially chapters 2 and 5.

MCCRACKEN, B. *The facts Come First, then the Change of Heart,* in *National Catholic Reporter* 22 (March 28, 1986) 21-28 includes a listing of teaching resources from primary through adult levels.

MURNION (ed.), P.J. *Catholics and Nuclear War. A Commentary on The Challenge of Peace. The U.S.Catholic Bishops' Pastoral Letter on War and Peace.* New York, 1983.

NCCB. *In the name of peace. Collective Statements of the US Catholic Bishops on war and peace, 1919-1980,* Washington, DC, 1982.

SCHNEIDERS, S.M. *New Testament Reflections on Peace and Nuclear Arms,* in P.J. MURNION (ed.), *Catholics and Nuclear War. A Commentary on The Challenge of Peace. The U.S. Catholic Bishops' Pastoral Letter on War and Peace.* New York, 1983, 91-105.

SENIOR, D. *Jesus' most scandalous teaching,* in J.T. PAWLIKOWSKI and D. SENIOR (eds.), *Biblical and Theological Reflections on The Challenge of Peace.* Wilmington, DE, 1984, 55-72.

SENIOR, D. *Enemy love: The challenge of peace,* in *Bible Today* 10 (1983) 163-169.

SHANNON, T. *War or peace? The search for new answers.* Maryknoll, NY, 1982 especially chapter 13.

VALETI, R.G. *100 Plus Peace Strategies (For Conflict Resolution and the Prevention of Nuclear War).* Fresno, CA, 1983.

Audio-visual Materials

The following are some of the audio-visual materials which are related to the chapter content. The list is not exhaustive, but is intended to give some initial suggestions for previewing.

If there be peace (film; 43m; Mennonite Central Committee;1975) relates stories of persons who are peacemakers in their daily lives throughout the USA and Canada.

Be not afraid (video; 28m; Sojourners; 1983) is a documentary of the 1983 Peace Pentecost in Washington, DC.

Blessed are the peacemakers III: Come, Lord, Spirit of Peace (filmstrip; 17m; Treehouse; 1972) aims at the conversion of heart necessary to a lifestyle of peacemaking.

Gods of metal (Film; 27m; Maryknoll; 1982) presents the interconnection between the arms race and third world development. Its emphasis is effective peacemaking actions from a Christian perspective.

Introductory Activities
The purpose of the introductory activity is to begin discussion on a more peaceable approach to living as well as to allow students/participants a chance to express their previous experiences and understandings of peacemaking.

1. What is my concept of a peacemaker? Do I want to be one?
2. What changes in my life, attitudes or behaviour will advance Christian peacemaking in our world?

Discussion Questions
The purpose of the discussion questions is to encourage students/participants to integrate the text and/or presented material into their own thinking and living.

1. Who is the enemy: qualities? characteristics? behavior? What in our world and lives facilitates the concept of the enemy?

2. What does love of enemy mean? Is it possible? Is there a difference between love of enemy and love of those who name us enemy?

266

3. What are personal and social barriers to peacemaking as a way of living for me?

4. Who are some peacemakers whom you have met? What did they do or say which struck you as being part of peacemaking?

Activities for Application and Integration

The following suggested activities provide opportunities for students/participants to carry the concepts of this chapter beyond the classroom. They are intended to clarify and integrate understandings into lived experience.

1. Write a 5 page strategy paper on the topic: How can I be a peacemaker in my career/profession/state of life.?

2. Interview three persons involved in various peace organizations. Ask them how and why they became involved in peacemaking organizations, what activities they have participated in, and what family and community reaction to their involvement has been.

3. Prepare a script and audio-visual materials for a 5-10 minutes presentation on love of enemy as it applies to Christian peacemaking at this time.

Spirituality Component

It is one thing to read and study about a theology of peace and quite another to become a person of peace. This spirituality component offers a series of Scripture readings with reflection questions which are closely aligned with the chapter topic. It is suggested that they be used for prayer and reflection over a series of days. The reader may wish to find another Christian with whom the prayer and its fruit may be shared or to journal one's growth as a peacemaker.

DAY 1: Colossians 3.12-17
What do I need to do so that Christ's peace can reign in my heart and in the body of Christ?

DAY 2: Matthew 10.12-15
Am I a greeting of peace to those homes I enter?

DAY 3: Jeremiah 29.7
This passage reminds us to pray for the peace of our cities and homes. How do I expect to carry this out?

DAY 4: Ephesians 4.1-6
What can I do to live in greater human and Christian solidarity with persons throughout the world?

DAY 5: Isaiah 52.7
How do I announce peace to my immediate and global community?

DAY 6: Romans 14.17-19
How do I plan to make my lifestyle more filled with peace and justice, so that the reign of God may become more present in my immediate and global community?

DAY 7: Micah 5.1-4
Micah describes the rules of land as one who is peace. How do I evaluate my own leadership for peace?

BIOGRAPHICAL SKETCH

Mary Elsbernd, OSF is a member of the Sisters of St. Francis of Dubuque, Iowa. Her undergraduate degree in French and German is from Briar Cliff College in Sioux City, Iowa. She holds a MA in Theology from St. John's University in Collegeville, MN. She received her Ph.D. and S.T.D. from Katholieke Universiteit Leuven in 1985 with a dissertation entitled *Papal Statements on Rights. A Historical, Contextual Study of Encyclical Teaching from Pius VI to Pius XI (1791-1939).* She has previously published articles in *Frau und Mutter, Sisters Today, Ephemerides Theologicas Lovanienses,* and *Haversack* as well as a co-authored essay in the recent Leadership Conference of Women (LCWR) publication, *Claiming our Truth. Reflections on Identity by American Women Religious.* She currently teaches courses in scripture, moral theology and social teachings within the Theology Department at Briar Cliff College, where she also serves as Interim Director of the Peace Studies Program.